Multicultural Education
as Social Activism

SUNY Series, The Social Context of Education
Christine E. Sleeter, Editor

Multicultural Education
as Social Activism

Christine E. Sleeter

State University of New York Press

Published by
State University of New York Press, Albany

© 1996 State University of New York

Printed in the United States of America

For information, address State University of New York
Press, State University Plaza, Albany, N.Y., 12246

Production by Diane Ganeles
Marketing by Fran Keneston

Library of Congress Cataloging-in-Publication Data

Sleeter, Christine E., 1948-
    Multicultural education as social activism / Christine E. Sleeter.
        p.   cm. — (SUNY series, the social context of education)
    Includes bibliographical references and index.
    ISBN 0-7914-2997-0 (ch : alk. paper). — ISBN 0-7914-2998-9 (pb :
alk. paper)
    1. Multicultural education—Social aspects—United States.
    2. Educational sociology—United States. I. Title. II. Series:
SUNY series, social context of education.
    LC1099.3.S587 1996
    370.19′6′0973—dc20   95-38596
                                                             CIP

10 9 8 7 6 5 4

Contents

Acknowledgments

No book is a solo effort. Many colleagues have given me helpful feedback and suggestions on one or more chapters in this book. They include: Carl Allsup, James Banks, Sari Knopp Biklin, Lynne Boyle-Baise, Maureen Gillette, Carl Grant, Susan Gould, Martin Haberman, Noel Ignatiev, Sandra Jackson, Kent Koppelman, Joe Larkin, Cameron McCarthy, Peter McLaren, Clara New, Jackson Parker, Diane Pollard, Lana Rakow, Evelyn Reid, and Barbara J. Shade. In addition to their helpful feedback, I am also very grateful to the efforts of James Scheurich and Lisa Wachtel in faxing and mailing me articles during the period of my transition between the University of Wisconsin-Parkside and California State University, Monterey Bay, when I was without ready access to a library for a period of time. Research reported in chapter 4 was supported by the Joyce Foundation of Chicago; I would like to thank Margaret Oliver for her help in collecting data, Susan Gould for her collegial relationship throughout the project, William McKersie and Angel Zapata for their encouragement on the research project, and the teachers who gave so much of their time to it.

I would like to thank the many students I have taught over the years, whose work and comments as they grappled with issues and assignments I tried out on them informed the ideas in chapters 6 and 7. I am grateful to Priscilla Ross for her encouragement and support in completing this book.

Portions of this book have appeared elsewhere in a different form. I am appreciative of the following publishers for their gracious and willing permission for me to use the following. Chapter 1 appeared in an earlier form in *Journal of Education*, vol. 171, 1989. Portions of chapter 3 appeared in *Keepers of the American Dream*, 1992, published by the Falmer Press. Chapter 4 appeared in *Educational Foundations*, Spring issue, 1992. Chapter 6 appeared in

Multicultural Education, Critical Pedagogy, and the Politics of Difference, published by SUNY Press. Portions of chapter 7 appeared in *Multicultural Education* magazine, vol. 1, 1994. Chapter 8 appeared in *Teachers College Record*, vol. 90, 1988. An earlier version of chapter 10 appeared in *Gender and Education*, published by the National Society for the Study of Education. Finally, an earlier version of chapter 12 appeared in *Kappa Delta Pi Record*, Winter issue, 1992.

CHAPTER 1

Multicultural Education as a Form of Resistance to Oppression

Multicultural education is a relatively new field that has faced a constant struggle for legitimacy, even though the issues it addresses regarding human difference, social justice, and the form education should take in a pluralistic society are as old as the United States. Conservative educators criticize or dismiss multicultural education as radical and misdirected. Twenty years ago, Harry Broudy (1975) argued that the stress on cultural diversity is divisive and will lock out minority groups from the system by failing to teach them "to participate not only in the culture of this country but also in the intellectual and artistic achievements of the human race" (p. 175). Recently conservative critics such as E. D. Hirsch (1988), Arthur Schlesinger (1992) and Diane Ravitch (1990b) have put forth the same objections, claiming that in their attempts to teach children about diverse groups, schools have produced culturally illiterate Americans who have little sense of a shared culture. Such criticisms are hardly surprising: since multicultural education challenges conservative beliefs, one would not expect it to garner much conservative support.

Of greater concern is its dismissal by many radical educators, since they also mount a challenge to oppression in society and schooling. Many critical theorists have located the main source of oppressive social relationships in the economy and relations of production and until recently rarely addressed issues of racial and gender oppression. Philip Wexler (1982), for example, in reviewing contributions by sociologists of school knowledge, repeatedly emphasized social class only:

> School knowledge reflects class interest. . . . School knowledge is the unequal representation of the experience and culture of social classes. . . . School knowledge is an organizational representation of different class languages. . . . School knowledge develops as cultural representation in response to the system needs of capitalism. (p. 278)

1

Such theorists have simply ignored multicultural education, partly because it typically has offered a much stronger critique of race than social class relations.

Growing numbers of other radical educators occasionally string together the words "race, class, and gender," recognizing the existence of multiple forms of social oppression. However, social class and class theorists still receive most of their attention, and they too have given little attention to multicultural education.

Some radical theorists in the United States have published criticisms of the field of multicultural education (Mattai, 1992; McCarthy, 1988; Olneck, 1990; Popkewitz, 1988). Radical theorists outside the U.S. have also criticized it, but since the history of and thought within the field differs somewhat from country to country, this book will concern itself with criticisms originating in the United States; reasons why will follow. Radical theorists criticize multicultural education on the grounds that it is part of the liberal, but not the radical, tradition. Their criticisms are important to attend to because, whether others voice them in print or not, they represent grounds for failing to take multicultural education seriously. They also illustrate problems in how the field is often interpreted today, which suggests directions it should take in its development.

In this book, I argue that multicultural education can be understood as a form of resistance to dominant modes of schooling, and particularly to white supremacy. As such, radical criticisms or tacit dismissals of it fragment progressive educational advocates and practitioners, which weakens attempts in this conservative era to challenge oppressive social relationships through schooling. But at the same time, as more and more white educators have become involved in the field, much work and activity has become disconnected from its political base. This book will attempt to clarify the field's political underpinnings particularly as they relate to challenging white supremacy. In this introductory chapter, I will review radical criticisms of multicultural education and then situate the field in its historic context.

Radical Left Criticisms of
Multicultural Education in the U.S.

Multicultural education has been a target of radical criticism in England, Canada, and Australia (e.g., Bullivant, 1986; Cole, 1986; Troyna, 1987). Recently criticisms of the field in the U.S. have been produced. Cameron McCarthy (1988) described multicultural education as "a body of thought which originates in the liberal pluralist approaches to education and society," and which is "a curricular truce, the fallout of a political project to deluge and neutralize Black rejection of the conformist and assimilationist curriculum models solidly in place in the 1960s." He went on to say that multicultural education attempts to "absorb Black radical demands for the restructuring of school knowledge and pedagogical practices," focusing instead on "sensitizing White teachers and school administrators to minority 'differences'" (p. 268). As such, it advocates a "benign pluralism ('We are all the same because we are different')" (p. 276). This benign pluralism has resulted in two faulty analyses on which he sees multicultural education as resting. First, McCarthy argued that multicultural education advocates moving racial minority young people into better jobs by promoting academic achievement through raising their self-concepts; this is a naive approach to the job market because it ignores institutional racist practices in the economic structure (p. 269). Second, he noted that, "By focusing on sensitivity training and on individual differences, multicultural proponents typically skirt the very problem which multicultural education seeks to address: WHITE RACISM" (p. 269).

His concerns are shared by Rudy Mattai (1992), who critiqued "the seeming inability of multicultural education to address the issue of race" (p. 66). He argued that multicultural education initially grew from the ethnic revival movements of the 1960s, in which racism was clearly the main concern. Since then, however, the discourse of multicultural education has shifted away from racism and toward culture, away from systemic oppression and toward individual attitude change.

Michael Olneck (1990) agreed with McCarthy and Mattai that multicultural education concerns itself mainly with individual differences and the primacy of the individual over the collective and that it depoliticizes race relations by focusing on expressions of culture rather than sociopolitical relations among groups. In describing multicultural education as emphasizing the development of positive attitudes and intergroup harmony, Olneck argued that it serves as a vehicle for social control more than for social change. He summarized his arguments as follows:

> Like intercultural education, dominant versions of multicultural education delimit a sanitized cultural sphere divorced from sociopolitical interests, in which culture is reified, fragmented, and homog-

enized, and they depict ethnic conflict as predominantly the consequence of negative attitudes and ignorance about manifestations of
difference, which they seek to remedy by cultivating empathy,
appreciation, and understanding. (p. 166)

These criticisms are important and need attention because they
indicate consequences of a disconnection between multicultural education and political action. In this book, I argue that such a disconnection is largely a result of white educators' reluctance to address
white racism. By white racism, I am referring to institutionalized
systems that are controlled by people of European descent and that
give those of us who are of European descent greater access than
groups of color to society's resources, and to the beliefs white people
use to justify such systems. At the same time, however, radical criticisms oversimplify the field of multicultural education and provide
grounds on which leftist educators and activists dismiss it. I will
argue that it is more productive to identify ways in which the field
works to challenge oppression and to amplify and develop those
dimensions of thought and practice. First, let us examine dimensions of the field's complexity that its critics tend to gloss over.

Complexities within the Field of Multicultural Education

Critics as well as advocates of multicultural education often
assume that it is a fairly homogeneous set of practices and that all
advocates subscribe to the same ends and the same models of social
change. As a result, critics often condemn practices that many multicultural education advocates also criticize or they condemn the
field for not addressing issues some of its theorists do address. The
field is often treated as static and homogeneous rather than dynamic
and growing, with its own internal debates. This is important to recognize, because there is much within the field that radical educators
should be working *with* rather than *against*.

First, the diversity across national borders must be recognized.
While there is considerable dialogue among advocates in the United
States, Canada, England, and Australia, the histories of race relations in these countries are sufficiently different that debates in one
country cannot simply be transplanted to another country. The
United States has struggled with race relations on its home territory
since its inception, in addition to sharing with England, Canada,
and Australia increasing diversification of its population due to

recent waves of immigrants of color. Not only did whites in the U.S. subjugate aboriginal people, as did whites in Australia and Canada; whites in the U.S. also imported large numbers of African slaves, whose descendants have lived here for about four centuries. The United States also colonized Puerto Rico and half of Mexico, absorbing Latinos into its borders while continuing to live next to sovereign Latin nations.

This history, which has helped shape relations among racial and ethnic groups in the United States, as well as dialogue about racial and ethnic relations, differs from that of other English-speaking countries. Only since World War II has Britain experienced a significant influx of people of color, while it historically had dominated people of color outside its borders through colonialism. Australia shares with the U.S. a history of whites subjugating aboriginal people, but only very small numbers of other groups of color have been permitted to immigrate there until recently. Further, aboriginal people in Australia are separated geographically from whites to a much greater degree than in the U.S., one consequence of which is that aboriginal Australians have even less input into non-aboriginal discussions of race relations than is the case in the U.S. Neither Canada nor Australia shares the U.S. experience of enslaving large numbers of African people, or of conquering and absorbing other nonwhite nations. Unlike the United States, however, Canada has a history of struggle between two strong European language and ethnic groups.

As a result of these different histories and cultural contexts, multicultural education in the United States today has a longer history and a more varied body of thought than the field has in other English-speaking countries, and race (as opposed to white ethnicity) has longer been at its core. In addition, the involvement among different groups in the debates about multicultural education differs from country to country. In the United States educators of color have always been at the forefront of the development of multicultural education, along with some Euro-Americans; in England and Australia, debates are carried on mainly by whites, and people of color are largely excluded. In the U.S., the federal government is not a participant in debates about multicultural education; in Britain, Canada, and Australia, the national governments have appropriated the term *multicultural education* to refer to recommended interventions that many argue are too weak and assimilationist (e.g., Green, 1982). These different cultural contexts have produced somewhat different alignments of educators who use the term *multicul-*

tural education. In Britain, for example, a lively debate is being waged between proponents of multicultural education and proponents of antiracist teaching. In the U.S., many proponents of multicultural education, such as James Banks (1992), Antonia Darder (1991), Sonia Nieto (1992), and Bob Suzuki (1984), *agree* with proponents of antiracist teaching, but do so under the umbrella of multicultural education.

Second, within the United States, one can distinguish between quite different approaches to multicultural education. These have been described and reviewed elsewhere (Sleeter & Grant, 1987, 1993), but will be summarized here. One approach, Teaching the Culturally Different, attempts to raise the achievement of students of color, although more through designing culturally compatible education programs than through simply raising student self-concept (e.g., Hollins, et al., 1994; Jordan, 1985; Shade, 1989). Partly because this approach does not necessarily address structural barriers to economic access, it is not the approach most advocates of multicultural education prefer. The second approach, Human Relations, aims toward sensitivity training, and teaches that "We are all the same because we are different" (Colangelo, Foxley, & Dustin, 1979; Tiedt & Tiedt, 1986). This approach does not address institutional racism; its intent is to improve the school experience itself more than to restructure society. This seems to be the approach that resonates best with the political beliefs of most white teachers (Sleeter, 1992).

The third approach, which we call Single Group Studies, includes Black Studies, Chicano Studies, Women's Studies, Gay and Lesbian Studies, and so forth. This approach teaches students explicitly about the history of the group's oppression and how oppression works today, as well as the culture the group developed within oppressive circumstances (e.g., Aguilar-San Juan, 1994; Lather, 1991). Ethnic studies and women's studies scholars have been re-theorizing academic disciplines from standpoints of groups other than that of Euro-American men (e.g., Asante, 1990; Harding, 1991). In contrast to the first two approaches, this one is usually overtly political and its adherents are often engaged in community politics, although to a lesser degree now than twenty years ago (Omatsu, 1994). The fourth approach is most commonly subscribed to by American multicultural education advocates (e.g., Baker, 1983; Banks, 1981; Gay, 1983; Gollnick, 1980), so we called it the Multicultural Education approach. Its processes involve redesigning schooling to make it model the ideal pluralistic and equal society. Its advocates concentrate on reforming many dimensions of the school process, such as curriculum, pedagogy, parent involvement, and tracking. Finally, the fifth approach, Education that is Multicultural and Social Reconstructionist, teaches directly about political and economic oppression and discrimination, and prepares young people to use social action skills (e.g., Grant & Sleeter, 1986a; Sleeter, 1991; Suzuki, 1984).

Advocates of different approaches debate with and sometimes criticize each other. It is important for those outside the field to identify which approach or approaches are actually being discussed, rather than assuming that all are alike. Both McCarthy and Olneck, for example, describe and cite mainly Human Relations ideas and sources. Neither mentions ideas associated with Single Group Studies or Education that is Multicultural and Social Reconstructionist, approaches within the field with which they and other radical educators might sympathize.

Third, one must distinguish between an approach as formulated by its main theorists, and superficial applications of it that one often finds in schools as well as in the literature. As James Banks (1984) has pointed out, quite often "the critics have chosen some of the worst practices that are masquerading as multicultural education and defined these practices as multicultural education" (p. 60). For example, the Single Group Studies approach as envisioned by its theorists examines a group's historic and contemporary oppression and also mobilizes its members as well as sympathetic out-group members for social action. But in schools this approach often takes the form of superficial study of the food, music, and dances of a group. Rather than condemning Single Group Studies, or the entire field of multicultural education for how an approach is often carried out in classrooms, it would be more productive to develop ways to strengthen its application and use.

Fourth, one can differentiate among advocates who address only race and ethnicity; race, ethnicity, and gender; race, ethnicity, and language; and multiple forms of diversity. Some theorists treat these as multiple layers of individual difference, while others treat them as multiple and connected forms of oppression. This is an important distinction. While the Human Relations approach stresses acceptance of a wide variety of manifestations of uniqueness, Education that is Multicultural and Social Reconstructionist searches for ways to build coalitions to combat oppression in its various forms.

Fifth, advocates often articulate their agendas for school reform using language that recognizes the resistance multicultural education typically encounters. Therefore, one cannot assume that advocates of multicultural education spell out their entire agenda in print and that one can infer all they are thinking or doing by reading the multicultural education literature. Multicultural education has been a highly political change strategy; many of its writings can be understood as attempts to mobilize particular changes in schooling, on the part of individuals who often would resist those changes. A large proportion of active advocates of the last three approaches are educators of color who have experienced a lifetime of white racism and know fully well that this is a major issue that needs to be addressed. But schools, as well as the colleges and job markets they serve, are controlled mainly by whites, and substantive reforms must have white support. Thus, advocates have had to address white educators in order to gain space within the curriculum to teach about the experiences of Americans of color and to reduce the obvious hostility schools often display toward children of color (Banks, 1992). Much of the multicultural education literature attempts to delineate very practical changes that could be made in classrooms (Gay, 1995). Having had considerable experience with white educators, advocates have known that whites do not usually listen to educators of color, particularly when they show emotion (Delpit, 1988). Thus, the politics of bringing about change has necessitated frequently couching arguments for school reform in language that white educators would attend to. Many advocates deliberately have chosen terms such as *human relations* because nobody opposes good human relations, while the term *multicultural* signals a red flag to many people, and the term *race* literally scares many more away. A friend who is African American and a school principal recently commented to me that she can get her white teachers to do more that is consistent with multicultural education when she does not use the terms *race* or even *multicultural education*. She finds this very frustrating because important issues simply go unaddressed, yet if she tries to address them directly, her staff retreats from her.

The strategy of appealing to whites through relatively benign language sometimes has been more effective than many recognize. For example, in Minnesota under the state's term *Human Relations*, Bob Terry developed a curriculum called "Foundations of Oppression" which is used by many teacher education programs. St. Cloud State University in particular has been able to develop a very strong campus-wide program in the study of oppression based on race, gender, social class, and sexual orientation (Andrzejewski, 1993). The same strategy has been used to create space in teacher certification programs for multicultural work in Wisconsin, Iowa, and Minnesota. Paradoxically, while terms such as *Human Relations* can be criticized for depoliticizing race relations, use of such terms can be politically quite effective. (As a colleague once put it, rather than looking for the sharpest needle, it is more strategically effective to look for the one that sews [Yamane, 1994].)

This is not to say that all advocates of multicultural education are radicals using benign language for political purposes. Many do indeed subscribe to limited visions of or naive theories about social change. But many activists who are working to make changes in education work with whatever points of entree they can gain in whatever fashion is acceptable to others with whom they work. In order to understand what any advocate really thinks or believes, one should interact personally with him or her.

Earlier I noted that criticisms of multicultural education by the left fracture a progressive potential coalition (often along racial lines) in a way that weakens it. It could be of great mutual benefit for those interested primarily in class, in race, and in gender oppression to work together as much as possible. Multicultural education can best be understood as a form of resistance to oppression; as such, it offers some help in formulating educational practices that challenge oppression. But the field also needs further development at both the theoretical and practical levels, partly due to changes in the social context in which multicultural education has been articulated.

Multicultural Education as a Form of Resistance

Over the last two decades, critical theorists have found themselves plagued by overly deterministic models of structural and cultural reproduction (e.g., Bourdieu & Passeron, 1977; Bowles & Gintis, 1976), and have explored implications of contradiction and resistance as a means of agency for social change. For example, Michael Apple (1982) argued:

> Functionalist accounts of the hidden curriculum—accounts that sought to demonstrate both that students, like workers, were effectively socialized and that the power of technical/administrative forms used by capital was unchallenged—were part of the very process of ideological reproduction I wanted to struggle against. (p. 24)

He went on to say:

> Clearly, then, workers resist in subtle and important ways, I believe. They often contradict and partly transform modes of control into opportunities for resistance and maintaining their own informal norms which guide the labor process. (p. 25)

Henry Giroux, among others, has explored the concept of resistance in some detail. He defines resistance as "a personal 'space' in which the logic and force of domination is contested by the power of subjective agency to subvert the process of socialization" (1988, p. 162). Resistance can take many forms, ranging from "an unreflective and defeatist refusal to acquiesce to different forms of domination" to "a cynical, arrogant, or even naive rejection of oppressive forms of moral and political regulation" (1988, p. 162). The power of resistance is its celebration "not of what is but what could be" (1983, p. 242) and the energy it mobilizes for social change. It is this resistance that provides an entree into education for social change; Giroux has argued the need "to develop strategies in schools in which oppositional cultures might provide the basis for a viable political force" (1983, p. 101).

Multicultural education can be viewed as a form of resistance to oppressive social relationships. It represents resistance to white supremacy and also (for many) to patriarchy. Multicultural education developed in the ferment of the 1960s and early 1970s, receiving its major impetus from the rejection of racial minority groups to racial oppression; it subsequently was joined to some extent by feminist groups rejecting sexual oppression. It was grounded in a vision of equality and served as a mobilizing site for struggle within education. However, due to changes over the past twenty years in the social and political context of multicultural education, many educators interpret its meaning quite differently today. Consequently the field needs to speak to oppression and struggle more explicitly now than it did in its inception.

Geneva Gay (1983), one of the field's major proponents and developers, has provided a useful discussion of the history of the field. She noted that it

> originated in a sociopolitical milieu and is to some extent a product of its times. Concerns about the treatment of ethnic groups in school curricula and instructional materials directly reflected concerns about their social, political, and economic plight in the society at large. (p. 560)

She went on to point out connections between the civil rights movement and the inception of multicultural education. In the mid-1960s, "The ideological and strategic focus of the [civil rights] movement shifted from passivity and perseverance in the face of adversity to aggression, self-determination, cultural consciousness, and political power" (p. 560). Racial minority groups actively proclaimed and developed consciousness of their own histories and identities. On college campuses this ferment took the form of demands for ethnic studies courses and elimination of stereotypic and derogatory treatment. Some of this energy was directed toward the public school curricula and to the "ethnic distortions, stereotypes, omissions, and misinformation" in textbooks (p. 561). At the same time, the movement was aided by social science research that undermined cultural deprivation theories and suggested that "the academic failure of minority youths was due more to the conflicting expectations of school and home and to the schools' devaluation of minority group cultures" (p. 561).

Gay describes the 1970s as "prime times for multiethnic education. This was an era of growth and expansion both quantitative and qualitative" (p. 562). During the 1970s "an avalanche of revisionist materials—including pedagogies, psychologies, ethnographies, histories, and sociologies" were created in the forms of "a wide variety of ethnic books, films and filmstrips, recordings, audio-visual packets, course outlines, and study guides" (p. 562). Conferences, workshops, and policies such as the Ethnic Heritage Act and the NCATE standards for accreditation supported this activity. The activity of the 1970s can best be thought of as a good beginning. Gay cautions that, while "theory was advancing, emerging, and evolving with apparent continuity," at the same time "multiethnic practice remained largely fragmentary, sporadic, unarticulated, and unsystematic" (p. 562).

In its inception, multicultural education was clearly connected with and attempting to contribute to a much larger social and political racial struggle, and many of its originators had their own roots in black studies (Banks, 1992). According to Banks (1984),

> A major goal of most ethnic revival movements is to attain equality for the excluded ethnic group. . . . Since the school is viewed by ethnic reformers as an important institution in their oppression, they attempt to reform it because they believe that it can be a pivotal vehicle in their liberation. (p. 58)

One task of the social movements of the 1960s was, as Michael Omi and Howard Winant (1986) put it, to create "collective identity by offering their adherents a different view of themselves and their world; different, that is, from the worldview and self-concepts offered by the established social order" (p. 93). Multicultural education's attempt to instill in children pride in their own racial heritage was a part of this larger task of creating new collective identities that emphasize strength and pride.

The social movements were directed toward equalizing power and legal status among racial and gender groups. Omi and Winant point out that "The modern civil rights movement sought not to survive racial oppression, but to overthrow it" (p. 94). Multicultural education's emphasis on cultural pluralism was an articulation of this vision of equality in power and rights among racial groups without resorting to separatism. Multicultural education's attempts to incorporate groups of color into curricula were part of larger attempts to make social institutions more accessible to and inclusive of Americans of color; the Brown decision and the Civil Rights Act of 1964 had opened the doors of white schools to children of color, but the histories and cultures of groups of color were still excluded.

Multicultural education workshops for teachers during the late 1960s and early 1970s (which was when I began teaching) conveyed the militancy of the broader social movements by dealing directly with white racism and trying to have teachers own and admit their own participation in and benefits from a racist system. Needless to say, such workshops often were not very popular among white teachers.

In the late 1970s and 1980s the political climate shifted: "For the first time in a sustained and programmatic way, setbacks in the domestic economy and U.S. reversals on the international level were 'explained' by attacking the liberal interventionist state" (Omi and Winant, 1986, p. 110). The civil rights movement had succeeded in placing race on the national political agenda and in attaining popular support for the idea (or at least the phrase) of racial equality. However, the right, which had suffered ideological losses during the 1960s, quickly began to rearticulate the nation's racial ideology. Omi and Winant describe this rearticulated vision: "With the exception of some on the far right, the racial reaction which has developed in the last two decades claims to favor racial equality. Its vision is that of a 'colorblind' society where racial considerations are never entertained" (p. 114). Its vision is also that of an individualistic society: "Racial discrimination and racial equality—in the neoconservative model—are problems to be confronted ONLY at an individual level, once legal systems of discrimination such as DE JURE segregation have been eliminated" (Omi & Winant, 1986, p. 129).

The left has lost considerable visibility and momentum, and some segments of the left have shifted strategies toward working within the system. Carlos Muñoz (1987), for example, described the shift in Chicano politics "that took place during the 1970s from a politics of militant protest to a politics focused on the electoral process and the two-party system" (p. 43). Manning Marable (1987) described rifts within the black community, concluding that, "The absence of a coherent Black left program and strategy, and the contradictory and sometimes antagonistic relationship between Black elected officials and their constituents, has created a political vacuum within Black America" (pp. 11–12).

To white America, the absence of mass protest, the presence of a small number of African American, Hispanic, and Asian women and men as well as white women in new positions (e.g., administrative jobs), and passage of civil rights laws all suggest that inequalities of the past have been remedied. This is not true, of course; the persistence of poverty and discrimination among historically disenfranchised groups is well documented. However, mainstream white America today is well versed in the right's rearticulation of a racial ideology and is fairly ignorant of or indifferent to limitations to gains made by racial minority groups and women during the past twenty-five years.

Within this context, many who are relatively new to multicultural education do not see it as directly connected with political struggle. Rather, they tend to see it as a means of reducing prejudice and stereotyping among individuals—as an attempt to learn to overlook differences in an effort to allow Americans of color to "progress" in the historic manner of white ethnic groups. This is not what multicultural education has meant to most of its developers and activists, but it is nevertheless a common interpretation. It reflects the fact that the language and recommendations in multicultural education have not changed to take account of changes in the political context.

When Carl Grant and I reviewed literature in the field of multicultural education (see Grant & Sleeter, 1985; Grant, Sleeter & Anderson, 1986; Sleeter & Grant, 1987), we expected to find an evolution from less radical to more radical approaches. Instead, we found all five approaches to exist side by side since the early 1970s, with theorists writing most frequently about the Multicultural Education approach and published teaching guides most frequently employing the Human Relations approach. The field as a whole demands changes in race relations today that are no less radical than demands of the 1960s.

What has changed is the manner in which the field is presented to teachers, and especially white teachers. Presentations that exposed teachers to racial anger have given way to more upbeat, practice-oriented approaches. To try to help white teachers understand multicultural concepts and to convince them to implement multicultural education, many educators begin with the concept of ethnicity and ethnic culture, having teachers examine their own ethnic cultures (e.g., Bennett, 1986). The assumption is that white teachers will see that the needs, feelings, and experiences of racial minority groups are not so very different from their own; this may, however, suggest that race is not different from European ethnicity. Teachers are taught to analyze textbooks for bias and to develop curricula that incorporate people of color and women. Teachers are taught TESA (Teacher Expectations and Student Achievement) strategies and increasingly cooperative learning to ensure that all their students are involved in whole-class instruction. Harold Hodgkinson's (1985) analysis of changing demographics is often used to convince teachers of the need to multiculturalize their teaching. What teachers are taking away from such workshops is a set of piecemeal strategies they can add occasionally to what they already do (Sleeter, 1992).

State support of multicultural education is another recent change. Increasingly it is becoming a state requirement for teacher certification, at the same time the teaching profession is becoming increasingly white and student populations increasingly of color and of poverty backgrounds. Omi and Winant (1986) point out that, "In response to political pressure, state institutions adopt policies of absorption and insulation" (p. 81). Multicultural education is gaining state legitimacy as a part of the preparation of teachers for culturally diverse classrooms. However, in the process it often becomes rearticulated and depoliticized. White teachers today commonly share McCarthy's and Olneck's perception of multicultural education. They interpret it as a form of individualism, a way of teaching "at-risk" children, and an extension of the ethnicity paradigm which suggests that "through hard work, patience, delayed gratification, etc., blacks [and other groups of color] could carve out their own rightful place in American society" (Omi & Winant, 1986, p. 20).

The 1990s are witnessing rollbacks of gains made during the civil rights movement. Affirmative action as well as funding for social programs is under attack; at the time of this writing it is possible that both will have been shredded by the time this book is published. Immigrants are increasingly vilified and denied services as well as legitimacy of the cultures and languages they bring; homelessness is being legislated as a crime rather than a symptom of insufficient jobs and affordable housing; and welfare recipients are subject to escalating hatred. In addition, public education at all levels is being cut. Conservative justification for increased racial and social class stratification is becoming increasingly popular, including justification on the basis of genetic grounds.

As we enter the twenty-first century, the field of multicultural education must develop in ways that are consonant with its original mission: to challenge oppression and to use schooling as much as possible to help shape a future America that is more equal, democratic and just, and that does not demand conformity to one cultural norm. It is essential that these goals be pursued in a politically powerful and strategic manner, given the growing hostility of the climate in which we are working.

Overview of the Book

This book attempts to connect political and pedagogical issues with personal experiences and reflections. I begin by reflecting on my own positioning as a white woman from a professional class background, in chapter 2. This book does not spring from nowhere: it grows from my own reflections on issues of difference and oppression, and those reflections are situated in my own lived experience. In chapter 3, I situate multicultural education debates politically. This chapter distinguishes among conservatism, liberalism, and radical structuralism, then discusses the political context of the 1980s and 1990s relative to debates about multicultural education. In chapter 4, I return to connections between personal conceptions of multicultural education and lived experience, exploring how several teachers constructed meanings of multicultural education from the fabric of their teaching experience as well as their own personal historic experiences.

Chapter 5 further probes the idea of social location by developing themes in minority position discourse that drive multicultural curriculum. In this chapter I attempt to distinguish narratives about America that are cosmetically multicultural but substantively colonizing from those that are multicultural and liberatory at their core. In chapters 6 and 7, I discuss my own attempts as an educator to help my teacher education students grapple with discourse rooted in the lived experiences of minority positions. Chapter 6 highlights teaching strategies that have made an impact on student thinking. Chapter 7 critiques the degree to which formal education can change how we think, given the profound impact of lived experience, vested interest, and social location; I focus my attention in this chapter on whiteness and white supremacy.

In chapter 8, Carl Grant and I explore how adolescents interpret their own lives relative to race, social class, and gender. We argue here that while formal schooling may not be able to completely transform how young people think, it plays a much greater role than educators often take responsibility for. Chapter 9 offers ideas regarding the teaching of science for social justice. This chapter came about as a result of being invited to talk with some science teachers about what multicultural education might mean for them. I have never been a science teacher, but through my examination of science teaching materials I can suggest directions for their use.

In chapter 10, I turn to complexities of power and position along multiple axes of power. In this chapter, I critique power relations in which white professional women often use our racial and class privileges to advance our own agendas at the expense of women of color and women from lower-class backgrounds. Chapter 11 returns to the issue of political power, using the metaphor of social movement to explore directions for multicultural education. This chapter moves from the classroom back to the larger society, linking the activism of the 1960s with the conceptual development of multicultural education literature in the 1990s. I close this book with the questions: What and whom is multicultural education for? Given very unequal power relations and our own locations in those webs of power, how can we participate in social change in ways that do not compromise the original intent of multicultural education? Finally, in chapter 12, I fantasize about the form multicultural education might take, presenting this fantasy in the form of a play.

CHAPTER 2

Gender as a Mediator of Racial Consciousness

Periodically I am asked about my personal process of grappling with white racism. In this chapter I will explore the fruits of some personal introspection, particularly as gender has served as a mediator within my racial consciousness. In chapter 3 I will complicate this analysis by arguing that awareness of sexism can block a substantive analysis of racial oppression. Gender can serve as a helpful mediator of racial awareness, although how such processes play themselves out is very complex. I will discuss how these two forms of oppression have played out in my life.

"Smart" and "Girl" as Mutually Exclusive

An ongoing issue throughout my life has been an attempt to reconcile my sex with my intellectual ability, in a society that penalizes smart women (Kerr, 1985). As a child and young adult, the conflict I perceived and experienced between my sex and my intelligence was often a source of personal pain. This pain probably helped me learn to empathize with experiences of marginalization; it also led me to develop coping strategies that I later used to deal with my fear of racial issues.

I grew up in a small town in southern Oregon. My ethnic background is mixed European, mostly German; about four generations back was a Cherokee woman. My father, a physician, died when I was young, leaving my mother to raise four children. At the time of his death I was too young to fully grasp what had happened, and my mother tried hard to minimize the impact of his death on us. As a consequence I grew up with a mother modeling strength and independence, although she also adhered to a traditional woman's role as

17

full-time mother (her father helped us out economically). I also grew up sensitive to other people's reactions to differences. When people heard that my father was deceased, they often expressed pity; to me, it was a fact of life, and my family was just fine, thank you. I didn't like to be asked about my family because of the reaction that often followed.

Growing up, one of my main difficulties was how to negotiate what I experienced as a conflict between being smart versus becoming popular with the peer group. The academically capable boys didn't seem to have to choose, but the girls did. Academic work came easily for me, and with it, adult praise. Attaining peer group popularity was always much more problematic. In junior high, for example, I tried out for cheerleading; my unsuitability was evident when I showed up with homemade pompoms that were not made correctly. I realized that the other girls had helped each other with theirs, but since no one apparently thought of me as cheerleader material, no one invited me to prepare with them, and I did not realize I had been excluded until tryouts. In high school I rarely dated and was rarely invited to parties. At school dances I stood on the sidelines with other wallflowers. To compensate for peer-group (mostly male) rejection, I excelled academically, which only aggravated boys' disinterest in me. (I have since been told by a couple of them than I scared them off by being academically smart.)

This feeling of marginalization was persistent and very painful. While it is also trivial, especially compared with the marginalization caused by racism, heterosexism, and poverty, I nevertheless experienced it for years as a hurtful inability to fit in because of personal characteristics I did not know how to change. I did have a few very close female friends, but as a girl, I felt like a failure. The pain and frustration were magnified by the apparent success my sisters had with the peer group.

My marginal position relative to the "popular" peer group from my side of town seemed to open me to seeking friends from other social circles. As a doctor's daughter, I felt most comfortable around professional class people. However, largely through my involvement in the school band, I made friends with a few peers from the "other side of town." One of my best friends in high school was a secretary's daughter from a working class neighborhood. I decided that if we could play our clarinets, commiserate about boys, take band trips, and go to the movies together, the different sizes of our houses or prestige of our family backgrounds was irrelevant. It wasn't, of course; upon graduating I went straight to a private college and she went to work.

As I got to know kids from the "other side of town," I also started wondering whether non-whites were actually much different from me. My hometown was over 99% white, so this was abstract speculation more than concrete testing. I had heard about a Black meteorologist who moved his family to town, but they were harassed so badly that they quickly left. I was aware of Mexican migrant workers who were termed "cheap labor," but I didn't know any. Questions about race surfaced when my mother took us to visit her family in California. My California relatives occasionally made derogatory comments about Black people as we passed them on the street. I would try to rise to their defense ("But you don't know that lady, do you?"), and would be quickly silenced ("Christine, be quiet, you've never lived around them"). I was not comfortable with categorical rejection of an entire class of people and hearing relatives occasionally do just that increased my discomfort. Of course I absorbed the racial stereotypes that everyone learns and also grew up tremendously ignorant of anyone who was not like me. However, since there were no African American, and very few Asian or Mexican American people in my town, the stereotypes I learned were largely abstractions, disconnected from real people. Rarely except when my family visited California was there occasion for an adult to point to a person of color and tell me what sense to make of that person or how I should act toward him or her. The racism I was raised with was grounded in taken-for-granted acceptance of white people as the center of the universe, but not active hatred directed toward real people. My racial and social class background conferred advantages on me of which I was unaware. For example, as a white doctor's kid who was doing well in school, teachers believed the best about me and treated me accordingly. Doors never closed to us, an experience I presumed to be universal.

When I went to college, I cultivated a strategy to cope with the incompatibility I perceived between being smart and female: I adopted the persona of an airhead and did my academic work secretively and only adequately. Quickly I became a cheerleader and a sorority girl and had dates every weekend. Few people around me were aware of my earlier academic track record, so few questioned this new persona. Ironically, this persona simply affirmed and legitimated the image that women are neither smart nor serious. For a while I thought I had succeeded in overcoming the problem of being a smart girl. It wasn't until I graduated that I realized that I had suppressed part of myself to make myself more "acceptable," and had not prepared myself for any identifiable future. In retrospect, the quality of my relationships with young men didn't improve, just the quantity.

I graduated from college with no game plan. Most women at my university spent their senior year pouring over *Bride* magazines, but I had no marriage prospects. I also faced the rejection of several women friends who had returned as feminists from a year abroad. Feminism would have been a helpful source of insight for me, except that I feared (without being able to articulate it) that to become a feminist would guarantee me a future as an "old maid."

At this point in my life, I still viewed being smart as a problem residing within me. Over the next ten years, I gradually constructed a critique of society and slowly began to accept myself. The processes involved exposure to feminist thinking, gradual growth in consciousness of sexism as I experienced it, and development of trusting relationships with men who were not afraid of smart women. For example, after graduating from college, while trying to figure out a direction for my life, I lived alone for a year in an apartment and worked as a secretary, spending considerable time in introspection. One day while talking with a young man, he asked if I lived with "a bunch of other chicks." I said I lived alone, and he looked at me strangely, then ended the conversation. This time, rather than blaming myself for being a nerd, I was angry: I wasn't a "chick," and my living space was not a party space.

Incidents of this kind marked the beginning of my conscious critique of sexism. In the broader social context the feminist movement was becoming quite active and while I had not yet become involved in that movement, I had some awareness of it. For a good while I regarded feminism as a position that would aggravate my unacceptability: if smart girls weren't desired, smart girls who critique patriarchy would be desired even less. The points of entry into feminism for me were concrete incidents; as I gradually connected those incidents with an alternative discourse (i.e., feminism), my self-acceptance and social critique strengthened. What kept me struggling to understand sexism was that in some ways, I simply did not fit the traditional prescribed woman's role. My tolerance in cooking and cleaning for other people wore thin before I ever married, causing me to question marriage as an institution. As I gradually developed satisfaction in professional success, I became increasingly critical of barriers women encounter as well as the choices society forces many women to make (such as the choice between raising a family and enjoying a professional life). The dominant partiarchal discourse simply could not interpret my life experiences in a way that fully supported my sense of self; I gradually learned that feminist discourse offered the social critique and self-affirmation I sought.

For me, gender acted as a mediator of racial consciousness, but not in a direct, straightforward manner. My awareness of racism began to develop when I moved to Seattle to become a teacher, although some groundwork had been laid earlier. I was an undergraduate between 1966 and 1970, a time when the nation was rocked by revolutions. My undergraduate experience was almost as sheltered as my childhood had been. The university I attended is located in a white Oregon town and was attended mainly by white, relatively affluent students. While the nation was confronting racism, the student revolution, war, and feminism, my classmates were worrying about the next football game or fraternity party. I didn't really get involved in the 1960s until the 1970s.

One significant college experience was a summer spent in Japan living with a family through the Experiment in International Living. I won't attempt to summarize all I learned, but will share some highlights. I learned what it means to be stared at because one looks different. I recall arriving in Tokyo International Airport thinking that all the people there looked alike. Gradually my eyes adjusted and Asians became highly individual and differentiated, and I was the odd one people stared at. Eight weeks later when I arrived back in San Francisco, I found myself staring at all the white people who, for a few minutes, looked alike.

I recall feeling extremely frustrated, after about three weeks, by my inability to follow conversations in Japanese. At the same time, over the summer my Japanese sister and I learned to communicate on a deeper level than our respective English and Japanese language skills would suggest. We developed a close bond across our differences that included trust, empathy, and inside jokes. I also learned to act as a participant observer in a different cultural context. There was so much I didn't understand. I learned to follow what I saw others doing and to assume that things made sense in their own cultural context, even if I didn't understand the reasoning or the context. I was not in Japan long enough to learn Japanese culture in any depth, but did gain a sense of the degree to which practices that at first did not make sense to me (such as taking off shoes in the house) made good sense in their own context. In addition, I returned from Japan with some awe about having found and shared common ground that I would not have anticipated with Japanese peers. For example, we spent hours singing Japanese love songs, not the traditional Japanese music (such as "Sakura") that I would have expected, but sort of a Japanese equivalent to Peter, Paul and Mary. Singing, eating, and playing games provided surprisingly (I thought) effective bridges for connecting across wide cultural differences.

Race and Gender

I moved to Seattle in 1971, where I lived until 1978. The urban education program in which I enrolled (for the reasons that Seattle seemed like an interesting place to live, and teaching seemed like a good job for a woman) was field-based, and we were encouraged to live near the school to which we were assigned. Much of the central area and south end of Seattle was quite racially diverse, and it was here that I spent most of the next seven years. During that time, I gradually established quality relationships with people of color (mostly African American), but following a sequence that reflects my own racial and gender baggage: 1) adolescents of color, 2) men of color, and then finally 3) women of color.

White adults generally feel threatened by adults of color because we are aware of contradictions in the broader society that we would prefer to deny. On the one hand, most of us don't want to be prejudiced, thought of as racist, or disliked personally, and don't approve of overt expressions of racial prejudice. We want to view racism as solved and ourselves personally as good people, as "good whites." We also want confirming evidence from people of color that we are not racist, and many of us are afraid of saying something wrong that might undermine our "nonracist" self-perception. At the same time, we are aware that whites collectively are better off on many indices of social life than are people of color. Further, the great majority of us are doing little or nothing to change that. We may not have started racism personally, but aside from trying to be friendly and fair with individuals of color we may encounter, we aren't doing anything to change it. When forced to think about it, many of us are uncomfortable being white in a racially stratified society that espouses equality. When surrounded by only whites, we can ignore this contradiction; being around people of color causes us to focus on it, to at least some degree.

When I began to teach in the early 1970s, I could not verbalize these thoughts, but I felt them. The subsequent relationships I formed with people of color depended heavily on how I processed my own feelings about racism and my whiteness, and what strategies I was able to use to attempt to deflect attention from my privileges as a white person.

The student body of the high school in which in which I completed eight months of field-based social studies teacher education was about 1/3 Asian, 1/3 white, and 1/5 African American, with small numbers of Mexican American and Native American students. I immediately fell in love with the students. I quickly got to know their names, and volunteered to spend lunch hour supervising basketball in the gym; I don't play basketball, but an adult needed to be present if the kids were to play. The strategy I adopted to deflect attention from my whiteness was to be an interested, friendly authority-figure. I was genuinely interested in the students, this was not a "put-on." But it got me past the antagonistic relationships that white teachers often experience with students of color.

My cooperating teacher used fairly traditional methods of teaching, mainly lecture and textbook reading. When I started helping students do their assignments, it struck me that they approached work as a mechanical task of finding the right sentence in the text to copy in answer to questions. Not long into the year, my cooperating teacher asked me to do a lecture on feudalism in Europe. I spent much of the night preparing. The next day, trembling, I began. My teacher sensed I had things under control so he left. As I stood at the front of the room, I saw students' eyes glazing over with boredom. This was not a new reaction on their parts, but it was one I could not continue to cause. So I stopped the lecture and asked them what they would be interested in learning. They suggested various subjects, then converged on "Women's Liberation" (a hot topic in 1971). I had them brainstorm sub-topics on the board, then divided them into small groups, each with a sub-topic to investigate. Needless to say, my cooperating teacher was very surprised when he returned, although he allowed me to continue.

The students worked enthusiastically for the next two weeks, then either presented oral reports (one group organized a guest speaker) or turned in written reports. Their work academically was mixed in quality, but they were responsive and inquisitive; we were not bored. In the process, I got to know them fairly well. What did I learn about feminism? I learned that high school students found gender issues fascinating, that I could keep my own name if I married later, and that some of my favorite male students had very sexist notions about women. One, for example, argued vehemently that the Bible states that women were created for the pleasure of men.

Of far greater importance, however, I learned that inner-city students would usually respond well to me if I showed a genuine interest in them. Over the next few years, as a substitute teacher and then as a classroom teacher, I had plenty of opportunity to get to know many, many inner-city adolescents. With few exceptions, I was able to establish good relationships with them by showing interest in them. Part of my interest was displayed by listening to them talk about themselves and their concerns, so I also learned a good deal from these encounters. The main exceptions to this were occasional assertive girls of color (usually African American girls), who seemed not to have much use for me and who I then felt threatened by, for reasons I will discuss later. For example, I volunteered to help another teacher with a lesson about Indian mythology. In the process of teaching it, I mentioned my own Cherokee ancestry. A female Indian student blasted me after class, saying she was angered by white people who claim to be Indian and haven't a clue what issues contemporary Indian people are dealing with.

Years later I realized that, much as I cared about these kids, I had no notion of preparing them for college, had accepted low academic expectations of them, and had almost no academic content knowledge about anyone other than Euro-Americans. I could get the students to do what I wanted, but what I wanted them to do embodied racism. Since that time, however, whenever a teacher of inner-city kids complains that they are unmotivated, I always ask what the kids are interested in and suggest that the teacher begin there.

As a friendly authority figure, I learned to form positive relationships with students of color fairly quickly. At this point, I had not begun to critique racism—I was not even sure what racism meant—but was able to get past my own racial self-consciousness with students well enough to enjoy teaching them and to learn from them.

Gradually, I began to develop friendships with African American men, mostly teachers. When I first moved to Seattle, I took with me a fear of African American men talking of Black Power. However, through encounters with colleagues at work and in the community, I learned to get past that fear by being a "cute" and likeable woman. Being "cute" could mean flirting and dating (a refinement of the airhead persona I had perfected in college) or simply having enough self-confidence to carry on a good conversation. In retrospect, the main issue I was confronting was my own self confidence in interracial contexts. To the extent I thought I could get others to overlook my unprocessed racial baggage by finding me "cute" and attractive, I used this strategy. Looking back, there is a good deal in this strategy to criticize. However, in the process of using it, I made some good friends and learned much about racial issues.

The most significant relationship was with Mike (pseudonym), an African American educator. We started dating, then decided to live together. One of the first problems was confronting my family. Until this time, my work in the inner-city could be viewed as a phase of social work; now I was crossing the line of a strong social taboo. It took months before I leveled with my family. They gradually accepted the situation better than I had anticipated, although they periodically voiced concern that if we married, what would happen to the children? I was angry that skin color was introducing problems of family acceptance; if he were white or if color were not an issue, our relationship would be addressed very differently. I was also angry that, while my family couched their reservations in terms of my welfare, their difficulty with the relationship was one of the largest problems I was facing.

I first began to understand institutional racism in the context of housing. We decided to rent a house together and proceeded to look for one. Prior to this time, I had never spent more than a day looking for a place to live. After we spent about two weeks looking unsuccessfully, Mike finally told me that nobody was going to rent to a mixed couple, and he should look for a place alone. He also anticipated that it would take a while to find a place. I had no notion of housing discrimination; it took a while to sink in how prevalent it was. I was incensed that anyone should discriminate against someone based on race; Mike was used to it and patiently looked until he found a house to rent, which was in a racially mixed neighborhood. At first I did not comprehend that it was racial discrimination he was facing, but I had to take that interpretation seriously for lack of any other reasonable way of understanding the difficulty he experienced locating decent housing.

In his work, Mike spent much time advocating for African American students in a desegregated school. In evenings we would often debrief from the day, and he discussed difficulties African American kids were having with the school. I gradually began to identify with their viewpoint, especially as I also got to know some of the African American students in the neighborhood who were attending predominantly white schools. I learned to think of a predominantly white desegregated school as white turf, onto which a small number of African American students were admitted. Being on someone else's turf, they were constantly under surveillance, constantly viewed with veiled suspicion, and constantly questioned regarding their academic ability. This alone created a kind of pressure that I had never experienced.

After a period of time with Mike, I felt somewhat marginal to the white community, which sensitized me to social and geographic racial lines. After I was hired as a teacher, I mentioned Mike to only a few people, fearing not just social ostracism, but being fired. A couple of white friends I had known from college moved to the Seattle area; when going to visit them I was conscious of crossing a geographic color line into white turf, which I sensed they were not comfortable crossing to visit me. I also became aware of areas of the city and surrounding countryside where Mike felt comfortable going, and areas he avoided in order to avoid harassment. I had never been aware of the strength of these invisible racial lines before; white people in this country can go almost anywhere with impunity, but I came to realize that African American people cannot.

For a long time, I felt uncomfortable around most women and assertive girls of color. With a few exceptions, most African American women I met were fairly cool toward me. I sensed before I was ready to verbalize it, that by living with Mike, I was taking something from African American women. But also I was aware that I could not use the same strategies with women of color that I could use with men to deflect attention from my racism. I couldn't flirt. For that reason, I felt as though women of color saw through me, right to my unprocessed racial baggage. If I was a recipient of unearned racial privileges, I sensed that the women knew it and would not overlook those privileges because I was either a friendly authority figure or a cute woman. These fears gained credence every time a woman of color either became angry with me (as the Native American student mentioned earlier did), ignored me, or looked at me with what I interpreted as disdain.

It is important to acknowledge that this kind of fear is not so much fear of a woman of color per se, but rather of my own unacknowledged racism. White people would like to be passive nonracists: "good" whites who are not contributing to racism, but who also are not changing our own lives to try to dismantle it. This is a position that is impossible to take, however. Whites benefit from white supremacy every day, and to do nothing is to accept the benefits, even if we are not aware of them.

Becoming actively involved in working to dismantle racism will change a person's life. It will change one's relationships with other people, particularly other whites. It will change how one spends one's time and energy, where one chooses to live, who one chooses to associate with, the stands one takes on issues, and so forth. Remaining uninvolved means conferring tacit acceptance on the status quo. The more aware of racism a white person is, the more fear one feels of either being recognized as racist, or of stepping out into the unknown as one changes much about one's own life, such as refusing to live in a segregated neighborhood or speaking out against racist statements friends make. With women of color, I felt as though I had no defense mechanism to hide behind.

For reasons I do not as yet understand, I became gradually more and more involved with multicultural education. Before leaving Seattle, I had reached a point where I couldn't go back and was ready to accept the challenges and changes that come with confronting white racism. In the process I began slowly to address my own white racial privileges. I eventually developed bonds with several women of color who seemed to like me as a person and who would level with me periodically about racial and race/gender issues. One does not, however, finish working through the impact of race, gender, and social class on one's own life. As I write this chapter, I do not claim to have finished working through my white racism, only to have made a commitment to stick with the issue.

Whiteness, Gender, and the Politics of the Personal

In my own life, gender provided a terrain in which I experienced pain and rejection, and through which I gained some practice critiquing the social context of oppression. Not fitting the peer group's ideal image of a girl, I experienced marginalization and self-blame, then the use of coping strategies that affirmed and legitimated sexist images of women, and finally self-acceptance along with social and cultural analysis. Gender also provided a repertoire of strategies I later learned to use in order to present myself to men of color in a manner that enabled me to dialog with some level of trust and self confidence. While I don't condone flirting as a way of opening up interracial dialog, that strategy helped me deal with some of my own fears.

As white people become aware of racial differences in the distribution of society's resources, we can either attribute those differences to presumed deficiencies of groups of color (e.g., of their homes, neighborhoods, cultures), or to racism in the workings of society. To the degree that we question the first attribution, we need to take the second seriously, although doing so implicates ourselves in racism. This is a position most white people find very difficult to accept because it suggests that we should act differently and that our lives are built on undeserved privileges. The personal discomfort we experience engenders collective behavior that has political consequences.

The easiest escape for most whites is simply to avoid close contact with people of color, particularly contact that might not affirm the white person's desire to be perceived as a "good" and "nonracist" white person. It is simply easier to gravitate toward other white people who will not scrutinize our unprocessed racial baggage, because they carry the same baggage, or toward people of color who also will not question us. With other white people, we can either not discuss racial issues at all, or shape them in a way that feels comfortable to us. The "Human Relations" approach to multicultural education is probably the most popular, especially with white teachers, because it is the easiest approach to shape around differences with which one personally feels least threatened (Goodwin, 1994). It gives us a way to act as "good" whites while avoiding white supremacy. In my own early involvement in multicultural education, I defined the issues as "Human Relations:" multicultural education meant getting along, developing awareness of stereotyping, and adding lessons about minority role models and contributions.

We may be willing to interact with individuals of color who inhabit white-dominant spaces and who do not critique race relations, or cause us to question our own white privileges. We are much less likely to seek out those who discuss racial issues critically, or to cross the invisible spatial lines that delineate turf of the "Other." We fear confronting the huge contradiction between seeing ourselves as good and fair versus acknowledging racial inequalities and advantages we gain through accepting and partaking of white supremacy.

To the degree that interracial contact brings out this fear, we usually retreat. Even when whites hear people of color express frustration with general patterns of white behavior, we often take that frustration as personal criticism, and retreat. We call on other white people to defend our own self-images and our view of reality that describes race relations without critiquing. Research on white racial identity development identifies two different directions white people can take after experiencing "disintegration", or a strong challenge to their earlier acceptance of race relations as they are. One can either continue to learn or retreat (Helms, 1990). When we retreat, our own personal baggage becomes very political, because we close our ranks to protect ourselves and our collective privileges. We use our collective power to maintain a status quo, and exclusion to maintain comfort with it.

The personal life experiences provided grist for learning. I was on my own a good deal, however, to interpret those experiences and figure out what to do on the basis of my interpretations. Over a very long period of time I gradually developed trusting personal relationships with people that provided the security I needed to venture into examinations of racism. I took enough criticism over time and learned that even though it may hurt or upset me, the pain of criticism is not lethal and the message is usually enlightening. While such personal relationships are indispensable, I would not wish to place the future of race or gender relations on the idiosyncratic bumbling that I've described. Later chapters of this book will discuss potentials of planned and deliberate forms of intervention to educate people.

What about Capitalism?

The ideological milieu in which I spent most of my life has been one in which capitalism is assumed and not critiqued. A major purpose in life, this ideology holds, is to acquire as much material comfort as possible, stockpiling excess money if one can so that one's excess wealth generates income on its own. I was raised to participate actively in capitalism, and it did not occur to me to name or critique it until graduate school. Indeed, my college education was paid for largely by stock dividends.

As a child I internalized a powerful framework for understanding and upholding capitalism. I learned to divide human social and economic systems into three worlds: democratic, communist, and undeveloped (never mind that these are not parallel constructions, I learned them this way and so have many of my students). I learned the following understanding of each. Democratic systems are best (most developed, most egalitarian, fairest, and most open) and are by nature capitalist. The only modern alternative is communism, which is totalitarian, imperialistic, and the enemy of freedom and democracy. To take communism or any variant of it seriously is to be unpatriotic. Undeveloped (Third World) countries may be neither democratic nor communist, but their poverty is a result of their lack of modern development. Systems existing prior to the development of capitalism were also undeveloped, and as such, not worth examining as potentially desirable models.

During the time of the "Cold War" the binary opposition of democracy versus communism was commonly used in everyday parlance to draw a distinction between "good guys" and "bad guys." The possibility that there might yet be other systems, that the economic system of the Soviet Union might be but one version of communism, that Third World poverty resulted from capitalist expansion, or that capitalism may aggravate rather than remedy economic disparities, was not discussed at all. The images above were simply taken as natural givens. I took them for granted and students I teach often do also.

It was not until I was a graduate student that I encountered any open critique of capitalism as an economic system, and I did not initially seek out this critique. I stumbled into it, having chosen a graduate school for its varied opportunities open to graduate students rather than the neo-Marxist orientation of some faculty. I still struggle with how to critique capitalism when I participate in it everyday. For example, my savings and retirement plans are based on investment portfolios chosen by the bank and the retirement systems in which I participate. Most Americans measure the success of any savings system by the interest or dividends accrued (the so-called bottom line), not by the social values embraced by companies in which money might be invested. Periodically I investigate social policies of companies in which I have some money invested (such as child care provisions and health care to employees), and if I know a company is part of a large multinational corporation, I withdraw funds. Yet I hesitate to investigate my bank, health insurance, and retirement company because I need these services to protect myself. I am a racist and I am also a capitalist because I benefit from racism and from capitalism. Yet I am also a critic of both systems, which produces a discomfort I live with.

Connecting white supremacy with capitalist expansion came even later for me, largely because discussions of racism are usually disconnected from analyses of the economic system. But this is an essential connection to recognize because it questions the idea that we can eliminate racism (or sexism) without also addressing issues of material accumulation and competition for scarce positions in a highly stratified world society. In complex ways, many of those fruits depend on exploitation of Third World people, immigrants, domestic workers, and the natural environment.

Capitalism has given people of European descent an identity and mode of living that we must critique and dismantle: whiteness.

Whiteness has come to mean ravenous materialism, competitive individualism, and a way of living characterized by putting acquisition of possessions above humanity. One need not be of European descent to participate in such a way of living. Nor do all people of European descent accept white supremacy and ravenous materialism. But it is a way of living that people of European descent constructed and sell, and one that we are persistently socialized to identify with and support. Whiteness—belief in the superiority of people of European descent coupled with the quest for gold—led to the European conquest of America and the institutionalization of American slavery. Whiteness today means consolidating economic resources in suburban enclaves, destroying indigenous knowledges and languages around the world, and teaching young people to value the "bottom line"—profit—above all else.

Implications

The processes described in this essay are not inevitable. One factor that was conspicuously missing in my own experience, although not absent entirely, was sustained instruction about racism, materialism, and competitive individualism in a context of interracial dialog and sustained instruction about patriarchy in a context of cross-sex dialog. Short workshops provided me with insights, but did not force me to stick with difficult issues. Workshops also do not allow for the development of trusting personal relationships that support risk-taking. For example, I participated in a week-long racial awareness training session the Seattle school district sponsored for teachers. It was conducted by a multiracial training team. The white trainer became very frustrated with our persistent externalizing of the issues (for example, discussing the reluctance of textbook publishers to change rather than our own resistance to change). Since the training was predicated on the assumption that we had no awareness of racial issues, and I was not starting at the very beginning, although I was also externalizing I was able to view myself as one of the "good" whites. The context of the one-week training session was not one in which I could process my own thinking in a trusting environment and then be pushed to grapple with painful issues while being supported through the process by someone who believed in me. When the training session was over, I remember noticing for the first time that greeting cards in local stores all featured white people—not an entirely worthless observation, but not a very pro-found one either.

Another process that, while not entirely absent, was in short supply in my experience was collaborative interracial and/or cross-sex work on political or cultural change issues. We need to learn not just to talk with each other, trust others, and accept ourselves, but also to engage in the work that will dismantle white supremacy, patriarchy, and poverty. Integrated action groups can engage in a great deal of personal processing in the context of developing collaborative strategies for making change. Childs (1993) discussed the value of "trans-communal cadres" which "bring together people from different groups to work on common issues." He argued that, "It is the shared experience of the process itself, rather than a prepositioned group location (e.g., ethnicity, race) that creates . . . collective identities and allegiances" (p. 48) and develops bridges across diverse communities.

Building bridges requires learning to construct positive self-identities that break with, rather than embody, social relations of oppression. As a white woman, this means learning a positive self-identity as an intelligent sexual being. It also means constructing a positive Euro-American identity that does not reproduce whiteness as discussed above. To break with whiteness, I must first distinguish between being a person of European ancestry and one who identifies as "white." My own European ancestry is sufficiently mixed that I do not identify with any particular ethnic community. I do, however, take some pride in contributions my ancestors made toward humanity, such as developments in medicine and creations of music and art. I am trying to develop a way of life that is sustainable, not dependent on acquisition of excess resources and power over other, and that is built on relations of mutuality with and respect for the rest of humanity.

Chapters that follow explore the issues of formal education and bridge-building in more detail. After examining political perspectives about diversity and inequality in chapter 3, I return to the question of how white teachers frame multicultural education from the vantage point of their own life histories in chapter 4. Multicultural education is not simply an academic issue, yet academic settings can be helpful sites for learning. In chapters 6 and 7 I examine possibilities as well as limitations of formal education for extending how white educators think about multicultural issues, drawing on my own experience as an educator. I will argue that as educators, we can help our students develop insights, pose questions, and locate and hear answers better than they did before working with us; but we are doing so in the context of lived experience, dominant modes of interpreting that experience, and vested interests. This does not by any means render our efforts as useless, but does temper the degree to which we can claim to "fix" social problems through enlightenment.

CHAPTER 3

Political Perspectives
about Difference and Inequality

In *The Immigrant*, Howard Fast (1977) wrote of his main character, Dan Lavette:

> He was 40 years old, and if anyone ever had, he had surely dreamed the American dream. . . . He had come out of nothing, and he had made himself a king, a veritable emperor. He ruled a fleet of great passenger liners, an airline, a majestic department store, a splendid resort hotel, property, land, and he dispensed the food of life to hundreds of men and women who labored at his will. . . . It was of his own making and his own doing that he controlled twenty million dollars of property. (p. 252)

For generations, Americans—particularly white Americans—have grown up believing that, with work, we can achieve whatever we want. Dan Lavette's success epitomizes the dream of millions, and while very few achieve it in such grandiose fashion, most Americans strive to attain some version of it. In his exploration of work life, Studs Terkel (1980) found many people, such as the following company president, to believe that U.S. society offers unlimited opportunities for individual striving:

> The American Dream is to be better off than you are. How much money is "enough money?" "Enough money" is always a little bit more than you have. There's never enough of anything. This is why people go on. If there was enough, everybody would stop. You always go for the brass ring that's always out there about a hundred yards farther. It's like a mirage in the desert; it always stays about a hundred yards ahead of you. (p. 38)

Most Americans are optimistic about their own prospects for getting ahead, and as chapter 4 will illustrate, we integrate our understanding of multicultural education into our own beliefs about the workings of society. James Kluegel and Eliot Smith (1986) summarized their findings of interviews with 2,212 Americans as follows:

> A clear majority of the American population subscribes, largely unreservedly, to the characterization of America as the land of opportunity. . . . On the one hand, Americans do express some doubts about equality of opportunity. . . . On the other hand, Americans express little doubt about their chances as individuals to make economic advancement. On the whole, they believe that no limits have or will impede their opportunity to make the most of themselves. The American public expects to have work careers characterized by steady advancement. The average American considers him or herself 'better than average' in terms of his or her prospects to get ahead. (p. 52)

How open is the social system to individual or group advancement? How do we explain the many obvious forms of inequality we see around us, such as rich and poor neighborhoods in our communities, unequal educational outcomes, or unequal earnings? By the time we become adults, we hold well-ingrained beliefs about the social system, human nature, and the character of various sociocultural groups, based on our own life experience as well as the ideology we have learned to use to interpret that experience. Usually, however, these beliefs are so taken for granted that we do not recognize them as beliefs, nor do we see the constraints they place on our interpretation of the world; rather, we regard such beliefs as "truth." Janice Peck (1994) explains:

> The power of discourses resides in their ability to impose these constraints and win participants' consent to abide by them. Power relations are enacted *within* discourse via these constraints, and are exhibited in struggles for control *over* discourse as a "mechanism of sustaining power" (Fairclough, 1989, p. 73–74). When a discourse has achieved such social dominance that these constraints are nearly invisible (as is the case with the Western discourse of "the individual"), it attains the status of "common sense" and "will come to be seen as *natural* and legitimate because it is simply *the* way of conducting oneself." (p. 91)

How multicultural education is framed depends on the political perspective in which it is understood.

In this chapter I examine three perspectives that may be used to interpret inequality: conservatism, liberalism, and radical structuralism; implications of post-structuralism are also discussed. I will then locate multicultural education in the increasingly conservative political climate of the 1980s and 1990s, suggesting how the field is interpreted, criticized, and reinterpreted within that climate. In chapter 4 I examine how several teachers situated multicultural education within their own political assumptions, largely either conservatism or liberalism.

Conservatism and liberalism dominate the American ideological landscape and are often viewed as the only competing alternatives that have legitimacy. Although conservatism and liberalism differ, in some fundamental respects they share common assumptions—assumptions that have attained the power of being accepted as "natural" by most Americans.

Conservatism and Liberalism

Most citizens of the United States and other Western capitalist countries share a core of beliefs that Michael Parenti (1978) termed 'Lockean ideology' (p. 43), key elements of which are individualism and civic rights. As John Locke conceptualized the ideal state of nature,

> First, it is a 'state of perfect freedom', in which men do as they choose within the limits imposed by the law of nature. Second, it is a state of equality for its inhabitants. No one has any more right, authority, or jurisdiction than does anyone else. Men are born equal in this way—not equal in capacity but equal in the rights they possess. (Harmon, 1964, pp. 246–7)

In the best possible world, individuals are free to pursue their desires and compete against one another in an open marketplace for self-advancement.

By nature, people differ, so what they attain also differs. Therefore, while rights should be equal, attainments are not. A class system results naturally from the differing abilities and strivings of a wide range of individuals, but that system should allow for individuals to move up or down. Most Americans interpret a capitalist economy as facilitating individual striving in a free market, allowing individuals to rise or fall according to their own effort. As Parenti (1978) put it, "The center (liberalism) and right (conservatism) share a common commitment to the capitalist system and the ongoing class structure and institutional hierarchy" (p. 48).

Because their unregulated striving would lead to a state of war, it is in people's best interests to establish consensus regarding laws that regulate their exercise of individual rights. When it is functioning properly, the larger society is viewed as a self-regulatory system in which individuals share consensus on its governing rules and everyone is able to attain a fair degree of happiness in accordance with his or her effort and abilities. This idea is basic to structural functionalism, a theoretical perspective conservatism and liberalism share.

> The structural functionalist is preoccupied with social integration based on shared values—that is with consensus—and he (she) conducts his (her) analysis solely in terms of the motivated actions of individuals. For him (her), therefore, education is a means of motivating individuals to behave in ways appropriate to maintain the society in a state of equilibrium. (Floud & Halsey, 1958, p. 171)

Education presumably promotes social cohesion and consensus and prepares young people to fill society's varied roles. Generally the roles themselves are not questioned; questions arise around the efficiency with which education systems prepare the young to fill these roles.

Americans who adhere to the 'Lockean ideology' divide into conservatives or liberals based on their view of human nature, their explanations for inequality, and their belief in the legitimacy of collective claims against the workings of the political economy.

Conservatism

From a conservative perspective, the good society places as few restrictions as necessary on individuals. All individuals, except those who are unfit (such as criminals or mentally ill people), should have an equal opportunity to compete against each other. Government should restrict individual competition minimally, but private institutions such as the family, the church, and various private associations should "instill a sense of personal discipline, courage, and motivation" into people and curb or control "the mistakes that people make" (Hoover, 1987, p. 33). Humans by nature are viewed as flawed and subject to immoral temptations, which are regulated best by institutions that preserve tradition, which in turn are best controlled by "good people: by the natural aristocracy of talent, breeding, and, very likely, wealth" (p. 34).

The purpose of schools is to "instill the traditional wisdom of the society" (Hoover, p. 34) and to foster social cohesion. Schools should develop character and morality, as well as identify the social roles for which various children are best suited and prepare them accordingly.

> As the high road to social mobility, [schools] sustain equality of opportunity. As sharpeners of the mind, they prepare rising generations for the responsibilities of citizenship. As purveyors of cultural understanding and technical skill, they further assimilation, national community, and the increase of the country's productive resources. As instruments for the discovery of new knowledge, they bolster expectations of material progress and ratify popular confidence in the powers of reason and science. (Balch, 1992, p. 21)

Tradition and reason define what count as culture and knowledge. From a conservative perspective, these are determined rationally rather than politically.

Conservatives regard inequality in school achievement and in attainment in the broader society as resulting largely from individual differences in natural endowment and effort. The sociobiology explanation for inequality traces differences in roles and attainments to biological endowment. Biological determinism has lost some legitimacy for explaining racial and social class differences in attainment, although the 1990s are seeing a resurgence of popular acceptance of this perspective. And it is still widely used to explain sex differences and sexual orientation, by construing sex "as a property of individuals. It may reside in their hormones or their psyches" (Rubin, 1993, p. 9).

The culturalist explanation for inequality holds that "the character and contents of Afro-American [or other] culture inhibits Black people [or other low-status groups] from competing with other people in American society" (West, 1987, p. 76). The habits, values, language, and lifestyles of people who are poor or people in inner cities, for example, are perceived as inferior or dysfunctional to life in a technological society. This problem can be corrected by replacing the culture of a "disadvantaged" group with one more suited for successful competition in public institutions, a task schools should perform. However, state intervention to remediate effects of "cultural deprivation" should be minimal so as not to reduce individual initiative.

Natural inequality rooted in genetics or culture may be exacerbated by discriminatory behavior of biased individuals. The prejudice explanation for inequality looks to interpersonal discrimination on the basis of prejudices and stereotypes. This dysfunction of the social system can be corrected by modifying people's prejudices to make them more inclusive and less stereotypic, which conservatives believe is an effective solution since irrational prejudices are inefficient and interfere with one's ability to capitalize on an open market. If people learn to interact with others as individuals based on personal characteristics they actually exhibit, society will work fairly and the market will operate smoothly.

Conservative interpretations of multicultural education might support the following. One would eschew critiques of society, favoring portrayals that highlight America's successes and greatness. One would seek strategies to reduce cultural differences, favoring school programs that steep youngsters in the "best" of traditional Western culture. In order to minimize prejudices and biases, schools might teach about similarities across difference, and positive contributions of diverse groups. One would champion individuality much more so than collective identities, however. Research oriented toward "diversity" might seek to establish biological differences that correlate with achievement differences (such as sex differences). Conservative interpretations would also evaluate various compensatory programs oriented toward enriching the knowledge base of culturally "disadvantaged" children, supporting only those that are low-cost and that seem to successfully assimilate the "culturally different." Further, color-conscious policies would be viewed as counterproductive in reaching the goal of a colorblind society, conservatives assuming that colorblindness is both possible and desirable. Conservative articulations of multicultural education will be returned to later in this chapter.

Liberalism

Liberalism shares conservatism's emphasis on establishing conditions for competition among individuals for mobility. However, it diverges from conservatism in its optimism about human nature. Liberals place more emphasis on rationality than do conservatives and are less concerned about rationality being undermined by genetic differences in capacity or moral depravity. As a result, liberals tend to reject sociobiological explanations for inequality and the concept of a "natural aristocracy".

One can identify two strands of liberalism: classical and reformist. Classical liberalism (emphasizing individualism regulated by the marketplace and only minimally by government) has one great flaw: to celebrate individualism is to accept extremes of economic inequality that leave some people far ahead of others in even the most basic prerequisites for a decent life. (Hoover, 1987, p. 63)

Contemporary liberal thinking is more reformist than classical. Reform liberals champion individualism but have some sympathy with claims that social institutions do not work fairly for some groups; they therefore support a limited degree of state intervention on behalf of such groups. For example, Alison Jaggar (1983) explained that,

> Liberal feminists believe that the treatment of women in contemporary society violates, in one way or another, all of liberalism's political values, the values of equality, liberty, and justice. Their most frequent complaint is that women in contemporary society suffer discrimination on the basis of sex. By this, they mean that certain restrictions are placed on women as a group, without regard to their individual wishes, interests, abilities or merits. (pp. 175–6)

Championing both collective claims and individual rights leads to contradictory beliefs. "On one hand, the 'problem' is framed as unequal rights among different social groups; on the other, the problem is identified as violating *individual* rights by locating people within, or identifying oneself with, those groups." (Peck, 1994, p. 100)

Interventions that reform liberals support reflect this belief in both individual rights and group claims. Like conservatives, they support state interventions that attempt to ensure that people will be treated as individuals without regard to group membership, and they support freedom of individual expression, even when the ideas expressed are racist or homophobic (Peck, 1994). But reform liberals also support state interventions such as affirmative action, which attempt to remediate effects of past discrimination, believing that at some point in the future they will no longer be needed and individuals will be able to compete as equals. "Reform liberals do not set out to abolish the marketplace, but rather to use governmental power to remedy the inequalities of opportunity that it produces" (Hoover, 1987, p. 62). Ultimately, they believe that cultural, attitudinal, and institutional dysfunctions that block the strivings of individuals can be corrected.

Reform liberals tend to follow two lines of thought in analyzing inequality related to schooling. One line is to examine and correct institutional biases in schools. For example, mainstreaming, followed by the Regular Education Initiative, has been premised on the belief that children with disabilities will gain more from school if unnecessary barriers to their integration with mainstream children are removed. Much of the research on gender equity focuses on biases in treatment of girls and boys in school (e.g., how teachers interact with students) or on gender differences in students' behavior and interests. Recommendations then outline strategies for gender equity in the classroom (e.g., Grossman & Grossman, 1994). The assumption is that biases within the institution of the school are significant enough to warrant correction *and* that doing so will solve equity problems.

The other line of thought is to examine the cultures children bring with them and to develop adaptations to the school culture so that teaching processes within the school build on children's strengths. Much of the research on learning styles and second language learning follows this line of thinking. Again, the assumption is that if the culture of the school builds on cultural strengths of children, achievement problems will be remedied. Reform liberals generally do not contextualize schools within broader institutional power relations, which is what radical structuralists do.

Before moving to radical structuralism, I should note that radical structuralists generally agree that the issues identified by reform liberals are important and generally support the teaching strategies liberals champion. However, radical structuralists view a focus on the classroom or school, disconnected from its social context, as myopic and argue that changing what takes place in classrooms will have only limited impact without concurrent changes in the larger context. The narrow range of possibilities within which liberals construct analyses of social problems serves the purpose of legitimating the social order by offering the illusion of significant activity, when in fact liberals do not entertain solutions that would radically alter the status quo. James Scheurich (1994) provides an example in his analysis of liberal policy discussions of the school failure of poor children of color. By constructing the children and their immediate environments as the problem rather than directing criticism toward white supremacy, male supremacy, capitalism, governmentalism, and professionalism, liberal policy analysts offer woefully inadequate solutions that relieve the dominant society from implication and that discipline the behavior of mainstream society by providing images of how not to behave.

Radical Structuralism

Radical structuralists contextualize human behavior within larger social structural relationships. Radical structuralists share a sense of optimism for cooperation and collective living that they believe is thwarted by individualism, competition, and rampant materialism (Hoover, 1987, pp. 83–4). The good life should be found in a synthesis of the welfare of individuals with that of collectives. Justice, liberty, and equality, which are fundamental to the American dream that both conservatives and liberals champion, ought to characterize the lives of all people, prevail across groups, and include material conditions and political power.

These "oughts" diverge from what "is," however. To understand contemporary life, it must be situated historically in struggles over power and wealth. Radical structuralists reject the individual as the main unit of analysis and focus on relations among groups, although they diverge in their perspectives regarding the relative importance of various forms of difference. Race, social class, gender, language, disability, and sexual orientation are each viewed by some theorists as *the* most significant difference around which people organize, while other theorists (particularly women of color) focus on multiple forms (Allsup, 1995).

Radical structuralists characterize society as involving continuous struggle for power among competing groups: "There is no ultimately good society, only a continual struggle to overcome specific obstacles to human fulfillment as these become apparent" (Jaggar, 1983, p. 208). Inequality across groups is more significant than inequality among individuals and results from collective conflict over power and wealth much more than from natural endowment or culture. It is human nature to protect vested interests, and the more resources groups have, the more they channel into maintaining and expanding their power. Human action is not entirely rational or individual, but rather is determined partially by location within systems of power. Radical structuralism interrogates systems of power "which reward and encourage some individuals and activities, while punishing and suppressing others" (Rubin, 1993, p. 34). As Martin Carnoy (1989) explained,

> The struggle of dominated groups to change the conditions that oppress them and the attempts of dominant groups to reproduce the conditions of their dominance are the key to understanding changes in the economy, in social relations, and in the culture. These changes, in turn, are reflected in state policies and in public schooling, both prime targets of conflict. (p. 6–7)

Radical structuralists argue that the ideology of individual advancement and individual rights obscures group conflict.

For example, in his analysis of modern social movements, Carl Boggs (1986) remarked that liberalism and the spirit of the American dream "depended in great measure upon a self-regulating market, abundant territorial space and natural resources, dynamic community life, and later, prospects for seemingly endless material growth" (p. 6). These conditions were never present for many people. But even for white middle class people,

> By the 1960s, . . . none of these conditions prevailed any longer, with the result that liberalism was finally transformed into a ritualized belief system barely masking a highly centralized and expansionist corporate system. In economic terms liberalism failed to generate any new priorities that could encourage a shift away from outmoded patterns of production, work, and consumption. (p. 6)

Because those in power have a vested interest in protecting that collective power, inequality cannot be addressed effectively through solutions that focus on altering chances for individuals.

Most social organizations, particularly the corporate world and the state, are structured primarily by groups with the most power and operate to their benefit. Unlike liberals, therefore, radical structuralists believe that the state cannot be relied upon to serve the interests of oppressed groups, since it operates primarily as an arm of corporate wealth (Parenti, 1988). Oppressed groups themselves must mobilize to challenge and restructure specific institutions that thwart their own interests. A problem, however, with much radical scholarship is that it lacks a notion of agency: by focusing on how dominant groups maintain relations of dominance, much of it says too little about how people resist oppression and bring about change. We must focus, then, on how "oppositional cultures might provide the basis for a viable political force" (Giroux, 1983, p. 101).

To be more specific, a radical structuralist analysis of racism interrogates white supremacy, examines how white people use our power to protect our privileges, and directly challenges white supremacy. A radical structuralist analysis of sexism interrogates male supremacy as well as the power of heterosexuals to silence alternative sexual identities and relationships. A radical structuralist analysis of social class critiques the distribution of wealth and the use wealthy people make of power to protect their class status. Rather than "haves" critiquing the behavior of "have nots," which is the direction of criticism and power exercised by conservatives, radical structuralists critique from the "bottom up." They critically examine the collective behavior of "haves" for the purpose of changing have/have not relationships. Those who are relatively advantaged under the status quo find such work threatening and generally resist it tenaciously. For example, as Scheurich (1994) noted, "it could reasonably be argued that overwhelmingly white suburban schools (substantially born of white flight from people of color) are training grounds for white supremacy" (p 308). This perspective would lead toward a radical structural analysis. Rather than problematizing white behavior, however, white people generally problematize the behavior of people of color. In chapters 6 and 7 I will address the question of teaching radical structuralist analyses to "haves," and in chapter 11 I will discuss social change as requiring community-based political work.

Many radical structuralists view education as crucial to the process of social change, since through education young people can learn to examine social relations and act collectively to create a more just social system. However, as a state-controlled institution, education is controlled by dominant social groups. Most radical structural scholarship in education has examined how power and control are reproduced in education. While such examinations are essential, they are insufficient since they typically offer little help in understanding how to challenge power relations.

This brings us to a fundamental question within which multicultural education is situated: How can educators act in a way that actually furthers social justice? As a field, multicultural education has tended to be action-oriented in that much of its literature is prescriptive. Multicultural education attempts to frame and advocate what educators can do. While theorists in the field are generally well aware of systemic oppression (especially racism), much of the literature in the field is naively prescriptive, offering suggestions for practice that decontextualize schools from larger structures of power relations. This is why many radical educators find the field wanting. As Lilia Bartolome (1994) put it,

> One of my greatest challenges throughout the years has been to help students to understand that a myopic focus on methodology often serves to obfuscate the real question—which is why in our society, subordinated students do not generally succeed academically in schools. In fact, schools often reproduce the existing asymmetrical power relations among cultural groups. (p. 176)

Later chapters in this book take up Bartolome's question.

Radical Structuralism and the
Challenge of Poststructuralism

Like many others (such as Lather, 1991, and McLaren, 1994), I find myself ambivalent about the growing popularity of poststructuralism and postmodernism (some writers differentiate these, others conflate them). "Postmodernisms are responses across the disciplines to the contemporary crisis of representation, the profound uncertainty about what constitutes an adequate depiction of social 'reality'" (Lather, p. 21). Questions postmodernists and poststructuralists grapple with include: How have electronic media changed and enabled the manipulation of our notions of "reality"? How is desire mobilized in the interests of power, and what implications does an analysis of desire have for previously-assumed rational action? How can individuals be understood as multi-sited rather than unified selves? As subjects rather than objects? How can we understand structures of oppression, given multiple forms and vectors of oppression (such as race, gender, sexual orientation), and the complex and contradictory ways in which these play out in everyday life? Given this complexity, where does power come from and how does it operate? Given the social construction of knowledge, how can we be sure of anything? These issues have many connections with multicultural education, although poststructuralists and multiculturalists give each other "only the most cursory nod of recognition" (Perez-Torres, 1994, p. 161).

While I grant these to be important questions, my hesitation echoes that articulated by Nancy Hartsock:

> Somehow it seems highly suspicious that it is at the precise moment when so many groups have been engaged in "nationalisms" which involve redefinitions of the marginalized others that suspicions emerge about the nature of the 'subject,' about the possibilities for a general theory which can describe the work, about historical progress. (cited by Nicholson, 1990, p. 9)

Does poststructuralism (or postmodernism) serve as a terrain on which white men can control and dominate critiques from the margins? Sometimes (although not always) when I turn down the volume and just watch the picture (i.e., observe how people interact and position themselves), I see the same traditional power relations being acted out. Yet at the same time, poststructuralism offers important analytic tools which I use in my own work.

Drawing on work by Teresa Ebert (1991), Peter McLaren (1994) distinguished between ludic and resistance (critical) postmodernism in an effort to retain insights of radical structuralism while also making use of insights of poststructuralism. (Perez-Torres [1994] made the same distinction between what he called neoconservative and culturally resistant postmodernism.) Ludic (neoconservative) postmodernists focus primarily on the endless variety of difference, the end of grand narratives, the fragmentation of texts, and the dispersal of power. There are no social structures or subjects, and structural analyses of oppression constitute grand narratives that have no validity. Difference is catapulted forward as the primary way of discussing social relations. I recall a colleague laughingly referring to his office as very postmodern because the colors, shapes, and contents formed a lively pastiche that had little apparent order. Ludic postmodernism "often simply reinscribes the status quo and reduces history to the supplementarity of signification or the free-floating trace of textuality" (McLaren, p. 198). In a fascinating analysis of how corporate America has seized ludic postmodernism, Henry Giroux (1993–4) critiqued Benetton's advertising campaign: "Difference in this sense poses the postmodern problem of maintaining the particularity of diverse groups while simultaneously unifying such differences within Benetton's concept of a 'world without borders'" (p. 18). Ludic postmodernism plays itself out in multicultural identity politics in which representation of differences triumphs over political organizing, and historical analyses of the contexts of contemporary social issues are minimal.

Resistance postmodernism, on the other hand, does not jettison insights of radical structuralism and historic analysis, but rather seeks to deepen our understanding of complexities of difference within relations of oppression. One cannot reduce relations of oppression to class, race, or gender, nor can one simply add these in a linear, additive fashion. On the micro-level, all of us participate in complex, crisscrossing relations of difference and define ourselves accordingly. At the same time, however, power and wealth *are* distributed very unequally across collectives. As Judith Butler (1992) argued, poststructuralist analyses question universals in terms of who defines them, for what purpose and what a given universal authorizes as well as excludes. But such analyses need not destroy agency or political work. "To call a presupposition into question is not the same as doing away with it; rather it is to free it up from its metaphysical lodgings in order to occupy and serve very different political aims" (p. 17).

Poststructuralist analyses can open up political debates around socially constructed ideas that are commonly viewed as natural givens. For example, in his development of "policy archaeology," a process for analyzing public policy, Scheurich (1994) argued that poststructuralism directs us toward analyzing how some problems and not others emerge in the public discourse as "problems," and how such "problems" and the range of socially acceptable "solutions" emerge from a larger grid of social regularities most people take for granted as natural. The grid itself may be very complex, comprising relations of race, social class, gender, and other regularized relationships, and is itself historically situated and not immutable. Thus, any analysis of a social issue must account for the ways that issue becomes articulated and acted upon at a given point in time, by a complex range of social actors who themselves are situated in particular contexts. Poststructuralism of this sort warns us not to replace one grand narrative with another, to recognize and tease out the nonsynchronous and multiple positions all of us hold, and to engage in "continuous critical negotiation" (Perez-Torres, 1994, p. 185) without erasing subjects, histories, and political engagement.

Most teachers, however, are never exposed to either radical structuralism or poststructuralism. Most Americans find themselves choosing between conservative and liberalism, the choice having been driven to the right through the 1980s and 1990s by the rise of conservatism.

The Rise of Conservatism in the 1980s and 1990s

By the 1980s many Americans were skeptical of their ability or that of their children to achieve upward mobility. Terkel listened to people describing their concerns and fears:

> The American Way, to me, has been one of chasing the dollar. You hear a labor leader say: "What's good for the company is good for us, because if they make a profit, we get more wages." That's bullshit. US Steel is making more profit. We're sure as hell not making more wages. . . . Buying a piece of land has always been the American Dream. Owning your own home. A kid, starting out today, it's beyond him. (1980, pp. 240–1)

> I think Reagan made it very accepted to be a white bigot. It's the most fashionable thing. Now they say: America is white. America isn't single women on welfare. Why should us taxpayers support these people who ride on our backs and bring this country down? I'm afraid of what's gonna happen to blacks in this country. There

are a fortunate few who will get over. But for the many, no way. . . .
The dividing line is becoming clear and the bitterness is growing.
You can't help but wonder why. (1988, pp. 67–8)

During the late 1970s and 1980s, U.S. citizens "experienced defeat in
war, the . . . resignation of a President, an inflationary peak of 22
percent, peacetime shortages of oil and gas, and the fall of Keyne-
sianism and the political alignment which it sustained" (Omi &
Winant, 1986, p. 137). As people experienced cutbacks and loss of
opportunity at the individual level, they were increasingly offered a
conservative portrait of the U.S. and problems.

The dominant discourse of the 1980s and early 1990s has been
conservatism, in contrast to the liberal discourse of the early 1970s.
Teachers do not have to read professional journals to encounter it,
although it is certainly prevalent there; all they must do is pick up the
newspaper or turn on their television sets. And while many people do
not accept the dominant discourse, they must search harder to find
alternative definitions of the state of the nation and of education.

Throughout the 1980s and 1990s, the media focused on three
related sets of "problems": eroding U.S. international hegemony and
domestic lifestyles, growing diversity of the U.S. population, and
declining morals among the U.S. population. Through the 1980s the
media proclaimed that the United States was falling behind other
countries in the international battles that Ira Shor (1986) termed the
"Trade War and Cold War" (p. 119), and that much of its loss was
due to schools. Many commentators emphasized the need for action
in order to retain international supremacy in not just trade and
influence, but also living standard. For example, an article in *Science*
magazine explained that, "The proper test of competitiveness, then,
is not simply the ability of a country to balance its trade, but its
ability to do so while achieving an acceptable rate of improvement in
its standard of living" (Hatsopoulos, Krugman and Summers, 1988,
p. 299). Further, commentators affirmed that "The United States
retains the highest standard of living of major nations" and that it
"should be able to maintain a living standard at least as high as
that of other advanced countries" (p. 299). U.S. citizens have long
regarded ourselves as superior to the rest of the world, with presumed moral and technological superiority justifying our wealth.
The conservative discourse of the 1980s and 1990s appealed to that
sense of superiority and our desire to remain "Number One."

This loss in international status and living standard is ascribed
to a variety of causes. Americans are told that "our society itself has

become uncompetitive" (Lamm, 1988, p. 9). Too many resources have been diverted in the wrong direction: "The U.S. spends almost 12 percent of the gross national product on health care—far more than any of our international competitors" (p. 9). Conservatives frame the health care crisis of the 1990s as a need to control costs much more so than as a crisis in distribution of health care. Conservatives also attribute loss of international trade supremacy to the overpay of American laborers, and corporations have moved thousands of jobs out of the country to cut labor costs. Eroding living standards are attributed to a variety of factors that include loss of family values, illegal immigrants and welfare mothers draining resources, and laxity on crime.

Further, "schools today [are] not preparing kids for jobs, they aren't even teaching them to read and write" (Perry, 1988, p. 70). Beginning with *A Nation at Risk* in 1983, a spate of education reform reports elaborated on the "rising tide of mediocrity" presumed to be spreading from the schools to the rest of society. In order to ensure that American citizens would be able to continue to pursue their dreams, international supremacy must be restored. School reform should play a role in accomplishing that, but on reduced budgets. As taxpayers saw their own earnings erode, they increasingly turned their frustrations toward schools and portrayed teachers and administrators as "fat."

A second "problem" U.S. citizens are told about is the growing diversity of its population. For example, a special issue of *Time* magazine (11 July 1988) placed actor Edward James Olmos's picture on the cover, under the caption "Magnifico! Hispanic culture breaks out of the barrio." Readers of *Time* magazine in April 1990 were told about problems confronting America as it moves "Beyond the melting pot;" the main problem would be learning to "maintain a distinct national identity" that builds on commonalities while embracing ethnic diversity (Henry, 1990, pp. 28–9). Generally diversity has been characterized as a growing problem that requires containment. Television airwaves conveyed images, for example, of uncontrollable hordes of Mexicans invading the southern border of the U.S. to steal jobs and other economic resources, "fanatic" Arabs terrorizing U.S. citizens, and impoverished Haitians attempting to bring their poverty as well as AIDS into the U.S. (Martinez, 1993). When Los Angeles erupted in 1992 in the wake of the verdict in the trial of white officers who beat Rodney King, riots were characterized as random expressions of ethnic hate.

Such media discussions of race and immigration usually frame Asians as the "model minority".

> In recent years, articles have proliferated in news magazines and
> Sunday supplements, proclaiming that Asians are "Outwhiting the
> whites," explaining "Why Asians Are Going to the Head of the
> Class," and touting "The Triumph of Asian Americans." (Suzuki,
> 1989, p. 13)

The reason attributed to the supposed success of Asians is their
embracing of traditional American culture and values:

> "It's no wonder," Reagan emphatically noted, "that the median
> incomes of Asian and Pacific American families are much higher
> than the total American average." Hailing Asian and Pacific Amer-
> icans as examples for all Americans, Reagan conveyed his grati-
> tude to them: We need "your values, your hard work" expressed
> within "our political system." (Takaki, 1989, p. 10)

Many Americans agree, believing that Asians prove that racism no
longer exists and anyone can attain the American dream; other
immigrants and racial minorities ought to follow their example.

A third group of "problems" Americans hear much about are
domestic social problems which many regard as outcomes of moral
lassitude: drug use, teen pregnancy, homosexuality, and a growing
underclass dependent on welfare. A panel issued a report in June
1990 that reviewed statistics on the state of youth in America, concluding that,

> America is raising a generation of adolescents plagued by preg-
> nancies, illegal drug use, suicide and violence, . . . [Y]oung people
> are less healthy and less prepared to take their places in society
> than were their parents. (Teens less healthy, 1990, p. 1)

If uncorrected, the result would be "a failing economy and social
unrest" (p. 1). These problems of morality are characterized as most
concentrated among the growing underclass, which conservatives
such as John Silber (1988) describe as "seemingly self-sustaining,
limited primarily to blacks and Hispanics though including individuals and families of all ethnic backgrounds" (p. 215). Silber characterized the tragedy of the underclass: they "no longer dream the
American dream. They do not imagine working hard and moving
from where they are to where they would like to be" (p. 215). Many
Americans blame the welfare system for the growth of an underclass; for example, Charles Murray (1984) argued that welfare policies and the expansion of welfare rolls during the liberal interven-

tionist state of the late 1960s and 1970s had produced a growing generation of dependants for whom unemployment and welfare had become a "logical" and comfortable lifestyle. Silber (1988) emphasized the decline in the American family brought about by women working increasingly outside the home, by the sexual revolution inflicting adolescents who are "so immature that they lack the knowledge and insight to protect themselves" (p. 216), and by television which uncritically presents children "with sex, with violence, the perverse and the sublime" (p. 217). He urged moral education and self-control as the solution to the growing underclass (echoing Reagan's moral solution to social structural problems: Just Say No).

By capturing the slogan "family values," conservatives heated up an attack on people who were not white, Christian, heterosexual, and conservative. For example, several towns across the U.S. as well as the state of Colorado passed anti-gay legislation, capitalizing on the prevailing ideology that frames sexual orientation as an issue of morality rather than civil rights. ("In response to a reader's request for stories on gay families, the editor of *Focus on the Family Monthly* writes that 'the Maker of families did not include homosexual groupings in His master plans for households'." [White, 1993, p. 8]). Abortion clinics became targets of conservative protests which at times included violence and even murder. Welfare came under attack increasingly, with some welfare cuts in states such as Wisconsin supposed to serve as incentives for families to stay together or couples to marry ("Bridefare"), and welfare reform became a major theme of election slogans and congressional debate in the 1990s.

Americans are being urged to pull together and work harder to reestablish U.S. supremacy in the international economic arena. The U.S. will be able to continue to manufacture some products if it improves technology and allows domestic wages to continue to fall (Nasar, 1988), but its future is in technological development and information management, not manufacturing. In the conservative New World Order, the U.S. is to become the "brains" of world economic production while much of the rest of the world, particularly the Third World, is to become the "brawn." The message is not usually explicitly stated this way; rather, we are told that manufacturing jobs are being exported to nations where wages are much lower, and jobs in the U.S. will increasingly require thinking and problem-solving skills. The American Hudson Institute, for example, predicted that the majority of new jobs in the 1990s "will require some form of education beyond high school" (Perry, 1988, p. 71). The dominant discourse suggests that Americans will work increasingly in "high-tech" careers.

Within this New World Order, the U.S. is to consolidate an economically imperialistic relationship with Third World countries; agreements such as NAFTA help pave the way. Conservatives have been cultivating an interest in cultural diversity but redefining how it should be treated. Cultural differences at home are to be stripped of political content and harnessed to help U.S. business abroad. Racial and ethnic minority students who conform to the demands of revamped schools and identify with business interests can look forward to careers representing American business internationally. Those who do not have no place in the future society; the "at-risk" ideology blames their failure squarely on their families and neighborhoods.

Education reforms of the 1980s were to provide more workers for this information economy: excellence became the main byword. In the reform reports of the early 1980s, excellence meant raising academic requirements for high school graduation, i.e., requiring more math, science, and computer literacy; teaching higher-order reasoning; lengthening the school day and year; demanding stricter discipline; making it harder to enter college (an interesting recommendation if most new jobs will require post-secondary education); and improving the quality of teachers (Shor, 1986, pp. 116–7). By 1994, these recommendations had taken the form of standards under the rubric Goals 2000, which

> requires the creation and federal approval of substantive content standards in subject-matter areas. . . . These national standards, which may be too limited or distorted to match the diversity of American lives, will prescribe the knowledge and skills that every student in the United States will be expected to master; and the success of both standards and students will be measured by performance tests approved by the federal government (Arons, 1994, p. 353–354)

On the heels of the first reform reports of the 1980s came a large volume of discourse about "children at risk" of failure in the revamped schools and economy. Although definitions of who is "at risk" varied, Richardson and her colleagues (1989) explained that, "The 'risk factors' or predictors that are statistically most often associated with school failure or dropping out are student background characteristics such as minority status, poverty, and language difference" (p. 4); pregnancy, drug use, and child abuse are also often cited as predictors of risk. By the 1990s, growing public reluctance to fund education diminished talk of reforms unless they were tied to cost-cutting measures.

Conservative Rearticulations of Multicultural Education

Multicultural education has been the subject of occasional conservative critiques since its inception, but the early 1990s saw a barrage of them, written mainly for the lay public. In the process of conducting a review of critiques of multicultural education in the U.S., I located two that were published in the 1970s, six published in the 1980s, and 51 published between 1990 and 1992, most written by conservatives (Sleeter, 1995a). Conservative renderings of multicultural education currently dominate conceptions that the lay public encounters.

Conservatives challenge not the multicultural education literature (they do not refer to it), but rather curricular changes and policies in schools and universities, particularly New York State's *A Curriculum of Inclusion* (a framework written by a task force to guide the development of new multicultural curricula), Portland, Oregon's *African American Baseline Essays* (a series of essays that explicate six disciplines from an Afrocentric perspective, designed to help teachers reconceptualize their own curriculum), Afrocentrism in general, and revisions of core curricula on several university campuses. Many conservative critics acknowledge that the U.S. is becoming increasingly diverse. Their argument is not so much whether education should acknowledge diversity, but what that should mean. Sandra Stotsky (1991), for example, explained that reasonable citizens "should applaud the integration of non-Western cultures and the histories of various minorities—women, Hispanics, blacks, native Indian communities—into our schools' curricula" (p. 26). However, conservatives are concerned that schools and universities are integrating such cultures and histories in a dangerous manner. They level four charges against multicultural education.

First, they regard it as the politically-charged extremist work of a fringe of loony radicals who subscribe to a "cult" and are foisting new policies on a public they do not represent. For example, in *U.S. News and World Report*, John Leo (1991) charged New York State's *A Curriculum of Inclusion* as having been prepared by "prescreened worshipers at the altar of multiculturalism" who do not represent "the views of most blacks, immigrants, or New Yorkers in general" (p. 12). Charles Krauthammer (1990) explained that multicultural education "did not start in the New York schools. It started at the elite universities"—Stanford, in particular. To Lewis Feuer (1991), multiculturalism is partly a product of African Americans who "repudiate the sciences they cannot master" during a time when scientific culture is dominant (p. 21).

Second, conservatives are concerned that an excessive emphasis on race and ethnicity is divisive and will tear the U.S. apart.
They regard the U.S. as "an entirely new experiment in politics,"
rooted in Western political thought, which upholds individual rights
rather than group claims:

> By recognizing and accepting man's natural rights, men found a
> fundamental basis of unity and sameness. Class, race, religion,
> national origin or culture all disappear or become dim when bathed
> in the light of natural rights, which give men common interests
> and make them truly brothers. (Bloom, 1989, p. 27)

The purpose of schooling in Western classical thought is to cultivate
reason so that citizens can rise above their own particular circumstances and participate rationally in a common culture. Europe is
"the *unique* source—of those liberating ideals of individual liberty,
political democracy, the impartial rule of law, and cultural freedom . . . to which most of the world aspires" (Schlesinger, 1992, p.
127). It is important to emphasize that conservatives underscore
not only these ideals, but also the claim that they are European in
origin, and that their underpinnings will be compromised if Western
classics lose favor. In spite of its imperfections, they regard the U.S.
as having become increasingly unified for over two centuries by a
common culture and by individual opportunity.

Some conservatives contrast two different forms of multicultural education. The form they advocate upholds individual rights
and the Western basis of U.S. institutions, but incorporates diverse
groups into its history and culture. The form they regard as divisive examines group status and cultural difference (see for example, Ravitch, 1990b; Schlesinger, 1991b; Stotsky, 1992). A spokesper-
son for what she calls "pluralistic multicultural education," Diane
Ravitch offered the California History-Social Science Framework,
which she helped to draft, "as an excellent full-length multicultural
curriculum" (1990a, p. 18). It teaches that the U.S. has always been
multicultural, although its main institutions are rooted in Western
civilization. It posits that Americans share histories of immigration
to North America, but over time have become united by "the moral
force of the American idea" (p. 19). As a pluralistic multicultural
curriculum, it includes diverse groups in a grand narrative of America's extension of equality and freedom to all. The attention contemporary minority group members are giving to ethnic origin, they
argue, subverts this trend toward inclusivity and commonality.

Third, critics argue that much multicultural curriculum is intellectually weak. They criticize curricula from kindergarten through the university level, but their main target is Afrocentrism, particularly the Afrocentrist claim that ancient Egypt is a part of Black Africa, with a second target being New York's *Curriculum of Inclusion*. For example, Arthur Schlesinger (1991a) wrote of New York's curriculum: "Its interest in history is not as an intellectual discipline but rather as social and psychological therapy whose primary function is to raise the self-esteem of children from minority groups" (p. 25); he dubbed Portland's *Baseline Essays* as "bad history" (p. 27). He patronizingly described Afrocentric thinking as having been developed as a result of blacks' deeply wounded pride, which "many generous-hearted people, black and white" have gone along with "out of a decent sympathy for the insulted and injured of American society" (1992, p. 73). Paul Gray (1991), writing in *Time* magazine, termed New York's report a "hatchet job on existing academic standards" (p. 13), and Feuer (1991) regarded the aim of cultural diversity in higher education as being "to entrench a place for the superficial and mediocre" (p. 21), advocating "ideological apologia for backward peoples" (p. 22).

Fourth, some conservative critics argue that multicultural education offers a poor critique of minority student underachievement, replacing old-fashioned work with gimmicks such as self-esteem exercises. In the process, it does not give minority students the intellectual tools they need to "make it" in the real world. For example, Irving Howe (1991) and Arthur Schlesinger (1992) argued that the traditional university curriculum, particularly the classics, stretches the mind: respected African American authors such as Richard Wright and Ralph Ellison read Western classics, and minority students today who are not assigned the classics are not well-served academically. Neither are Spanish-speaking students served well by bilingual education because it retards acquisition of English and encourages segregation.

Conservatism Critiqued

Compared to the postwar economic boom, the 1970s and 1980s were a time in which Americans had to learn to settle for less: fewer jobs were available, prices rose, real income of a large portion of the population fell, and white middle class families experienced some of the hard times with which poor families had always lived. This downward spiral resulted from corporate restructuring of the global economy; transnational corporations, based mainly in the U.S., Western Europe, and Japan, established global factories "in which a single manufacturing process is broken down into many steps that are divided among workers in different nations (or different areas of a single country)" (Kamel, 1993, p. 185). A combination of factors including the computer revolution, intensified competition for profit, saturated markets, and rising "costs" of domestic labor led large corporations to abandon domestic labor markets and relocate to areas "where workers will accept lower pay and harsher working conditions" (p. 186). This is an inherent crisis of capitalism itself, since as markets have become saturated, consumption is not keeping up with production. However, as more power and wealth have become concentrated in a small elite, that elite has been using its power to intensify its control rather than redistribute wealth.

Further, Americans have been less bound together by consensus than they had been in the recent past.

> Commonly held concepts of nation, community and family were transformed, and no new principle of cohesion, no new cultural center, emerged to replace them. New collective identities, rooted in the "new social movements," remained fragmented and politically disunited. (Omi & Winant, 1986, p. 119)

The strategy of containing discontent by appealing to patriotism has been invoked with vigor, and disenfranchised communities have been pitted against each other. For example, Martinez (1993) argued that, "The myths [about immigrants] are intended to prove that the very real deprivation experienced today by the U.S.-born should be blamed on immigrants—that largely impoverished 2–4 percent of the population" (p. 25).

Whites increasingly fear losing control over access to the best positions. Shor termed the 1983 reform agenda as "a crisis in white mediocrity and as an elite reaction against minority advances" (p. 143). The decline in SAT scores had served as "proof" that students were learning less in school, although much less publicized results of the National Assessment of Educational Progress did not support this claim. But while test scores of white students either declined or remained roughly the same over the 1970s, depending on which test or sub-test one examined, test scores of African American and Latino students rose on both the SAT and the NAEP. Further, in the early 1970s, college-going rates of students of color rose dramatically. The non-white population was growing faster than the white population;

if good opportunities are shrinking and education really brings social mobility, Americans of color may out-compete white Americans with growing success. A white acquaintance told me recently that the main thing she learned by taking a multicultural education course is that birth control among whites has yielded a dangerous consequence: lower white birthrates. In her view, the growing proportion of the population who are of color threatens white security.

But Americans of color know their own economic status has not improved in over two decades for a variety of reasons, despite gains in education. Even Asian Americans, viewed as the model group who had 'made it', are not nearly as successful as the media suggests. In Wisconsin during 1980, for example, 18 percent of Asian families were living below the poverty line, while only 5 percent of white families were in the same condition (Applied Population Lab, n.d.). The media spotlights individual Asians who do well in school and attain good jobs, and corporate America applauds upwardly mobile young Asian professionals, dividing them from "the legacy of grassroots organizing" in Asian American communities (Omatsu, 1994, p. 40). Poverty-ridden urban Asian neighborhoods, for example, or extreme difficulties many Asian immigrants have faced are rarely noted. Further, the fact that Asian Americans still have to attain more education and work longer hours than whites in order to achieve comparable earnings is rarely mentioned. Some of the most outspoken critics of misinformation about Asian Americans have been Japanese Americans, the group often touted as most successful (for example, Jiobu, 1988; Omatsu, 1994; Suzuki, 1989; Takaki, 1989).

To mask its attempts to reassert white dominance, conservatives use the language of fairness and equality: "Its vision is that of a 'colorblind' society where racial considerations are never entertained in the selection of leaders, in hiring decisions, and the distribution of goods and services in general" (Omi & Winant, 1986, pp. 113–4). Conservatives imply that there was a time prior to the civil rights movement when merit rather than race and gender was the sole criterion for mobility, while failing to acknowledge how many doors were firmly closed to those who were not white men. The racial ideology of colorblindness is not only ahistorical, it also assumes that people today will behave in a colorblind manner, when there is abundant evidence that this is not the case (Raskin, 1995). The racial ideology of conservatism and renewed white supremacy has been rearticulated in "code words . . . which refer indirectly to racial themes, but do not directly challenge popular democratic or egalitarian ideals," such as "busing," "choice" and "reverse discrimination" (Omi & Winant, 1986, p. 120). The principle of individuality is reasserted; group claims to equality are decried as unfair. In fact, "most civil rights remedies and mechanisms for achieving racial inequality are now considered to discriminate against whites" (p. 132).

Conservatives also implicitly blame women for many of the nation's difficulties: teachers—"the women who teach the children who fail" (Grumet, 1988, p. 23), mothers who fail to perform "their" role at home because they enter the workplace, and poor women who depend on welfare for survival. Ruth Sidel (1986) quoted a study published in 1931: "'Truancy, incorrigibility, robbery, teenage tantrums, and difficulty in managing the children' all stemmed from a 'mother's absence at her job'" (p. 55); the same sentiment was echoed in the 1980s in discussions of latchkey children. And teenage girls, especially African American girls, are implicitly blamed for the rise in adolescent pregnancy and the growth of the underclass.

As a product of the civil rights movement, multicultural education has the potential to unsettle, disrupt and challenge racism, rule by wealth, and curbs on democratic decision-making. Through the 1970s and 1980s, advocates fought to be noticed and taken seriously. By the 1990s, conservatives were not only taking multicultural education seriously, but trying to rearticulate it or mobilize public opinion against it. But their criticisms have some serious weaknesses.

First, conservative critics ignore the body of literature on multicultural education as well as research and theory it builds upon, produced largely by scholars of color, feminist, and critical scholars. None of the critiques refer to work by James A. Banks, Geneva Gay, Carl Grant, Sonia Nieto, or Henry Trueba, for example. While conservatives criticize multicultural curricula as weak on scholarship, by failing to address literature on multicultural education, they display this very weakness in their own work. Instead of working with educators of color, conservatives (the great majority of whom are white) position themselves as spokespeople and advocates for both the broad American public in general *and* racial minority groups in particular. A strategy they use is to sprinkle their writings with the names of scholars of color such as W. E. B. DuBois, Carter Woodson, Frederick Douglass, and James Comer, who, they imply, agree with their viewpoints.

Second, conservative discussions of multicultural education offer little analysis of inequality today, framing their discussion mainly around unity versus dissension and defining equality only as equal rights of individuals before the law. For example, Schlesinger (1992) wrote that racism has been a "great national tragedy" in U.S. history (p. 19), but it has been largely overcome: "The American synthesis has an inevitable Anglo-Saxon coloration, but it is no longer an exercise in Anglo-Saxon domination" (p. 118). Conservatives are angered by what they regard as excessive criticism of Europe's role in the conquest and enslavement of Third World people. To argue that Europeans do not have a monopoly on cultural vice, they advocate that everyone's "warts" should be presented equally. Absent from their writings is a recognition of the growing frustration that many Americans have experienced over the past twelve years, as poverty rates have risen, jobs have left the country, and funding for various social programs has been cut. Rather, conservatives seem to conceptualize ethnic and racial conflict as stemming from excessive group pride.

Third, conservatives assume their own viewpoints to be apolitical, conceptualizing them as rooted in intellectual training that enables one to rise above ones own particular circumstances in order to make an objective assessment. They deride multicultural education as "political," and many then go on to bifurcate the "political" from the "academic," such as in the following passage: "Yet one of the most contentious issues in education today is what the words 'multicultural education' mean and whether the content of such programs serves academic or political ends" (Stotsky, 1991a, p. 26). This issue is embedded in a fundamental assumption of traditional Western thought: that intellectual engagement with its classical ideals enables an individual to transcend personal vested interest in order to speak dispassionately for the whole society. How does one critique ones own thoughts and actions for self-interest? One does that within the framework of classical Western philosophy. If one attempts to critique ideas from outside that framework, or attempts to critique Western philosophy itself, one is being political, not rational, engaging "thought police" to try to get everyone to think uniformly.

David Theo Goldberg (1993) wrote that a great irony of modernity is the Western assumption of a universal "subject" that fails to take race seriously and in so doing, solidifies racist exclusivity. By conceptualizing humans in moral and rational terms only, assuming their ability to transcend political, economic, cultural, and geographic boundaries, Western thinking has reduced racism to an irrational

psychological response, while at the same time, positioning Western actors as the world's most advanced. We see this line of belief in
the conservative criticisms of multicultural education, which argue
that multicultural curricula displace Western classics and that discussions of race in such curricula are political and irrational.

Multicultural education was not a popular target of conservative criticism until about 1990, even though it has been around since
the mid-1960s. As long as it took the form of sporadic practices in
schools (largely those populated by students of color), scholarly writings, and occasional conference themes, conservatives could ignore it.
As soon, however, as it began to make an impact on white schools
and major universities, it could no longer be ignored. In a "tug of
war over who gets to create the public culture" (Kessler-Harris, 1992,
p. 310), people of color were making gains, in an increasingly unstable time. Hugh Price (1992) observed:

> Note the coincidence between the erosion of earnings among work-
> ing-class people—white, black, and Latino—and the rise of stri-
> dent multiculturalism. The social compact in America between our
> society and its working people—white and minority alike—is dis-
> solving. . . . Those manufacturing jobs that once provided dignity
> and decent wages for high school graduates and dropouts alike are
> vanishing. All are victims of a new world industrial order that is
> redistributing manufacturing jobs and redefining the economic role
> of our communities. (p. 212)

Given this instability, who will non-white Americans align themselves with: white corporate America and its European ties or black
and brown America and their historic ties with the Third World people who increasingly constitute "cheap labor" in the American world
economy?

Domestically, white middle America is uneasy about its own
future and rather readily can be led to pin its fears and anxieties on
the threat of "diversity." Internationally, the "U.S. is now embarked
on an effort to establish its supremacy as the world power, primarily
through militarism. . . . To do this requires a sense of national unity,
of a country united behind war and militarism" directed against
Third World nations (Platt, 1992, p. 133). Education, as Noam Chomsky (1987) has argued, serves as an important form of ideological
control and is increasingly under the purview of the state. He
observed that the ideological spectrum of the intelligencia in the
U.S. has gradually narrowed; most academic work now serves the

purpose of manufacturing popular consent for U.S. military aggression and capitalist expansion. I would suggest that multicultural education threatens that ideological consensus, opening questions about both domestic and international issues that the political elite would rather not have examined publicly.

To shut down such questioning, conservatives appear to be constructing for the lay public an image of a multiculturalist that draws on their racial prejudices, in a manner similar to the "ugly feminist" image conservatives periodically resurrect in order "to checkmate power" following successes of the women's movement (Wolf, 1991, p. 19). Playing on racial stereotypes and fears, conservatives suggest that multiculturalists consist of a frenzied mob of anti-Americans trying to destroy the U.S., who are joined by "ugly" feminists and Third World immigrants, and led by angry, intellectually weak African American men. This image is designed to destroy public support for multicultural education and mobilize opinion to support a conservative definition of how young Americans should be taught to view the U.S., its diversity, and its position within a hierarchical, capitalistic global order.

Conclusion

Having experienced considerable conceptual growth and some limited gains in affecting schools, the field of multicultural education currently is buffeted by critiques. Those of us who work in it find ourselves walking a tightrope between naming issues accurately and antagonizing potential supporters. The left would, correctly I believe, have the field develop a much more explicit critique of white racism, capitalism, and patriarchy, using analytic insights of radical structuralism and poststructuralism.

As the gap between "haves" and "have nots" in U.S. society widens and conditions among the poorest (and darkest-skinned) deteriorate, there appears to be a tendency across the general public to accept inequality as natural and to adopt conservative viewpoints explaining inequality. Many teachers, in fact, believe that racism and sexism were solved during the civil rights movement and ascribe today's problems to moral degeneration among the poor (Kozol, 1991; Sleeter, 1992). As the ideological orientation of U.S. politics and the media continues to move to the right, and as the need for grassroots mobilization intensifies, it becomes increasingly important that social justice issues are addressed clearly and comprehensively through radical structuralist and post-structuralist viewpoints. Yet it is very difficult to name social justice issues squarely in the context of the right's characterization of the field as un-American and dangerous. In that context, how do today's teachers think about multicultural education? Chapter 4 examines this issue.

CHAPTER 4

Resisting Racial Awareness:
*How Teachers Understand the Social Order
from their Social Locations*

As student populations become increasingly racially and culturally diverse and the teaching force becomes increasingly Euro-American, interest in training teachers in multicultural education is growing. Many educators conceptualize this task as helping them "unlearn" negative attitudes about race, develop positive attitudes and a knowledge base about race and various racial groups, and learn multicultural teaching strategies. This chapter shows that the task is more complex than that: as white women, many of whom have worked up from working class origins, teachers already have considerable knowledge about social stratification in America, and it tends to be fairly conservative. They integrate information about race provided in multicultural teacher education programs into the knowledge they already have, much more than they reconstruct that knowledge.

Various theorists have examined teachers as upwardly mobile members of the working class (Lortie, 1975; Ashton & Webb, 1986), as women (Grumet, 1988; Pagano, 1990), and as working class women (Apple, 1987), focusing on how they construct their understanding of reality from these social class and gender locations. Teacher race has been examined mainly by comparing how white teachers and teachers of color interact with and teach children of color (Irvine, 1988; Simpson & Erickson, 1983). Teacher race is seen as an issue mainly when teachers display overt prejudice toward children of color, expect less of them than they do of white children, or fail to understand them.

In this chapter, data are used from a two-year ethnographic study of thirty teachers, twenty-six of whom are white, who participated in a staff development program in multicultural education. These data illustrate how social class and gender life experiences inform white teachers' understanding of the social order and how they use that understanding to construct an understanding of race. The teachers' perspectives about social inequality and multicultural education is examined in relation to the theoretical perspectives discussed in chapter 3.

Background of the Study

This chapter probes teachers' understanding of multicultural education and society in general. Data are drawn from a two-year study of thirty teachers who voluntarily participated in a staff development program in multicultural education (Sleeter, 1992). The teachers were from two contiguous school districts; they taught preschool through high school (most taught grades 1–6) and were from eighteen schools in which at least one-third of the students were of color (mostly African American or Latino) or from low-income families. The teachers had taught between four and twenty-nine years; the average was fourteen years. Twenty-six were white, three were African American, and one was Mexican-American; twenty-four were women and six were men. Seven taught special education, two taught English as a Second Language, and the rest taught in the general education program.

During school year 1987–1988, the teachers were released to attend nine all-day sessions held at a staff development center located between the two school districts; they also attended three after-school sessions and a dinner meeting. During school year 1988–1989, eighteen teachers chose to continue to participate and attended five all-day sessions at the staff development center. A list of session topics is included in Table 4.1. The topics were selected by a steering group composed of African American, Latino, and white educators from the local community and university on the basis of interests teachers expressed in the first session. The sessions were led mainly by consultants with expertise in particular topics. Although the sessions differed considerably from one another, most used a combination of lecture, discussion, and practical application.

For example, Session #3 began with a two-hour multimedia presentation by an administrator from a local district, describing changing demographics in the U.S. and local region and suggesting implications of these changes for how Americans define ourselves.

Table 4.1
Schedule of Sessions

FIRST YEAR

Full-Day Session #1:	Introduction, Assessment of Interests
Full-Day Session #2:	Building Home-School Partnerships
After-School Session #1:	Star Power Simulation
Full-Day Session #3:	Race, Ethnicity, Social Class, and Gender in Society
Full-Day Session #4:	Ethnic Learning Styles and Racism Awareness
Full-Day Session #5:	Community Resources
After-School Session #2:	Discussion
Full-Day Session #6:	Working with Curriculum and Instruction
After-School Session #3:	Teachers as Leaders
Full-Day Session #7:	Cooperative Learning
Full-Day Session #8:	Library Resources for Multicultural Education
Full-Day Session #9:	Dropout Prevention Programs, Motivation and Self-Esteem, and Sharing

SECOND YEAR

Full-Day Session #1:	Action Research and School-Based Change
Full-Day Sessions #2–4:	Teachers selected 3 from the following:
	Working with Your Staff
	Making Curriculum Multicultural
	Cooperative Learning
	Building Self-Esteem
	Parent Involvement
Full-Day Session #5:	Wrapping up and Organizing for Change

After a short break, a university professor contrasted Euro-American and African American struggles for assimilation and success in the United States by addressing the question: if European ethnic groups were successful, why are Americans of color and particularly African Americans not following the same pattern? Another university professor discussed gender differences in how people attribute their successes and research on how teacher-student interaction patterns in the classroom reinforce these gender differences. During a subsequent hour provided for open discussion, the teachers talked mainly about sexism. For the last half-hour, teachers viewed a videotape on bilingual education, which related directly to the morning presentations.

Session #4 was not as crowded with information. The morning was facilitated by a university professor who discussed the creation of culturally compatible classrooms. She began with a lecture on achievement and learning and cultural effects on information processing strategies. She then involved teachers in an activity in which they drew their ideal classroom using crayons and newsprint. The facilitator had teachers share their drawings, then used them to discuss cognitive styles among children from racial minority groups, especially African Americans, and how their styles conflict with the teaching styles found in most classrooms. She included in her talk many specific recommendations for teachers. After lunch, a panel of three professional women of color discussed their own experiences with racism as they grew up. The panel was followed by a discussion in which the teachers reacted to what the panel members said.

The sessions themselves drew most heavily on the language of liberalism, although some facilitators also drew on conservative ideas about social class and some drew lightly on radical structuralism. Although in Session #3 the European ethnic experience was contrasted with that of African Americans, many concepts used in other sessions reflected those of the ethnicity paradigm.

Research was conducted using a variety of methods, mainly classroom observation and interview. Three one-hour observations were conducted in teachers' classrooms during the first year, and two during the second year, totaling 121 hours. In the classroom observations, data were recorded on time use and instructional strategies, curriculum-in-use, teacher-student interaction patterns, student seating patterns, classroom decor, instructional materials, and decision-making patterns. Most of the staff development sessions were also observed. Each classroom observation was accompanied by an interview; a total of 125 interviews were conducted.

Over the two-year period, observable changes in classroom teaching were fairly limited. I will describe them here briefly to provide a context for examining how teachers defined multicultural education. The curriculum and room decor in most classrooms was about as multicultural, at the start of the program, as published textbooks are (Sleeter & Grant, 1991). About half of the teachers tried using or developing some multicultural curriculum on a sporadic basis, mainly incorporating "little things" into existing lessons. Eight wrote and taught one new unit or some lessons, mainly in elective subject areas such as art, music, and home economics or in special education. Four used a multicultural calendar they had received in the program, and six taught one or two lessons from books they acquired in the program. The quantity and quality of classroom decorations representing human diversity stayed much the same over the two years, although about half reported preparing displays with diversity in mind, to which they drew my attention during observations.

To respond to student learning styles, half of the teachers gradually increased their use of cooperative learning and cut back on individual seatwork and whole-class recitation, which dominated their teaching. While at the beginning of the program they spent an average of 11% of observed time using small groupwork, by the end this proportion had doubled. They reported that students found cooperative learning much more interesting than individual seatwork and seemed to learn better when it was used. Five teachers reported supplementing print, such as using more oral reading.

Most of the teachers interacted with students in a very warm and friendly manner throughout the two years, but there were some changes in their distribution of attention to students. Over the two years, with the exception of one observation following a session on gender patterns in teacher-student interaction, boys received a disproportionate share of questions and praise (e.g., in the first observation, boys comprised 54% of the students but received 61% of the questions and 68% of the praise). At the beginning of the study, teachers distributed questions and praise in proportion to racial representation in the classroom. Over the first year, they gave a growing proportion to African American students and particularly African American boys. But by the second year, patterns were about the same as they had been at the beginning of the study.

One-third of the teachers reported trying new strategies to improve home-school communication, mainly sending or phoning home positive messages, getting parents to help more with homework, and looking for ways to make parents feel welcome in the building. Five teachers worked on long-range plans to strengthen home-school relationships; their work was inspired by other involvements in their buildings, although they used ideas they had gained in the program.

Although some observable changes occurred, the program's impact on classroom teaching was fairly limited. This was not because most of the teachers found it useless. Teachers frequently commented on how "excellent" the consultants were and how much they enjoyed the sessions. Although some felt they were getting few ideas they could use in their classrooms, several said they found sessions to be practical and "solution-oriented," and many described the program with unqualified enthusiasm.

During one of the interviews, twenty-six teachers were asked to discuss their goals for teaching and their thoughts about how multicultural education contributes to those goals. In other interviews, teachers were asked to discuss their personal and professional backgrounds and their reactions to the staff development sessions. Data for the discussion below are drawn from these interviews. I first discuss how the teachers defined multicultural education in relationship to their goals for teaching. Teachers' life experiences are then examined as upwardly mobile members of the working class, as whites, and as women to show how these experiences informed their understanding of multicultural education.

How the Teachers Saw Multicultural Education

Their perspectives on multicultural education were categorized into four groups: those who saw it as irrelevant, those who saw it as human relations, those who saw it as building self-esteem among out-groups, and those whose perspectives defied classification.

Conservatism: Multicultural Education as Irrelevant

Seven teachers saw multicultural education as irrelevant to their work. They described their main goals as promoting academic achievement and individual development; two flatly stated that their main goal was to get students to perform at grade level. Those who also discussed individual development defined it within the parameters of grade level achievement. For example:

> We have the district goal that they must attain certain things before they're promoted, but each individual then besides that should be getting some goals. . . . Like, if they have reversals, I know one little boy, oh, really a lot of reversals and that was my goal, to make sure that by the end of the year, hopefully, that he would be improving a lot.

They wanted their students to think, solve problems, and feel confident in their ability to achieve.

> I would like the students to understand that . . . I am teaching them problem solving through the content approach and processes approach and . . . thinking on their feet, to know what you should do if in fact you encounter a problem.

* * * * *

> I try to accomplish the goal of having every child leave my class
> with a spirit of self-confidence, knowing that they can believe in
> themselves and do whatever they set out to do if they have enough
> determination and self-confidence.

For the most part, they believed that everyone who works hard can achieve their goals; they felt optimistic about society. Those at the primary level believed that if they made learning fun and gave students plenty of reinforcement, they would achieve. Secondary level teachers admitted perplexity about some of their students; they believed many were failing because they came from families that simply did not encourage and support achievement and learning.

Conservatives view inequality as natural, resulting mainly from individual differences in natural endowment and effort. These teachers who saw multicultural education as irrelevant drew on the culturalist and prejudice explanations for inequality that West (1987) discussed. They described students' homes like the following teacher did:

> Where are they coming from? . . . What's going on in their brains,
> you know? Because sometimes I realize how irrelevant it is to stand
> up here and talk, and I have a very close family, . . . [my husband
> and I] have been very strong disciplinarians and we encourage the
> work ethic. . . . I realize how foolish and presumptuous [it is] to
> think all these kids are coming from the same thing. . . . Just to
> have a totally helter skelter house where there is nothing regular
> and the people who are your parent figures come and go and—you
> don't know, you know what I mean, just what is going on in their
> brains and where they are coming from.

They used the prejudice explanation when trying to be colorblind, wanting NOT to be among those who discriminate unfairly. All seven were white. They did not find multicultural education useful mainly because of its stress on color, believing that acknowledging color or other ascribed characteristics would either reinforce limiting stereotypes or excuse people from performing. They emphasized paying attention to individual needs, not group membership:

> You know, this has been a constant, boring—I have never really
> thought about Asian Americans or Blacks until I got into a multi-
> cultural course. I just treat them as children.

As long as they saw their own expectations as appropriately high and their treatment of children as caring and unbiased, they did not see themselves as interfering with children's progress and thus saw no need to change what they were doing. The only use they saw in multicultural education was its insights into culturally-different students that might help them teach more effectively, such as information on learning styles or parent involvement.

Liberalism: Multicultural Education as Human Relations

Six teachers saw multicultural education as human relations. They described two main goals for teaching: promoting academic achievement and helping students get along with and appreciate each other. For example:

> Academics, I want them to be as near grade level as possible, which for some kids isn't a problem, but for a lot of other kids it is a very big problem. . . . With behavior, it's important for me that they learn to work together, so that's some of the reason I'm doing the cooperative learning.

They saw multicultural education as relevant to the extent that it gave them strategies for addressing both achievement and interpersonal relations in the classroom. Like the teacher above, they were quite interested in cooperative learning because it can address both goals.

They also expressed some interest in infusing multicultural content into lessons to help students understand each other better, to the extent time would permit without compromising academics. This infusion usually took the form of adding little things "when it comes up." For example:

> We try to talk about different cultures when it comes up. The English curriculum, with literature especially, like Anne Frank. Grammar, not nearly as much. But the calendar idea, putting different days on the board and the holidays, we do things for Women's History and Black History Month.

In addition, some taught lessons on individual differences to help foster good relationships among students.

These six teachers were all white. But unlike those who saw multicultural education as irrelevant, they were comfortable thinking in terms of race and color and attached positive feelings and images to racial diversity. They also recognized a connection between race, student self-image, and student-student relationships. As one teacher said, "You've had these groups going to school together and still have a lack of understanding." Therefore, they sought strategies and content to add into their daily lessons that would address these concerns. Their orientation toward children seemed to be very humanistic: personal fulfillment, inner peace, and harmony seemed to be of greater value than mobility or material gain. For example, one described multicultural education as an "atmosphere . . . of openness and acceptance;" another had served in the Peace Corps and emphasized the tragedy of war in her teaching; and another was active in a peace organization in her personal life.

I categorized these teachers as having a liberal orientation because their discussions of students' home cultures focused on positive as often as negative characteristics, and they did not describe themselves as colorblind. This suggested that they acknowledged worthwhile meaning in racial group membership. In addition, they occasionally criticized conservative national policies such as military build-up, and conservative political leaders such as former President Reagan.

Multicultural Education as
Helping Members of Out-Groups to Cope

Eight teachers were interested mainly in developing self-esteem among their students and preparing them to survive and cope in a somewhat hostile society and saw multicultural education as fostering empathy for the personal struggles of society's out-group members. The main feature that distinguished them from those with a human relations orientation was that they taught in special programs: English as a Second Language, special education, alternative education, art, and "at-risk" students. With the exception of the art teacher, all of their students were "behind" in one or more areas and were struggling in school. Their goals for students focused on their struggles for success:

> I work a lot on improving their self-image and their self-esteem. And I think that's probably my main goal, and I think that if I accomplish that, the other things will come along, the academics will come along and the social skills will come along.

> * * * * *

> The one goal is to help them to identify where they need to work, and help them to be successful, . . . helping them to realize a little success and then to build on that success.

These eight teachers (seven white and one African American) saw multicultural education as helping children cope, particularly those who had encountered many difficulties in life:

> There are a number of us who really try to fight all the negative things and so forth, but the negatives have been so many, so powerful.

They discussed the importance of being sensitive to individual needs and feelings, optimistic about the worth of those whom others have rejected, and flexible toward students.

They differed among themselves in their attributions of students' academic difficulties and their theoretical perspectives about social inequality. Their views ranged from conservatism to glimmerings of radical structuralism. For example, an elementary special education teacher saw lower class students' homes as the main source of their difficulties, commenting that, "I don't know how much love goes on in most of the families or how much attention they get at home." The ESL (English as a Second Language) teachers saw their students' difficulties as stemming from the fact that they were having to learn a new culture; once they learned it, they would be able to compete successfully. Several teachers saw their students as encountering negative experiences in many areas of their lives, including school, due to inflexible attitudes and institutional procedures. A special education teacher saw the whole of society as stacked against her students:

> Our society is basically built on not being able to handle differences. And that's why these kids can't get through school. That's why we have these little red-necked teachers who will not see anything but their own little box.

On the basis of her experience in special education, she was beginning to develop a radical structuralist critique of social institutions.

More Complex Perspectives

Five teachers (three white, two African American) discussed multicultural education in ways that were more complex and harder to categorize than the other teachers. These were some of the teachers who had showed the most interest in it; their own insights had come in fits and jumps. They were in the process of active growth, and their discussions were less systematic than those of other teachers. In my lengthy interviews with them, they often responded to questions by discussing in detail a new idea or insight without necessarily integrating it with other comments they had made. At times some of them espoused conservative perspectives, at times all five took liberal perspectives, and some occasionally expressed radical structuralist insights.

For example, an African American teacher's main goals were to teach students what is morally right and to help them become strong enough to overcome life's inevitable barriers.

> My attitude is right now that in America we are raising a genera-
> tion of wimps and followers. That's generally the way I feel.
> Because if we were not, . . . the drug problem would not be as preva-
> lent as it is. Kids are not strong enough to resist their peers or
> resist other people who talk them into it.

Multicultural education meant not sheltering students from tough realities they would face. It also meant believing in the capabilities of children from low-income and minority backgrounds and helping them develop the moral strength to succeed and do the right thing. His discussions mixed together culturalist explanations of poverty with institutional explanations of racism.

A white home economics teacher described multicultural education as "something that has to be incorporated into everything." To think through how to do that, she developed a very creative unit about culture and clothing, which examined the relationship between climate, local cultures, and clothing design. She saw a relationship between multicultural education and not only achievement and intergroup relationships but also issues such as world hunger, about which she was in the process of thinking through how to teach.

Summary

Most of the teachers' conceptions of multicultural education emphasized individuality and success within the existing social system. They differed from each other mainly in the extent to which they saw race and culture as helpful factors to consider in preparing children to compete successfully. They also differed in their assessment of their own students' chances for success and their estimate of the kinds of support and help their students needed. Theirs were mainly debates between conservatism and liberalism. Several had adopted the conservative "children-at-risk" discourse, in that they focused on characteristics of students that hinder their success (culturalist explanations of inequality) rather than characteristics of institutions that block attempts to advance.

I took a course back last fall, I believe, which was . . . basically understanding at-risk kids and not really multicultural, but you know, they would be included in both of those scenarios. They are at risk, many of them, because of either their background, the level of acceptance they receive from school, or just basic lack of understanding.

With few exceptions, most of the teachers did not link multicultural education with a collective social movement aimed at redistributing resources across groups. For them, it was a tool for addressing problems they saw in their classrooms: tensions among groups of students, boredom, and failure.

Teachers as White Upwardly-Mobile Women

Most of the teachers were enthusiastic about the program because they were acquiring much new information. What I came to realize, however, was that they were adding that information into conceptions they already had about the workings of the social system, rather than reconstructing those conceptions. Their interpretations of what they were hearing minimized institutional racism and racially-based conflict in society's reward structure.

As Martyn Denscombe (1980) and others (e.g., Densmore, 1987; Gitlin, 1983) have argued, teachers' perspectives stem partly from the structure of their work as teachers. I examine their work context in detail elsewhere (Sleeter, 1992). But in spite of the structure of their work, teachers have some autonomy in their classrooms. They decide what to do with that autonomy based on how they frame problems and issues. How they frame diversity and inequality results from their own experiences within particular racial, gender, and class locations. Although most of the teachers had been insulated from perspectives and experiences of oppressed racial groups, they had constructed a fairly well-developed conception of the social order based on their experiences as white women and upwardly-mobile members of the working class.

Mobility through the Class Structure

Liberalism values individualism and hard work; the image of pulling oneself up by one's own bootstraps is taught to American citizens from their early years. Patricia Ashton and Rodman Webb (1986) noted that,

> The life experiences of most teachers demonstrate their allegiance
> to the ethic of vertical mobility, self-improvement, hard work,
> deferred gratification, self-discipline, and personal achievement.
> These individualistic values rest on the assumption that the social
> system . . . works well, is essentially fair, and moves society slowly
> but inevitably toward progress. (p. 29–30)

Several teachers described life experiences that had taught them
that one can work one's way up the class structure through persistence and hard work. Twenty-three discussed their parents' occupations. Four of their fathers had held jobs that normally require college education: pharmacist, engineer, manager of a company, and
minister, and two fathers had owned small businesses. The fathers of
the other seventeen had worked as laborers of various sorts, such as
a factory worker, railroad laborer, welder, farmer, and fire fighter.
Most of the teachers had raised their own social class standing by
earning college degrees. Further, at least twelve had completed a
master's degree when the study began, and three more were in the
process of doing so. Volunteering to participate in this project was
part of this broader pattern of bettering themselves through education.

Most who were white believed that anyone else who worked
and struggled could also achieve success. For example, one had
grown up in a poor family in Chicago. He had joined the navy at
age 17 "for a place to sleep and a place to eat." Of nine siblings, he
was the only one to work his way out of poverty; he was driven by
"the inner feeling of wanting to be successful." He did not know why
so many other people do not have that same drive; it had worked for
him so presumably it could work for other people.

Several teachers talked about their own European ethnic backgrounds (or that of their spouse), and their grandparents' and parents' work ethic. For example, a daughter of Italian immigrants commented:

> One of my pet peeves, that I know if you want to work, you can
> work. . . . I know what my father did when he was in need, . . . and
> we didn't have the free lunches and we didn't have the clothes that
> other kids wore.

She went on to describe her father working two jobs, and the family
pitching in to do agricultural work; as a result, without government
help, she had been able to attend college and establish a fairly comfortable life. Opportunity is there, if people will only work.

Many Americans regard their own social standing as higher than that of their parents. While most social mobility has been due to an expansion of middle class jobs and widespread improvement of the living standard of Americans in general, people tend to attribute their own improved status to their individual efforts. As Kluegel and Smith (1986) point out,

> while the most common pattern is stability of class position from one generation to the next, upward mobility has also been common and outweighs downward mobility by roughly two to one. . . . Even those who have not been mobile have benefited, on the whole, from the aggregate improvement in living standards that has taken place since World War II. (p. 24)

Attributing their own family's improved life to individual effort rather than broader social changes, many people then blame those whose lot has not improved greatly.

None of the teachers who had been born into the working class identified with it or discussed strategies to raise the class as a whole. One's social class of origin, unlike one's race or gender (usually), can be left behind. The teachers who did so successfully saw in their own example the best strategy for confronting social class inequality: working one's way up into another social class. By extension, group membership should not matter, at least in considering life chances. How group membership may affect individual mobility is a subject of debate between liberals and conservatives, but both agree that individual mobility is desirable. Radical structuralists, on the other hand, focus more on group relations and ask not how to leave behind one's group of origin but how to strengthen the position of the group as a whole.

Teachers as White

Teachers bring to their work a worldview that is constructed within unequal racial relationships, but they usually do not recognize it as such. Kathleen Weiler (1988), based on a study of white teachers, observed that,

> [A]s whites they are in a position of dominance and thus do not identify themselves by race, since white privilege is so much a defined part of U.S. society that whites are not even conscious of their relationship to power and privilege. In U.S. society, white is the norm; people of color are defined as deviating from that norm and therefore their race becomes an issue. (p. 75–76)

White people and people of color grow up in different locations in the racial structure. According to David Wellman (1977),

> Given the racial and class organization of American society, there is only so much people can "see." The positions they occupy in these structures limit the range of their thinking. The situation places barriers on their imaginations and restricts the possibilities of their vision. (p. 235)

Most whites live in racially homogeneous neighborhoods, families, social groups, and churches, and consume media that are dominated by whites. Most whites spend little or no extended time on non-white "turf," although they may incorporate a few people of color into their own worlds.

The worldviews of whites tend to support white privilege, but do so in ways that whites interpret as natural or as fair. Wellman argued that a contradiction whites face is how to interpret racial inequality in a way that defends white interests in publicly acceptable terms. Generally, sociobiological explanations for inequality are not acceptable today, so whites construct alternative explanations. They "resolve the contradiction by minimizing racism. They neutralize it" (p. 219).

Most of the white teachers in this study had fairly little exposure to the life experiences and worldviews of Americans of color. All but one had grown up in white neighborhoods. Eighteen had virtually no life experience with Americans of color outside of their experiences as teachers and, in some cases, formal instruction about racial diversity. They acquired firsthand experience with Americans of color mainly by having children of color in class.

The other eight white teachers had somewhat more substantial life experience with racial diversity which they had acquired through travel, outside interests, or involvement in school-related projects. For example, one had served two years in the Peace Corps in Thailand and had traveled in the Middle East and Europe; another had been an exchange student in Mexico City one summer, living with a wealthy family but witnessing much dire poverty. Travel can expose teachers to other people's perspectives and ways of life, but does not substitute for experience with American racial minority groups. Two white teachers had attended multiracial schools, one had grown up near an African American neighborhood, and one participated in a summer program for students of color that required extensive home visits.

Travel and contact experiences can sometimes help whites realize how much they do not understand about race relations and sensitize them to injustices and to perspectives and experiences of other groups. One white teacher described her first teaching experience in a university town:

> I . . . taught in the highest minority school I've ever been in, it was 95% Black. And to my surprise, that's when my commitment began. I didn't like the fact that the university community didn't know there was a Black school there. And they didn't. And I knew there was something wrong.

However, such experiences can also help whites get past the discomfort people feel around other racial groups without opening them to alternative perspectives. A few of the white teachers commented that they were raised "to be open to anybody" and "without any prejudice," yet their discussions revealed a limited understanding of racism.

Over half of the white teachers had taken a course or a workshop in multicultural education. Four had taken a required course as part of their preservice education, three from African American professors. They said the course had raised their awareness; but one commented that the professor had been "really big into Black culture," and another described the course as a "hostile experience." Eight had participated in workshops when their school district was desegregated. What seemed to have stuck with them from the workshops were awareness that curriculum materials should include diverse people, some background information about minority groups in the community, and familiarity with multicultural education terminology. One emphasized having learned that,

> I didn't feel that there was the prejudice that I had been led to believe, especially in the elementary teachers. I know I've heard many people say, I don't like it when you say you're colorblind, because you shouldn't be colorblind, but I really believe that elementary teachers feel that kids are kids, . . . 'cause people would say, Well, what's your minority breakdown? And teachers would really have a rough time saying, you know. It was like asking how many of your kids are wearing glasses. And so really, I'm not denying that there's prejudice but I just don't think it's as strong in the school system as people really assume.

A few other teachers had attended courses or workshops on other topics, such as Southeast Asians. Some found such courses interesting and signed up voluntarily for more. But at the same time, most were uncomfortable with what they perceived as racial anger; they sought similarities among groups and wanted concrete classroom applications that they could add to what they already did. Many did not see a need to change what they did radically and were offended by strong suggestions that they should.

As the staff development program progressed, several white teachers tried to minimize race by negating it altogether. The seven who advocated a colorblind perspective clearly were trying to negate race. Five tried to show interest in race by criticizing the project's emphasis on some racial groups—African Americans and Latinos—to the exclusion of others such as American Indians, Arabs, or Japanese. Most white teachers had an unresolved dilemma: how to accept all children regardless of race while explaining their difficulties in school without seeming racist. Some directly used culturalist explanations that blame the "culture of poverty," asserting that race was not the issue. Several tried to ignore culturalist explanations, but unconsciously used them anyway for lack of another explanation for children's classroom behavior and achievement; they first mentioned the racial or socioeconomic composition of their students, then immediately described their problems:

> Well, we have quite a mixture [of students.] We have two Vietnamese children. I have a mulatto. I haven't counted the Blacks. I have a few Spanish, a couple Spanish. And the majority of them do come from a low socioeconomic class. But then I do have a couple of them, about four, from the higher middle class, you know. So it is quite a motley crew of kids, and you've got your middle straight down. There's twenty-seven and they aren't the brightest group that I've had. . . . It's basically an average, low average class.

For the most part, teachers did not have a convincing alternative framework for thinking about racial inequality.

The teachers of color, on the other hand, held different perspectives. All four had moved north from southern states, where they had grown up in segregated neighborhoods and attended segregated schools. All four had experienced racial discrimination while growing up and had learned about family experiences with it; they did not have to be convinced that racism exists. For example, one described discrimination his ancestors had experienced in Texas, as well as what he had experienced as a child:

> I remember my third grade teacher telling that we were animals
> because we didn't know how to eat with a knife and a fork like
> white children, because . . . we ate with tortillas. . . . I wanted to
> take German in high school, and they . . . would not let me take
> German, I had to take, as a foreign language I had to take Spanish.
> Jesus Christ, it doesn't make sense, I could read, write and speak
> Spanish because we did it at home!

All four had been angry but learned to keep going.

> There are roadblocks, there are obstacles, there are some people
> who will throw obstacles in front of you or try to keep you from
> achieving, OK, you don't have to hate them to get back at them, you
> just have to do what you need to do, . . . Go on and achieve what you
> want to achieve.

Their parents' education levels varied from not having completed elementary school to having earned a college degree, but their parents
had stressed the importance of education, and the teachers of color
understood that most families of color value education. They identified
with their ethnic community and tried to serve it through their work.

The main difference between the white teachers and the teachers of color is that the latter flatly rejected conservative explanations of racial inequality. Further, although they recognized racism
as it is expressed through personal attitudes, they did not reduce it
to attitudes. Neither did they accept culturalist explanations for
racial inequality, although two articulated culturalist explanations
for social class inequality. None of the teachers of color offered a
radical structuralist interpretation of race relations, but they had
insights that would support that perspective, such as a recognition
that whites consistently erect barriers against people of color. Further, they had been involved in social protests during the civil rights
movement, understood that many of the battles being fought then
were still not won, and could see a relationship between multicultural education and social movements for racial equality.

In their investigation of how Americans view inequality,
Kluegel and Smith (1986) found most Americans to believe that
opportunity for economic advancement is widely available, and that
inequalities are due mainly to unequal efforts and talents. But they
also found that,

> The largest and most consistent group disparities in expressed
> doubt about the workings of the American stratification order are

those between blacks and whites. . . . [N]either the disparity by
status nor by sex is so large or so consistent across beliefs as that by
race. . . . [B]lacks are the group of Americans that come closest to
being "class conscious" in the Marxian sense. (p. 289)

The teachers in this study illustrate racial disparities in perspectives about how society works. White Americans generally are not
victims of racial discrimination, as are people of color. Whites do
not experience as barriers institutional rules and processes that
oppress other groups. Further, whites usually do not experience the
strength and resilience of racial minority communities and families.
As I argue in more detail in the next chapter, spending their lives on
white-dominated turf enables most whites to develop an experience
base that allows them to deny or minimize racism.

Women in a Gendered Profession

Two white women teachers discussed their interest in feminism, which might suggest that a feminist analysis of society would
cause them to question the ideology of individualism and equal
opportunity. Although the program focused much less on sexual
than racial discrimination and since most of the teachers were
women, it is worth wondering to what extent their experiences with
sex discrimination sensitized them to other forms of discrimination.
Contrary to what may seem obvious, the data suggest that women's
unexamined experience with sexism limits their understanding of
social stratification by encouraging them to believe they understand
discrimination. I can only speculate on this, since the idea did not
occur to me until after I had finished collecting data, but my speculation fits patterns in the data.

In the first session of the program, teachers discussed and
rank-ordered topics of interest to them. Very few indicated an interest in studying gender equity, although it was one of several topics
suggested to them. Their relative lack of interest seems to have
stemmed from a perception that they already understood it. The
most lively exchanges among the teachers occurred when men made
sex stereotypic statements or accepted instances of obvious sexism,
and the women challenged them. For example, in a session on cooperative learning, a technical education teacher mentioned having
only one girl in class. Two women immediately asked what he would
do next year to change that. He replied, "I have no idea," and went on
to say that he uses four different rooms, so students can hide and do
things other than work. He was teased heartily, but some women

grumbled about sexism in the distribution of students to vocational courses.

An Attitude Assessment that was administered at the beginning and end of the first year provides some insight into this (Grant & Sleeter, 1986, p. 270). It asked teachers to respond on a Likert-type scale to 100 items, which I analyzed by categorizing items by race, language, social class, and gender, then computing mean scores (1 = low, 5 = high) for each category for pre- and post-assessments. Since the interview data proved much richer than data from this assessment, I did not test the scores for statistical significance. However, I was struck by the high mean scores for items about gender. On the pre-assessment, average scores for items on race, language, and social class were 3.54, 3.32, and 3.70 respectively; on the post-assessment they rose to 4.05, 3.83, and 3.96 respectively. The average score for items on gender on the pre-assessment was 4.44, and on the post-assessment, 4.49. These scores suggest that the teachers entered the project already sensitized to gender to a much greater degree than issues of race, language, and social class.

But the women's understanding of sex discrimination was most likely a liberal understanding, locating sexism mainly in biased attitudes of individuals who limit the opportunities of other individuals by treating them stereotypically. A speaker on gender equity reinforced this view as she discussed how patterns in teacher-student interaction encourage boys and discourage girls. The main solution to sexism from a liberal perspective is to try to eliminate sex stereotyping and sexist practices in social institutions, so that all may strive for their dreams as individuals, without regard to sex. From radical structuralist perspectives, liberalism leaves several problems unexamined and contains some contradictions. For example, by stressing the value of careers men of wealth have dominated, liberal feminism tacitly accepts disdain for manual labor and work involving care of the body. Liberal feminism does not offer a critique of the economic structure or the relationship between the economy and the state, which leads to naive assumptions about the neutrality of the state and ignorance of the role of capitalism in women's oppression. From a radical structuralist perspective, liberal solutions to discrimination would end neither sexism, racism, nor class oppression.

However, the very having of a theory of sexism can suggest to its holders that they do indeed understand one form of discrimination and need only learn how that theory applies to other forms. Thus, to the extent that women are consciously aware of sex stereotypes that other people articulate and that have limited their own choices, they feel they understand sex discrimination and do not need to analyze it further. Conflating experience with theory precludes the development of a deeper understanding of that experience than one would construct through the categories of meaning that are readily available (Scott, 1992). The teachers constructed theories of sexism by interpreting their personal experiences through frameworks that were already familiar to them (such as liberalism) without scrutinizing such frameworks themselves. Transferring their understanding of sexism to racism led them to focus mainly on stereotyping and on persevering in spite of the hurt other people's stereotypes may cause a person. In this way, women's unexamined experiences with sexism in the context of a discourse rooted in liberalism strengthens their own adherence to liberalism as a generalized perspective for understanding social inequality and gives them a framework for thinking about how discrimination in general works.

The lives of the women teachers, however, had been structured by gender in ways they took for granted. Historically teaching has been one of the few socially acceptable routes many women have had into public life and paid work. Madeline Grumet (1988) argued that women enter teaching in an effort to move out of the domestic sphere and develop their own potentials and identities as individuals.

> Bonded, interminably, it would seem to her mother and then to her child, the woman who survives the demands of these relationships to work in the world as a curriculum theorist, school administrator, or teacher is often engaged in the project of her own belated individuation and expression. (p. 28)

As teachers, women experience the contradiction between being controlled by a male bureaucracy that has hired them to bring children under control, while they themselves are seeking growth, achievement, and productivity.

All of the women in this study were married, and most had children of their own. Fifteen were asked about their own mothers' work. The mothers of six had been full-time homemakers (one had taught school before she was married, then quit), the mothers of seven had been homemakers and had also held clerical jobs, and the mothers of two had been farmers. Becoming teachers, all of them had taken on full-time work in the public sphere, which their mothers had not done. In a sense, they had rejected gendered limitations on their lives that their mothers accepted.

However, the women teachers with children all described a pattern of balancing and usually deferring their careers to the demands of childbearing and mothering, and in this sense their lives had reproduced traditional gendered patterns. Some were consciously aware that they had initially chosen a different career. For example,

> My dad was a pharmacist, . . . and my mother had been a teacher, but she taught for maybe three years and then they were married and it was not acceptable for a pharmacist's wife to work, so she was at home. . . . I really wanted to go into pharmacy, but my mother told me that I should leave that for my brother, that it would be a good idea for me to go into nursing and teaching. Being an obedient child, I did. My brother tried to go to school and he did not like anything that had to do with pharmacy, not the math or chemistry that I enjoyed, and so he never did go into pharmacy.

Many described career patterns that were checkered by moves due to husbands' work and stops and starts due to childbirth. The following story was typical.

> I taught kindergarten, went back to school, worked in a child development lab while I was in semi-graduate school. My husband . . . [was] doing some graduate work, but then I taught so he could finish. That's why I didn't finish my program. . . . I taught there three years and that was the extent of my teaching at that time because I started a family and chose to be at home for 12 years. And just a fluke, I turned in a sub application the day before Thanksgiving, and on the following Monday I had a call saying, We have a kindergarten opening quite unexpected. Your sub application is here, would you like to apply for a job.

But at the same time, most of the teachers showed an active interest in continuing to learn, grow, and create, within the bounds of their gendered lives.

For example, one teacher developed an interest in Indian art that she pursued with determination:

> I got very interested in Indian art. . . . My poor ex-husband had to crawl out of and into every settlement that the Indians inhabited, whatever the height of Indians had ever been, and he had to go hiking in there because Shari was interested in it. And this last summer, my husband and I were in Arizona, because I'm very interested in this group of Indians.

But, like most of the women teachers, her teaching career was inter-
rupted periodically by family demands. Even the fact that she was a
teacher rather than another kind of professional was due mainly to
following her husband and taking what job she could get in the town
in which his job was located.

The teachers seemed to accept their gendered family responsibilities and career choice. Many of them were very bright and capable and, within a context that was shaped and limited by their gender, they had sought opportunities for growth and achievement. As
Weiler (1988) discussed, we see in the career choices and patterns of
women teachers "a logic of existing social structures and ideology"
that subordinates women's lives to men's careers (p. 89). A critical
examination of their own lives could form the basis for a radical
structural analysis of gender oppression, but this becomes personally
very threatening.

Conclusion

Anthony Giddens (1979) advanced his analysis of social theory on the premise that, "every social actor knows a great deal about
the conditions of reproduction of the society of which he or she is a
member" (p. 5). Regardless of how little experience with racial or
cultural diversity teachers have had, they enter the classroom with
a considerably rich body of knowledge about social stratification,
social mobility, and human differences based on their life experience. The analogies the white teachers in this study drew between
what they knew about racism and what they knew about sexism,
class mobility, and the European ethnic experience tended to minimize or neutralize racism and multicultural education's implications
for action. However, from the teachers' perspectives, they were
accounting for racial discrimination, not ignoring it. The teachers
participated in as many as fourteen all-day sessions of multicultural
education. Classroom observations and interviews suggested that
they took from the staff development sessions information and teaching strategies to add into their thinking and their work, but that
few (if any) substantively restructured their perspective about racial
inequality or classroom teaching.

Of the twenty-six teachers in this study who discussed the relationship between their goals for teaching and multicultural education, seven saw it as irrelevant, basing their arguments on a conservative understanding of society—that all Americans have fairly

equal opportunity to achieve upward mobility, and that those who do not progress well are hindered mainly by their own efforts or deficient home backgrounds. Two more who were concerned with struggles of out-groups also articulated mostly conservative perspectives. However, these two probably rejected the sociobiological explanation for racial inequality and, in so doing, regarded themselves as relatively progressive. All nine were white, but their sex and social class backgrounds were diverse. The women acknowledged their own experiences with sex stereotyping, one doing so at some length, but saw this as inescapable and too easily used as an excuse for not trying. Those who had grown up in socioeconomically poor homes had pulled themselves up and, as a result, believed anyone else could do the same. They maintained that life is not easy and advancement requires work and at times a tough skin, but in general opportunity is open to everyone.

The remaining seventeen teachers interpreted multicultural education broadly within a liberal understanding of society. Ten—all women—focused on personal and interpersonal connection. The six who defined multicultural education as human relations showed interest in interpersonal relations more than in how social mobility works and willingly addressed the social and personal ambiance within their classrooms. Four of the eight teachers who focused on the struggles of out-groups were also interested mainly in nourishing students' self-esteem and interpersonal relationships. When asked about social processes outside the classroom, they acknowledged discrimination and at times showed anger about unfairness. But they were concerned more about helping children cope with the world than teaching them to change it. Their interpretation of multicultural education was feminine in their emphasis on connection, community, and feeling (Gilligan, 1980). It was not yet politicized, however; like the feminist teachers Kathleen Weiler (1988) studied, they valued "the creation of a classroom where 'it's okay to be human' in terms of relationships," but unlike them, had not "developed a commitment to raising issues and questioning accepted social values and ideology." (p. 113–114).

The rest, whom I have classified broadly within liberalism, brought some degree of political criticism to their understanding of multicultural education. The teachers of color brought their awareness of institutional racism; two special education teachers brought awareness of how schools institutionalize failure. The other white teachers brought life experiences they began to connect with political criticism for reasons the data do not suggest.

But for the most part, the teachers' perspectives took as given the social context of the individual and asked how to prepare the individual to live within that context. Most further assumed that, with some variations, society's rules apply similarly to everyone; the rules may not always be fair, but they are acceptable, and processes for setting them are fair.

It is important to note that the teachers in this study were a self-selected group. They volunteered to participate because they believed multicultural education might be useful to them. The proportions advocating conservative and liberal perspectives (as well as radical structuralist glimmerings) are probably rather different from those of the teaching profession at large, where it is likely that a much higher proportion subscribe to conservatism.

Teacher educators who work with teachers in multicultural education need to confront teachers' political perspectives, doing so in a way that accounts for, rather than dismisses, the experiential basis of those perspectives. In chapter 6 I will share thoughts about doing this. First, however, we will examine differences between dominant and "minority position" discourses. Themes in the dominant discourse tend to resonate with the life experiences of many educators, blocking our ability to "hear" oppressed voices clearly.

CHAPTER 5

This Curriculum is Multicultural . . .
Isn't It?

During the 1960s, textbooks clearly featured experiences and viewpoints of white middle class and elite people, mainly men. Over the past twenty-five years textbooks have gone through phases of active revision and on the surface appear to be pluralistic. If one thumbs through almost any textbook published over the past ten years, it appears well integrated. Many teachers, too, work to make their curricula multicultural and become puzzled or frustrated when the fruits of their efforts are criticized.

What constitutes a multicultural curriculum is a political decision that is grounded in everyday politics over who gets to define what "America" means. As Catherine Cornbleth and Dexter Waugh (1995) argue, debates about multicultural curricula are nested within the "'America debate' about how the United States of America should be, or can be, redefined to encompass our increasingly diverse population" (p. 4). As noted in chapter 3, conservative think tanks and spokespeople have become increasingly active in this debate, with battles having been played out at the state level in both California and New York and at local levels in many communities.

Teachers do not necessarily align themselves with conservative think tanks, yet often manage to produce multicultural curricula that adhere to white, conservative renditions of the U.S. This results from filtering "diversity" through taken-for-granted ideas about what that should mean. Often the result of such work are curricula that are integrated, but in a colonizing sense: they add representations of diverse groups into grand narratives that still privilege the positions and perspectives of those who dominate control over power and wealth (Sleeter & Grant, 1991). Spivak (1990) described them as, the rationalist narratives of the knowing subject, full of a certain sort of benevolence towards others, wanting to welcome those others into his own—and I use the pronoun advisedly—into his own understanding of the word, so that they too can be liberated and begin to inhabit a world that is the best of all possible worlds. (p. 19)

What differentiates a "colonizing" multicultural curriculum from one that reflects genuine concerns and perspectives of oppressed groups? In this chapter, after briefly reviewing some concerns about attempts to create multicultural curriculum, several themes will be outlined that are common to "minority" discourses and differentiate them from dominant discourses. Then I will suggest implications of this discussion for multicultural curriculum construction.

Curriculum and Worldview

When creating a multicultural curriculum, educators tend to preoccupy themselves with what to add to the curriculum: which literary selections, which historical figures, which artistic representations, and so forth. The questions that too often are not addressed are: Who decides? What is the nature of the curriculum into which these "additions" are to be made? Whose stories are actually being told? In his critique of multicultural liberal arts curricula, San Juan, Jr. (1992) asked: "Are we witnessing the return of tokenism writ large, integration recuperated, races separate but equal under the same roof?" (p. 28)

The multicultural curricula many educators and textbook publishers end up creating are too frequently colonizing, Eurocentric, patriarchal curricula in disguise, still structured around a worldview rooted in the European immigrant experience (King, 1992). Or, as Rey Chow (1992) put it, uncritical (ludic) postmodern multicultural curricula allow " 'the others' to be seen, but would not pay attention to what they say" (p. 114). The same old traditional grand narrative—the overall picture and story that emerges as the "universal" story that presumes to account for and tie together all "substories"—remains intact and unquestioned. Several largely unstated themes structure the grand narrative of curricula fashioned within this worldview; these are summarized on Figure 5.1.

Such curricula implicitly stress individualism, upward mobility, broad social consensus, and the legitimacy of the status quo. They

Figure 5.1
Themes in a Eurocentric, Patriarchal Curriculum

The United States is the land of wealth and opportunity; it is open to all who try; anyone can get what he works for.

American history flowed from Europe to the East Coast of North America; from there it flowed Westward.

American culture is of European origin; Europe is the main source of worthwhile cultural achievements.

National ideals are (and should) consist of individual advancement, private accumulation, rule by majority as well as by market demand, loyalty to U.S. government, in addition to freedom of speech.

Some social problems existed in the past, but they have been solved.

Most problems society faces have technical solutions, for which science and math offer the best keys.

Americans share consensus about most things; differences are individual and can be talked out (usually in one story).

Other places in the world may have poverty and problems, but the U.S. does not; we tend to solve other nations' problems.

America is basically white, middle class, and heterosexual; white wealthy men are the world's best thinkers and problem-solvers and usually act in the best interests of everyone.

present a new grand narrative of U.S. history, its identity, and its diversity, reducing difference to family heritage and customs from the "old" country, such as food, holidays, folktales. By omission, such curricula imply that race, sex, social class, and other forms of difference no longer structure access to resources, although historically these may have been "problems." Diverse groups stand in equal status to one another, differentiated only by "old world" customs in which anyone can participate. Even lessons about role models, by focusing on individual achievements and ignoring the status of the group or barriers confronting the group, suggest that the system is open equally to anyone who will try. For example, I have seen women's studies lessons that focus on "famous women," without much suggestion that sexism still exists, nor analysis of it. Disability-awareness lessons often describe characteristics of people with disabilities without critiquing the social context that reinforces barriers. Diverse groups are incorporated into a grand narrative that describes, rather than questions, the social order.

Many students reject that curriculum. For example, white teachers who attempt to teach a multicultural curriculum are often puzzled when students of color object. "That just don't sound right" (Gates, 1992, p. 77). Students sense—accurately—that parts of their world are being rearranged to fit into the same old Eurocentric, patriarchal worldview. Some of the details may ring true, but the overall main ideas do not.

Critics of the canon critique the worldview underlying the dominant discourse; questions about which role model to add, which literary selection to add, which historical events to highlight, are the wrong questions. For example, Mudimbe (1988) examined the structure of colonial discourse about Africa, which has "tended to organize and transform non-European areas into fundamentally European constructs" (p. 1). Colonial discourse is rooted in an epistemology that posits a universal "sameness" among people based on western norms. Assuming a universal "man," westerners placed everyone within their own narrative of human history. Western discourse has explained differences among people in relation to a social Darwinist conception of history, in which cultures evolve through a hierarchy from "primitive" to "modern." Western anthropologists and historians, as well as casual tourists, when encountering "others," created inventories of cultural objects and practices that differentiated "them" from "us," and that

> formed part of the series of oppositions and of the levels of classification of humans demanded by the logic of the chain of being and the stages of progress and social development. Explorers just brought new proofs which could explicate "African inferiority." (Mudimbe, p. 13)

Historically, the entire project of fitting "others" into "our" worldview helped give legitimacy to the political project of colonizing the rest of the world for European use.

Whether one is speaking about multicultural curricula that add in American "Others" or Third World "Others," the result is still colonialist if the underlying worldview structuring knowledge and action is not transformed and a single master narrative is not abandoned. As Perez-Torres (1993/94) argued,

> Multiculturalism does not simply involve the recuperation of "lost" traditions in order to prove the richness and diversity of "America," . . . Rather, multiculturalism interrogates which traditions

are valorized and by whom, which are devalued and by whom, which serve to empower marginalized peoples, which serve even further to disempower, which traditions provide strength, how traditions provide agency, when traditions provide knowledge. (p. 171)

In an emancipatory multicultural curriculum, voices from the margins are fully heard.

Among academicians, ludic postmodernism has offered an alternative to traditional western narratives in its:

> rejection of or debunking of modernism's epistemic foundations or metanarratives; a dethronement of the authority of positivistic science that essentializes differences between what appear to be self-possessing identities, an attack on the notion of a unified goal of history, and a deconstruction of the magnificent Enlightenment swindle of the autonomous, stable and self-contained ego that is supposed to be able to act independently of its own history, its own indigenist strands of meaning-making and cultural and linguistic situatedness, and free from inscriptions in the discourses of, among others, gender, race, and class. (McLaren, 1994, p. 196)

As argued in chapter 3, it is quite possible to create a ludic postmodern multicultural curriculum that features multiple perspectives, but has no organizing structure that provides a basis for organized action for or against anything. This is the "diversity" curriculum that celebrates a benign pluralism in which "all differences can be understood; all differences can be overcome" (Perez-Torres, 1994, p. 169). It is the "diversity" curriculum that "articulates race [and other forms of difference] in terms of private virtue, not collective responsibility" (San Juan, Jr., 1994, p. 23).

To provide a basis for critique of domination and action aimed toward building a more just society, a multicultural curriculum can neither add difference into one grand narrative that pays homage to present social arrangements nor reduce difference to chaos. It must, rather, elucidate crucial differences in perspective and experience in a way that supports genuine dialog across borders of race, ethnicity, gender, sexual orientation, and class and that galvanizes organized work toward a shared project of a just community. I share Spivak's (1990) recommendation that an activist critic is "an essentialist from time to time. . . . You pick up the universal that will give you the power to fight against the other side" (p. 12). Further, "it's not a question of waging war on narratives, but . . . looking at the limits of narration" (p. 19). In other words, we must create narratives and constructs that will enable us to act, while maintaining awareness of the limitations inherent in any set of narratives.

This chapter suggests that groups occupying minority political positions have grappled with several themes and issues that differentiate their discourses from those who occupy dominant positions of power. Examining these themes and issues provides a means of linking minority discourses in a meaningful way, and juxtaposing them against dominant discourses. This juxtaposition provides some direction for creating authentic multicultural curricula. In what follows, I do not claim to represent the writings of all oppressed people, since perspectives of individuals vary widely, some taking quite conservative views. Rather, I will highlight themes in articulations framed within a critique of collective subordinate positioning.

Minority Position Discourse

Since the late 1960s and early 1970s, scholars in departments of ethnic studies, women's studies, disability studies, labor studies, gay and lesbian studies, and cultural studies have generated an enormous amount of research and theorizing. Not only has a great amount of information about diverse groups been retrieved, but scholars have been mapping out new conceptual frameworks within and across various disciplines (Lauter, 1991).

On what basis might we posit shared concerns across "that uneasy, shifting set of alliances formed by feminist critics, critics of so-called minority discourse, and Marxist and poststructuralist critics generally, the Rainbow coalition of contemporary critical theory" (Gates, 1992, p. 17)? Abdul JanMohamed and David Lloyd (1987) wrestled with this question in the context of a conference on "The Nature and Context of Minority Discourse." They argued that, on the one hand, premature integration of discourse

> is exactly what is to be avoided at present. Those who argue for the creation of canons of various ethnic and feminist writing do so with the full awareness that formations of *different* canons permit the self-definition, and, eventually, self-validation that must be completed before there is any talk of integration. For, to date, integration and assimilation have never taken place on equal terms, but always as assimilation *by* the dominant culture. (p. 9)

On the other hand, oppressed groups share minority *positioning* relative to the dominant society, which is a *political* rather than *cultural* issue, and thus share "the effects of economic exploitation, political disenfranchisement, social manipulation, and ideological domination on the cultural formation of minority subjects and discourses" (p. 11).

In what follows, I will suggest six related themes that differentiate minority discourses from the dominant discourse that result from historic and contemporary experiences of occupying minority positions viz a viz the dominant society. While considering these themes, it must be borne continuously in mind that the experiences and perspectives of diverse groups are very different, are still in the process of being defined, and can never be pinned down to one final definition. In addition, the following cannot be taken as suggesting harmonious agreement across groups, although I believe that continued coalition-building is an important project for effecting social change. While diverse groups grapple with several common questions and issues, the manner in which these are worked out varies widely.

Centering: Who is the Story About, and Where and When does it Begin?

A discussion I had with a history student illustrates how the reference point with which one centers and begins a story shapes the entire subsequent story. This student was attempting to explain why Mexican Americans are not in the U.S. history curriculum prior to the Mexican War. He argued that one might study what happened in Mexico before the U.S. colonized half of it, but that is not U.S. history; U.S. history concerns what happened within the political borders of the United States and, prior to its founding, what happened in Europe that shaped that founding. I countered that from a Mexican American (and Indian) perspective, history goes back to the ancient Mayas and Aztecs, and the U.S. colonization is a relatively recent event in a long history. As we talked, we realized that the student's starting place was the founding of the political system of the United States; mine was the beginning of civilization in the territory of Mexico. Both of us were arguing for very different histories, centered very differently. We were also arguing about the validity of diverse perspectives on U.S. history. This was not a question of U.S. history versus Mexican American history but rather a question of who defines how to tell U.S. history, and from what vantage point.

The remaining themes in this chapter begin with how one defines who one is talking about and where and when the story begins. A group's American story may begin in Asia and move east, in Latin America and move north, in Europe and move west, or on the North American continent thousands of years ago. The center or centers with which one begins gives direction to the backbone of the narrative. Thus, it is essential that we learn to identify how a narrative is centered and by whom, in order to recognize whose perspective informs it and what insights as well as limitations might accompany that perspective.

For example, when beginning African American history with slavery, one disconnects African Americans from African civilizations and renders any future progress as simply better than the past. An Afrocentric perspective, on the other hand, redefines the starting place of African American history from slavery to ancient Africa: "All knowledge results from an occasion of encounter in place. But the place remains a rightly shaped perspective that allows the Afrocentrist to put African ideals and values at the center of inquiry" (Asante, 1990, p. 5). In so doing, a centered African American curriculum frames the American experience as part of a diaspora of highly cultured African peoples, preceded by strong precolonial African civilizations. A historical trajectory would envision the future of people of African descent as reclaiming the self-determination, prosperity, and intellectual creativity that is in Africa's past. Afrocentrists' tug-of-war with EuroAmericans over ancient Egypt is important because Egypt historically has been regarded as a highly sophisticated and stable civilization. Not only has Afrocentric scholarship reconceptualized the starting place and subsequent narrative of African American history; it also challenges that of European and EuroAmerican history (Bernal, 1987).

Questions about what it means to "center" can be answered differently, depending on whose experience one wishes to consider. For example, American Indians center time differently than do Europeans or EuroAmericans. Allen (1986) pointed out that, "the tendency of the American Indian [is] to view space as spherical and time as cyclical, whereas the non-Indian tends to view space as linear and time as sequential" (p. 59). In the highly acclaimed novel *Ceremony*, Silko depicted the main character Tayo as he grappled with the cure of a "time/space disorder" resulting from the white man's witchcraft (Shanley, 1991, p. 251). Thus, the story of the Americas cast within an Indian framework is a multilayered, cyclical story of endurance and connection in the face of sustained genocide.

The dominant society framed people with disabilities, as well as people who are gay/lesbian, as individuals with certain characteristics without any particular community or history. Carol Padden and Tom Humphries (1988) discussed this problem with respect to Deaf people (using lower-case "d" to designate a physical condition of the individual and capital "D" to designate affiliation with the Deaf community):

> Ways of living proposed for Deaf people that ignore their past, that attempt to remove, either directly or indirectly, their historically created solutions, are not possible lives. . . . When deaf children are denied connections with Deaf people, . . . they lose access to a history of solutions created for them by other people like themselves. (p. 120)

When one begins framing a narrative with the Deaf community, or when one begins with the gay and lesbian community, the story is not so much a story of people with certain characteristics, as it is a story of communities claiming voice against a hostile society.

Gerda Lerner (1992), in her consideration of women's history, reconceptualized centering from a chronological issue to one of women's personal and political development. In the introduction to *The Female Experience*, she asked: "What would history be like if it were seen through the eyes of women and ordered by values they define?" (p. xix). She argued that the traditional periodization of U.S. history is largely irrelevant for telling the stories of women, and therefore orders women's history "from the personal to the institutional, from self and family to group and society" as women gradually created a feminist consciousness (p. xxiii).

There is danger, however, in reifying groups in order to recenter narratives. For example, which women are we talking about and who decides? In order to reframe patriarchal narratives, how often will white women continue to "once again construct women as a monolithic group whose common experiences are more important than our differences?" (hooks, 1993, p. 2). Identifying how narratives are centered means becoming keenly and critically conscious of who defined the narrative, starting with whom, and about whom. Such critical consciousness does *not* mean that we reject or disbelieve bounded narratives and look for the "correct" one—there is no correct one. That is the point.

If different groups define very different starting places, and even define the notion of starting place differently, how do we synthesize experiences? Perhaps we don't—or do so within limits. At present, the most important lesson to teach is that narratives depend on how they are centered; there is no universal center or starting place. If we learn this one idea well, we may learn to become more vigilant of the trajectories of interpretation we encounter, construct, or try to impose on others. For purposes of curriculum construction, an alternative to teaching one grand narrative would be to teach several narratives, each centered within its own context and each examining similar phenomena from different perspectives. Such study would help young people learn to recognize that starting places do differ and provide very different vantage points for considering our histories, and it would help them to grasp where someone else is "coming from."

For example, how might one's own community look historically from the perspective of Native American people who have lived in the region? White Yankees? African Americans? The gay community? Are there multiple historical narratives within the African American community, and why? Within the white community? What are the main differences between historical narratives, and what do those differences suggest about the lives of diverse peoples? Exploring these kinds of questions leads to the next theme of a multicultural curriculum.

Social Construction of Theory

Students usually encounter knowledge in school as a set of fixed facts, which presumably corresponds to something "real" and "out there," to be memorized and accepted as true.

> For example, a social studies teacher says, "On May 29, 1985, Ronald Reagan was president." The truth value of this statement is highly certain and is determined by the condition that on May 29, 1985, Ronald Reagan was president. When a social studies teacher says, "The Reagan administration made a complete commitment to supply-side economics," we are less certain about its truth value, because it is not clear what conditions would make the statement true. Textbooks are filled with cases like this. (Cherryholmes, 1988, p. 53).

Assumptions, interpretations, and judgments that someone made are very often delivered to students as neutral and firm facts. Further, schools reinforce the assumption that knowledge is something that can be discovered in an objective manner by those who are trained formally to discover it. These assumptions about the nature of knowledge rest comfortably within classical western thought and western thought's value for rationalism and positivism.

Challenges oppressed groups level against the curriculum are challenges to worldviews and theories that serve the purpose largely of explaining and justifying the social order. As those who benefit most from the status quo theorize about various dimensions of being, theories tend to explain "how things are" in a manner that renders the existing social order as inevitable and legitimate. For example, in his analysis of the AfroAsiatic roots of Greek culture, Martin Bernal (1987) contrasted the Ancient theory, which traced Greek cultural roots to Egypt, with the Aryan theory, which holds that Greece emerged from no significant roots. Bernal argued that the Aryan theory was advanced in the eighteenth century when Europeans were colonizing people of color around the world and needed justification to do so. Not only did Europeans rewrite theory, but they also reworked notions of what counts as valid evidence, limiting it to that which was archaeologically verifiable and excluding evidence from linguistic analysis, mythology and legend, and analysis of literary texts. Much curriculum is built on Aryan theory, supporting the belief that Europe is the unique source of the world's best civilizations. Bernal's argument and evidence suggest that such a rationale for European supremacy and colonization rests on a faulty foundation.

Even something as "factual" and neutral as a documentary reflects the values and perspectives of the creator: the film-maker chooses what to film, at what angle and depth, for what audience (Trinh, 1991). Nor is the dichotomy of science versus myth tenable. Teachers, as well as the broader public, commonly regard the fruits of Western science to be irrefutable fact and Third World mythology to be fiction that even elementary children can approximate in their creative writing. But, as Paula Gunn Allen (1986) argued with reference to Native American mythology, "Labeling something a myth merely discredits the perceptual system and worldview of those who are not in accord with the dominant paradigm;" dominant group conceptions define "myth as synonymous with lie" (p. 102). From Third World perspectives, what is termed "myth" tells truths differently from Western science; both modes of thought attempt to represent reality, but in very different ways.

Many contemporary intellectuals regard French deconstructionists as having invented processes for examining theory as a social construct. Such examinations have long been a part of the projects oppressed groups undertake in an effort to critique and dethrone regimes of truth that justify marginalization. A classic example is Gilligan's (1982) critique of moral development theory, in which she argues that Kohlberg's theory is rooted in the male experience (I would add, the white male experience) and does not capture (white) women's development.

Many people resist challenges to prevailing theories, believing that dismantling established "truth" would bring chaos. But the process of questioning theory is not meant to invoke chaos. Indeed, as Rosaldo (1989) noted, a vision of impending chaos impels people to accept as true much that need not be accepted (p. 100). Rather, the process is one of creating new ideas, frameworks, and spaces for work that suggest a different social order.

In the multicultural curriculum, young people can begin to grasp the social construction of theory by engaging in theory construction themselves. As one creates knowledge, one comes to understand issues such as how varied degrees of verifiability are, how theory simplifies reality, how arbitrary some "facts" actually are, and how ideas can be subject to questioning and reexamination. In addition, students can examine social uses to which theories have been put, in order to develop a basis for evaluating the worth of theories for themselves.

Subjugation and Liberation

> [H]istory is the version of events told by the conqueror, the dominator. Even the dominators acknowledge this. What has more feelingly and pragmatically been said by people of color, by white women, by lesbians and gay men, by people with roots in the industrial or rural working class is that without our own history we are unable to imagine a future because we are deprived of the precious resource of knowing where we came from: the valor and the waverings, the visions and defeats of those who went before us. (Adrienne Rich, cited by Gaard, 1992, p. 31)

The curriculum gives us a past and names our present in order to help us conceptualize a future. For those who perceive the past and present as legitimate, the future should bring more of the same. Thus the dominant curriculum valorizes the existing social order and the traditions upholding it. Euro-Americans (particularly men) who are relatively well-off are usually terribly naive about (and often indifferent to) the conditions groups other than themselves live. Most Euro-Americans define our own privileged experience as normal and curricular representations of it as apolitical. "Others" are then added in, represented in ways that do not disrupt the status quo. For example, in its portrayal of Indian people, the dominant media are

> projecting a carefully-perfected image that the system of colonial oppression no longer "really" exists. Culmination of the process will rest on inculcating the population at large with a subliminal "understanding" that the only "genuine," "authentic," "representa-tive," and therefore "real" Indians are those who "fit in" most com-fortably. (Churchill, 1992, p. 10–11)

Representations of Indian people that cast Indians as historic figures only, and representations of white people that are either completely removed from white-Indian relationships or that portray whites as supportive of Indians fit within a worldview Euro-Americans find comfortable.

Groups occupying minority positions, on the other hand, strive to redefine knowledge for the purpose of collective liberation from domination. Such intellectual work is not new. For example, in 1827, Samuel Cornish and John Russworm wrote, in the first issue of the first African-American newspaper:

> We wish to plead our own cause. Too long have others spoken for us. Too long has the publick been deceived by misrepresentations, in things which concern us dearly, though in the estimation of some mere trifles; . . . Is it not very desirable that such should know more of our actual condition; and of our efforts and feelings, that in forming or advocating plans for our amelioration, they may do it more understandingly? (Bennett, 1982, p. 174)

Minority position curricula provide the intellectual offensive for social and political struggles for liberation and cultural integrity (Cortada, 1974). Such curricula should arise from real life condi-tions of struggle and speak directly to "basic questions of power and oppression in America" (Omatsu, 1994, p. 26).

Groups that are positioned in society differently define subju-gation and liberation in somewhat different terms, but share a desire for liberation that contrasts markedly with the dominant society's desire to justify existing social arrangements. Labor studies, for example, envision a world in which the organization of work does not place large segments of society under the control of a wealthy elite. Traditional curricula usually portray business and corporate leaders

1986). Developing collectives requires networking individuals, politicizing their interpretation of their lives, and creating identities in which people can see themselves. Publications such as *Disability Rag* (a magazine produced by and for people with disabilities) were created for this purpose.

Another task is generating politically strategic alliances of groups who differ but share common concerns. Felix Padilla (1985) asked how various Latino ethnic groups can forge a larger "Latino" collective. He studied the formation of Latino ethnic consciousness in Chicago, arguing that a collective identity had to be constructed before Latinos could exercise political power effectively. He viewed identity formation as both a political response to structural discrimination as well as an articulation of a common cultural legacy. He found Latino identity to be situational: individuals identify either with a specific ethnic group (such as Mexican Americans) or a wider Latino collective, depending on the issue confronting them. It has been necessary for Latino community leaders to convince Latinos that they share common interests, to provide settings in which members of different Latino ethnic groups can mix, and to mobilize cultural symbols (particularly language) that bind groups together.

Creating politically strategic collectives is complicated work. Part of what complicates this process is that people are members of multiple groups (i.e., racial groups, gender groups, etc.). Further, these multiple memberships are situated in criss-crossing lines of privilege and power, positioning members of broad categories very differently relative to one another. Creating alliances requires self-critique around issues of power. For example,

> Women's Studies must divest itself of white-skin privilege, racism, and the feminist insistence on the primacy of gender; Ethnic Studies must divest itself of male-centered scholarship, sexism, and heterosexism, and must lend credibility to gender as a valid, viable, and necessary category of analysis. (Butler, 1991, p. 9)

Reconceptualized categories can also become new essentialized categories that obscure important differences within a collective and over time can become depoliticized. Cameron McCarthy (1995) criticized the essentializing of Afrocentric identities which posit similarities based on national origin and deny complex differences among African Americans. Biddy Martin (1993) critiqued constructions of lesbian identities that assume "there are no differences within the 'lesbian self' and that lesbian authors, autobiographical subjects, readers, and critics can be conflated and marginalized as self-identical and separable from questions of race, class, sexuality, and ethnicity" (p. 277). Recognition of differences within collectivities must move not toward fragmentation, however, but toward solidarity. As Cameron McCarthy and Warren Crichlow (1993) put it, "subaltern educational activists must begin to see racial difference as one (not the only) of the starting points for drawing out the various solidarities among subordinated minorities and working-class women and men over our separate but related forms of oppression" (p. xxi).

Curricula produced by the dominant society—even those that appear multicultural—hinder rather than help the process of critiquing and constructing collective identities. Most curricula take dominant categories and borders for granted as natural or legitimate. Texts define citizens as individual Americans, and "groupness" as culturally interesting but politically irrelevant. Teachers become bogged down in debates over terminology for groups, and, feeling uncomfortable in contexts in which they are minorities anyway, prefer to claim that race doesn't really exist; we are all just Americans, gender is biological and personal, and so forth.

A different departure point for curriculum construction would begin with the premise that collective identification is important and to construct inquiry around questions such as: Why do Native American leaders regard Indian identities as important? How do Indian people define Indian identities in the 1990s? What does it mean for identities to be political in addition to being cultural? How do indigenous people view current national borders?

A Group's Identity is Found in its Own Literature and Arts

The dominant society constantly creates and recreates images of oppressed groups through various media—movies, television, scholarly articles, stories and proverbs, literature, and art—which rationalize different groups' positions in society. Sucheta Mazumdar (1989) listed identities the dominant society has constructed of Asian American women: "the depraved prostitute in nineteenth-century San Francisco; the quiet, courteous and efficient Asian female office worker today. Asian women in America have emerged not as individuals but as nameless and faceless members of an alien community" (p. 1). Ward Churchill (1992) termed the dominant society's construction of Native American identities as *Fantasies of the Master Race*, created to convince the public of the legitimacy of colonialism. The dominant society has defined the working class as "middle class," with interests aligned to capital and private gain, and labor unions as passe and un-American. The poor have been given identities as criminals, welfare queens, and drug-abusers, which validate the status quo and blame the lower class for their condition (Aronowitz, 1992).

Constructing authentic identities—how group members actually see and define themselves—is a major project of literature and artistic products a group creates about itself. Gates (1992) describes this as a process of writing "themselves into being": appropriating language and art forms to construct one's own self-image, in light of the negative, inaccurate, and twisted images the dominant society has imposed (p. 57). Consider the difference between the identities of women in most popular movies versus women's identities in the movie "Thelma and Louise." Most movies construct women as love interests, seductresses, office workers, or mothers and wives; even if women hold other roles such as lawyer, their sexuality and relationships with men usually predominate. In contrast, Thelma and Louise, whose identities were constructed by women, rejected sexual control and decided to die rather than conform. The dominant society's definitions of diverse groups are powerful and pervasive; it takes effort and work to "get man off your eyeball," as Shug put it in Alice Walker's *The Color Purple*, because the "man's" (white male power structure's) viewpoint is projected constantly (Gates, 1992, p. 68). Images women encounter are usually mediated by men: in texts and media and through teachers, fathers, and lovers; as a result, women's search for identity is marked by uncertainty (Pagano, 1990). In writing *A Room of One's Own*, Virginia Woolf grappled with women's voice in text, naming women's uncertainty and desire to define one's own identity.

Deaf culture encoded in sign language is another example of a medium in which a collective has brought itself into being. Padden and Humphries (1988) described a folktale French Deaf people tell about themselves, which "has come to symbolize, in its retelling through the centuries, the transition from a world in which deaf people live alone or in small isolated communities to a world in which they have a rich community and language" (p. 29). Through sign language, Deaf communities and identities were created; Deaf theater has now become a rich medium for elaborating personal, cultural, and political dimensions of Deaf identities.

Language becomes an issue of contention because the language which is used to name experience and identity helps to shape that which is named. In their discussion of "real vs. fake" Asian American literary traditions, Chin, Chan, Inada, and Wong (1991) discussed how forced acculturation into the English language is partly a process of stripping identity: "They did not teach us English for us to make the language our own. They gave us English to force us to define ourselves in their terms" (p. 238). Because language is the medium through which we name ourselves and our world, language minority groups resist giving up language and the definitions of self and the world that language encodes.

Reconstruction of imagery and identity is an on-going process, given the hegemonic milieu in which oppressed groups work. West (1993) discussed the tightrope African American artists and intellectuals walk between the quest for mainstream approval in order to gain access—with White approval's accompanying bondage, the problem of oversimplifying one-dimensional reductionism (such as reducing identity to race only), or the personal pleasure of aestheticism.

> The main aim now is not simply access to representation in order to produce positive images of homogeneous communities—although broader access remains a practical and political problem. Nor is the primary goal here that of contesting stereotypes—although contestation remains a significant albeit limited venture. . . . Black cultural workers must constitute and sustain discursive and institutional networks that deconstruct earlier modern black strategies for identity formation, demystify power relations that incorporate class, patriarchal, and homophobic biases, and construct more multivalent and multidimensional responses that articulate the complexity and diversity of black practices in the modern and postmodern world. (p. 19)

Multicultural curricula often incorporate material from the repertoires of art forms produced by diverse groups. When out-group members decide what to put into the curriculum, their selections and presentations often reproduce those of the dominant society and run contrary to perspectives that group members themselves articulate. The selection of literature that a white female teacher makes to depict Asian American male identity may not at all represent identity as Asian American men define themselves. We all make curricular selections and interpretations based on what we view as worthwhile. The implication here is that curriculum constructors cannot create curriculum without working collaboratively with those whom we are attempting to include. Only by maintaining vigilance over our own biases and opening ourselves to definitions other groups are creating for themselves, can we create an authentic multicultural curriculum.

Even then, deciding how to represent any group is far from straightforward, since identities are always "in the making." A different beginning point is to assume that the curriculum cannot present fixed, "correct" representations of any group. Rather, it can help young people pose and examine questions about representation. How do Mexican Americans represent themselves in various media? If we read stories by authors such as Rudolfo Anaya, Sandra Cisneros, and Teri de la Peña, what different kinds of images and identities do we encounter? How do different members of the Mexican American community critique those representations and why? What kinds of representation build bridges of hope and action? Engaging students in questions such as these offers much more promise than attempting to pin down which images to teach as "true."

Dominant group members often feel left out of such discussions. Some of my white students respond to discussions of such issues by saying plaintively, "I guess I don't have a culture." One response is that, of course, dominant groups have a culture, which is represented in mainstream media constantly. Fish do not see water, not because it does not exist, but because it surrounds them constantly. A second rather different response, however, is that we do lack strong representations of ourselves in ways that reject domination, materialism, and impersonalism. *USA Today* hardly provides me with an identity that speaks to anything meaningful, but representations like those it projects surround me daily. Noel Ignatiev (1993) distinguishes between being white and being American. To be American is to be fully human and free from participating in domination; it is to develop genuine connections with a community and with nature and to place human connection above material gain. To be white is to cultivate the drive to consume and dominate. Those of us in dominant positions have the task of constructing identities and representations of ourselves that reject participation in racism and that are genuinely nurturing and sustaining.

Oppressed Groups are Durable, Strong, and Active

If we live an a free and open society—an assumption the dominant society makes—why do some groups fare better economically, educationally, and politically than others? The main commonsense explanations the dominant society offers focus on characteristics of groups: strengths and abilities of Euro-American male leaders and thinkers and deficiencies of "have not" groups, such as in culture, morals, will, language, or family. These assumed virtues and deficiencies become the stuff of stereotypes, part of the rationale for the underrepresentation of many groups in the curriculum. Multicultural curricula that maintain the dominant society's perspective try to cover over the deficiency orientation by adding on talented individuals who "made it" and bits of folk culture.

Minority discourses, conversely, develop depictions of strength, wisdom, and the ability of a group to get things done. What role did African Americans have in the abolition of slavery, and what difference does this make? Most curricula suggest that slaves were passive and powerless and that a few great people, particularly Lincoln, ended slavery. If this were true (which it was not), what implications would it have for solving problems the African American community faces today? It would suggest that the masses should wait for a few great men, particularly the President, to solve things—if indeed there is anything to be solved that cannot be corrected by getting young African Americans to work harder.

A reading of African American history gives quite a different picture, highlighting the active role many African Americans, both slave and free, played in ending slavery. Lerone Bennett (1982) described this work as the "expressions of the tenacity of spirit of a people who never stopped testing the wall, sending line after line into the breach, losing many and paying a frightfully high price for the handful who managed to slip through" (p. 177). Over time, this tenacious work contributed to the end of slavery, which presents quite a different image of African Americans, with very different implications for the potential of African American people to tackle current issues.

Minority discourses develop strengths, wisdom, creativity, and durability of groups—present as well as past. Allen (1986) pointed out that Indian history, properly understood, shows that Indian people endure: after 500 years of systematic policies of genocide (by disease, murder, forced sterilization, severe impoverization), Indian people are still here, and still creating. Women, when they have access to athletic opportunities, are now breaking Olympic records that men set years ago (Linn & Hyde, 1989). Women have the capability to do whatever we want, but the institutional context we inhabit tries to limit us. Asians are neither quiet nor passive. In their introduction to the anthology *Making Waves*, the editors explained that, "we are not afraid to rock the boat. Making waves. This is what Asian American women have done and will continue to do" (Asian Women United of California, 1989, p. xi).

It is impossible to depict oppressed groups as strong and active without situating them within oppressive contexts. (If we are so

> No matter what devices are contrived to bring about equality, it is
> clear that they require money-transfer, and the largest source of
> money is the portion of the population that possesses the most
> money. (p. 223)

And the most power and authority. Now imagine what multicultural critical pedagogy might mean if one is teaching those with the
most, rather than least. Banks (1988) recognized that curriculum
for powerful groups needs to differ from that for oppressed groups.
He explained that the "Enlightening Powerful Groups" model of curriculum should attempt "to modify the attitudes and perceptions of
dominant ethnic groups so that they would be willing, as adults, to
share power . . . and willing to take action to change the social system so it would treat powerless ethnic groups more justly" (p. 182).
However, he expressed pessimism that one could achieve significant
change by trying to educate powerful groups and saw more hope in
strategies to empower oppressed groups.

While I agree with his emphasis on empowering oppressed
groups, I believe there is value in attempting to educate others who
(like me) are white and relatively secure economically. This is a challenge I have struggled with for several years, and it presents an
enormous challenge. As Carolyne White (1988) put it, the pedagogical challenge is "how to foster critical inquiry by influencing students to question their assumptions about school and society while
avoiding the potential danger of inadvertently fostering indoctrina-
tion or nihilism" (p. 88). Early, I recognized an unsatisfactory but
common dichotomy in pedagogical orientations that Elshtain (1976)
described as the "coercive" classroom versus the "non-authoritarian" classroom. Teachers who wish to critique structural oppression
want their students to learn to engage in the same form of critique.
The greater the likelihood their students will find social critique
threatening and foreign, the greater the tendency of the teacher to
control the selection and flow of ideas, which many students experience as coercive rather than liberating. This coercive pedagogy con-
tradicts the participatory mode of critical teaching. So, many teachers instead construct a non-authoritarian classroom in which
students are invited to create knowledge by sharing their own perspectives and feelings—which often are not critical at all. For Elshtain, liberatory classrooms are neither non-authoritarian nor coercive, but involve shifting relations of power as students engage with
ideas they may find threatening; the long-range goal is construction
of "a theory of human liberation" that includes all of us (p. 110).

So again, how does one do that? How, for example, does one involve a class of male and female white students from mainly middle class backgrounds in a critique of various forms of oppression and, at the same time, help them to construct for themselves insights grounded in emancipation of other people?

Feminist poststructuralist work alerts us to complexities of this challenge. In raising questions about multiple identities within subjects, and the interplay between rational thought and desire, such works probe subtle and often unanticipated dynamics that occur in classrooms in which critical or feminist pedagogies are employed (Ellsworth, 1989). "Feminist poststructuralist discourse views the struggle over identity within the subject as inseparable from the struggle over meanings of identities and subject positions within the culture at large" (Orner, 1992, p. 74). This does not mean that critical and feminist pedagogies are impossible, but rather they are more complex than often recognized (Lather, 1992).

In the fall semester of 1992, I assigned a class of twenty-two undergraduate preservice students a paper, in which they were to ask a "Why?" question involving some aspect of race, social class, and/or gender that they genuinely did not understand. They were to attempt to answer the question from a perspective of the oppressed group(s) the question was about, with relatively little direct help from me. All of the students were white; sixteen were women and six were men. They ranged in age from about twenty-one to thirty-five and in social class from working to middle class.

Their papers surpassed what I would have expected several years ago. In most preservice teacher education classes, if one poses a question such as, "Why do children of poor families disproportionately not complete school?" one is likely to receive answers that focus on inadequacies of their families and communities, changes in the moral climate among students over the past three decades, or the problem of gangs. My students learned to proceed quite differently. In this chapter, I will frame the teaching problem I addressed in a theoretical context, describe what the students learned to do, describe my own teaching processes, then discuss further complexities of this work.

Repositioning Perspective

Figure 6.1 juxtaposes two perspectives about the nature of society and the nature of "have not" groups which derive from different

Figure 6.1
Perspective about Inequality

	DOMINANT POSITION	"MINORITY POSITION"
Nature of Society	Fair, open	Unfair, rigged
Nature of "Have not" Groups	Lack ambition, effort, culture language, etc.	Strong, resourceful

positions in an unequal social order. The dominant perspective holds that society is free and open to anyone who tries to advance, although one may encounter barriers one must work to overcome. To explain inequality, "deficiencies" of "have not" groups are high-lighted: deficiencies of language, effort, education, culture, family, and so forth. "Minority position" perspectives, which were discussed in chapter 5, hold that society is unfair and rigged to favor groups with power. "Have not" groups are more accurately understood as oppressed; they may lack access to society's resources, but culturally have generated a considerable reservoir of strengths.

As I discussed in chapter 4, teachers enter teaching with some ideas about diverse American groups and about why groups occupy different social positions, based on their lived experience and the ideology they have learned to use to interpret those experiences. It is very possible, in fact, to study the "Other" and retain one's own ideas about justice and the existing social system. When multicultural education is reduced to teaching about "other" people, educators are usually allowed to retain their perspective and theories about the workings of society.

The pedagogical approach I will describe aims to help students learn that there is more than one perspective and learn to use a "minority position" perspective to examine school issues. When attempting to teach "minority position" perspectives, teachers often bombard students with them, leaving intact the assumption that there is one correct interpretation of society: the teacher's interpretation. This creates what Elshtain termed the "coercive" classroom, which many students resist. Partly what students resist is the implication that the sense they have made of their lives is wrong. I have found them far more likely to entertain another perspective, as long as it is not presented as the only "correct" one.

Embedded within the project of attempting to reposition perspectives, however, is the recognition that students' perspectives are not singular. As feminist poststructuralists remind us, each student can learn to engage in a "minority position" perspective regarding some issues and in some circumstances, but retain a dominant perspective in other situations. Further, to the extent that my pedagogical process is "liberating," it is not necessarily liberating my students. Rather, my work attempts to connect students with discourses that others find liberating, so that when they enter the classroom as teachers, they will recognize and hear (and, one hopes, begin to act with) the words and visions of disenfranchised people.

Preservice Students Construct
Minority Position Perspectives

During their second semester with me, twenty-two preservice students posed "why" questions about a variety of issues. They formulated their questions on the basis of personal experiences or observations; most opened their "Why?" papers with very specific examples of the questions they addressed. Most of their questions had to do with race and culture; some involved gender issues. Their sources of information were mainly interviews with people who are members of the group(s) their questions involved; papers also drew on scholarly articles written by members of such groups. I will share examples of their work, then discuss the teaching they had experienced.

Four young white women wondered why African American males experience difficulties in schools. Their papers explored a variety of factors; their conclusions differed but fit within the context of an observation one made:

> The "black male crisis" becomes reified in isolation and addressed outside the full cultural, historical, political, and economic contexts of African-Americans' lives. Eurocentric formation of the issue defines it as a "black" issue, thus making it both the product and the responsibility of black people.

One of the papers focused on African American community self-help strategies, noting that white society, though creating problems that impact on the African American community, cannot be relied on to help. Another examined African American males' cultural coping a diverse faculty; at the time I was teaching the students described here, about half of the teacher education courses were taught by faculty of color. Most of the teacher education faculty taught in inner city schools and lived at some time in their professional lives in inner-city neighborhoods. To varying degrees, courses exposed students to minority (primarily African American) intellectual thought, feminist thought, specific multicultural teaching strategies, and the repeated experience of learning and taking directions from a person of color. In addition, field experiences for methods courses were often in culturally diverse classrooms. Thus, the strategies I used were supported in various ways outside my courses, in a context rich with thought rooted in "minority position" perspectives.[1]

Within this context I worked with critical pedagogy. Critical pedagogy questions the teacher's power over students in the classroom. Initially, some teachers interpret this as meaning that the teacher should exercise no more power than each student. Shor (1982) described a more helpful view, which he termed "the withering away of the teacher":

> One goal of liberatory learning is for the teacher to become expendable. At the start and along the way, the teacher is indispensable as a change agent. Yet, the need to create students into self-regulating subjects requires that the teacher as organizer fade as the students emerge. (p. 98)

The process I will discuss is predicated on this transfer of power. Initially, I used my power as teacher to make assignments, organize activities and discussions, present material, evaluate work, and so forth. However, over the two courses, spaces for student authority enlarged. The following discussion is organized in relationship to five kinds of strategies, more so than order of their use (a chronological description of some of what follows appears in Sleeter, 1995b).

Graphic, Emotionally-Charged Portrayals of Inequality

Social reconstructionism, multicultural education, and critical pedagogy rest on the assumption that society faces a crisis of grave proportions that impacts very disparately on different groups (Stanley, 1992). Some students come to school aware of a crisis they experience in personal terms; many, however, come unaware of any major crisis in American life. As noted above, Americans who perceive themselves as relatively well-off construct a perspective that explains and legitimates their own experience by denying that groups differ in social position. I begin, therefore, with a graphic portrayal of crisis and throughout the two courses, provide real and vicarious experiences with disenfranchised groups.

Students' first assignment is to read *The Education of a WASP* (Stalvey, 1989), which is an autobiography of a white middle class woman as she relearns how race in the U.S. worked for African Americans during the 1960s. It opens with the author's brief description of her life and her naive beliefs about the fairness and justice of American society. It then chronicles her experiences and the change in her perspective over a four-year period as she became increasingly involved with struggles within the African American community. She describes how she learned about institutional racism in a variety of areas: housing, schooling, media coverage, job opportunities, and so forth. Over the four years, Stalvey crossed a color line that most white Americans never cross and learned firsthand how African Americans experience the U.S. from the other side of that color line. The book provides my students with a vicarious experience with racism as African Americans experience it and with a white reexamination of what racism is. Overwhelmingly, students react strongly to the book.

This first experience should provoke an emotional jolt, clearly illustrate unequal conditions, and provide a range of concrete examples of structural inequality that can be used for analysis later. Initially students are caught up in their emotional reaction, and many do not identify any structural factors at all in the text; they will need help doing so later. I believe this first experience should not be fictional. If it challenges their thinking and provokes discomfort, many students try to dismiss the text (as dated, fictional, exaggerated, and so forth).

In the second course, students complete a fifty-hour field experience. I used to place them mainly in urban classrooms, but shifted toward placing most students in urban community organizations, such as community centers, field-based tutoring programs, or minority-run social service agencies. Placements are those in which the population being served as well as running the agency represent a low-income minority group. I seek placements in which my students will have specific service work to do under the direction and supervision of a staff person, and their work will allow them to talk informally with some of the clients (usually children and youth). Here, students usually find themselves actually seeing many conditions Stalvey (1988) described. For example, several students assigned to help with one agency's food bank and energy assistance program assume that, for the most part, the rules for distributing social rewards work fairly for everyone. The book illustrates that, in the 1960s, they clearly did not: African Americans and whites followed two different sets of institutional and social rules that were set by white society.

This is the crux of what I try to have students realize: Their own social reality, and their interpretation of that reality is valid within limits. But the entire social order is structured around boundaries that define different sets of rules for different categories of people. People are categorized socially on ascribed differences (that for the most part are visible, such as sex or skin color), with images of effort, ability, and desire projected repeatedly through media in such a way that the dominant society explains inequalities with reference to characteristics of people rather than rules of institutions. Thus, the realities we experience and the viewpoints we construct within those realities are quite different.

In *The Education of a WASP*, the author gradually discovers a wide range of informal as well as formal rules of society that apply differently to African Americans and whites. She also discovers the degree to which her own ideas about race and about African Americans as well as whites had been shaped by her absence of contact with African American people and persistent contact with highly distorted media imagery. After students have read the book, I have them analyze it in small groups, filling in the framework in Figure 6.2 with examples. We then discuss their difficulty in using this framework and their reactions to it.

A simulation that helps illustrate this framework is Star Power (Shirts, 1969). In the simulation, students become divided into three groups based on points accumulated in a trading game, with the highest group eventually given power to make rules governing the game. Invariably, they use this power to further their own advantages; the other two groups use various coping and resisting strategies, such as cheating or refusing to play. In the discussion that follows, I try to help students move from their own experience in the simulation to broader issues of unequal power, rule-making, and social behavior. The simulation provides the class with a shared vocabulary and shared set of experiences that illustrate concepts in Figure 6.2, although they typically need help connecting these with real-life issues in the local community.

In the remainder of the first course, we practice using the framework, focusing on the institutional and symbolic levels of analysis. I tell students that my goal is to help them learn to pose questions and examine factors within the context of the framework. I explain that doing this will challenge much of their thinking, but it will also help them understand where other groups are coming from. Ultimately, their personal beliefs are their own business; as a teacher, my responsibility is to help them see a different perspective.

Beverly Tatum (1992) described her use of research on racial identity development to help students acknowledge and transcend their emotional reactions to learning about racism. This research postulates stages that whites and people of color experience when confronting racism and reframing their perspectives. As students are confronted experientially and vicariously with inequality and "minority position" perspectives, many feel very threatened and use predictable strategies to deal with their feelings. I have found it very helpful to share this work with students, broadening the discussion to gender, social class, and other forms of oppression. Doing so validates their discomfort, gives them a shared language to discuss their feelings, and provides a "roadmap" of growth they can anticipate.

I also use Figure 6.1 in class with students to contrast dominant and "minority position" perspectives. For example, after they have been in their community field experience for a period of time, students often become very upset about the living conditions of those about whom the students have come to care. I ask the class to construct an interpretation of what they are seeing from a dominant perspective and a "minority position" perspective, filling in Figure 6.1 with examples. During this discussion some students begin to connect the language and interpretative frameworks used in class with the dominant ideology as it appears in textbooks, newspapers, and so forth, and "minority position" discourse as articulated by groups such as Black Power advocates, feminists, and labor unions.

Reflective Writing

Those who use both critical and feminist pedagogies often discuss the benefits of reflective writing, especially journals (Bigelow, 1990; Liston & Zeichner, 1987). Writing allows students to define issues, express feelings, and develop descriptive texts for analysis. In addition, "Creating personalized narratives is also a way of guarding against the rampant intellectual imperialism so prevalent in teaching, whereby outsiders provide the packaged and commodified answers to the issues that are nonquestions for teachers" (Smyth, 1992, p. 296–297).

Students in my courses complete two different kinds of reflective written work. In the first course, they are to keep a journal. I have structured the journal with specific assignments, although some students go much beyond that. The assignments mainly ask students to relate concepts or insights from the course to examples or incidents in their own lives. For example, I may ask them to reflect on a reading assignment and to write about any relationships they see between the text and their lives. I collect journals periodically and write comments or questions. Although a few students complete only a minimal amount of writing in the journal, most take it seriously; in some cases the journal develops into an active, personal dialog between the student and me.

The second form of reflective writing occurs in relationship to the field experience. I provide students with guides for conducting a wide array of mini-ethnographic investigations, such as suggested interview questions or guides for observing language use. Students are to select three of these (or design their own) and collect data. When writing the assignment, they are to interpret and reflect on what they learned, particularly focusing on what it means for them as a teacher. Quite often these assignments, too, become vehicles for personal communication between the student and me, as I write questions for them to consider and sometimes suggestions for further work.

There is far more one can do with reflective writing than I have described here. For example, some teachers have students share their written texts for broader analysis. Still, most students tell me that the reflective writing described above is very helpful, mainly because it forces them to think and to seek connections between their own experience and ideas discussed in class.

Tapping into Sources that Bring
Minority Position Perspectives

Commonly students perceive ideas and sources of information (such as textbooks) that draw on dominant perspectives as "normal" and those that use "minority position" perspectives as biased and political. Commonly also, they have had little exposure to "minority position" discourse, with the exception of excerpts on the news or courses taught by a few faculty members. I try to help students to realize that no discourse is ideologically neutral; "minority position" discourses are sophisticated and often richer with strategies for addressing social problems than dominant discourse, and they can learn to access such discourses themselves.

Throughout the teacher education program, in addition to my courses, students are exposed to African American intellectual thought and (to a lesser degree) intellectual thought of other groups. Thus, it is not incumbent on one course alone to attempt this huge teaching task. I engage students in explicit instruction and practice in accessing and using "minority position" sources to answer questions.

As students pose questions, ranging from the mini-investigations they share with the class to the "Why? " papers they write, we talk about where and why one might go for information. Figure 6.3 illustrates distinctions I make when discussing sources of informa-

Figure 6.3

	IN-GROUP MEMBER	OUT-GROUP MEMBER
Child		
Adult in community		
Scholar		

tion. The two vertical columns distinguish between in-group and out-group members. The importance of this distinction can be illustrated by comparing two articles about the same event or issue, written by an in-group and an out-group member. I require that at least some sources for "Why? " papers be in-group members with respect to the question the student is investigating. The three horizontal rows illustrate different perspectives one might encounter: a child's perspective, the perspective of an adult community member, and the perspective of a scholar who has studied an area of investigation. We discuss unique insights each of these perspectives might offer and fill in each cell of the figure with examples of sources. Then, in small groups, prior to their "Why?" paper investigations, students help each other generate a list of reasonable sources of information.

Before I worked with students on source selection, they typically sought answers to questions from in-group children and out-group adults (usually teachers) or scholars (such as textbooks, mainstream journal articles). The result was usually an elaboration of a dominant perspective. When challenged to seek information from in-group adults and scholars, students usually find themselves engaging with "minority position" perspectives. Initially many find this threatening (a few try to circumvent such engagement) and difficult (few have ever read an African American or Latino journal). However, students also report finding more insight and potential solutions from in-group adults and scholars than from any other source.

Collective Knowledge Production

Ultimately, for critical pedagogy to be empowering, it must involve "a process of knowledge production" in which students work together to generate their own text (Gore, 1992, p. 68). This is different from having students write traditional papers; papers are usually a private experience students share only with the teacher and require students to seek published knowledge from "experts" rather than actually creating their own interpretations. When working with peers to create text about social issues, students educate each other in ways that I cannot by sharing examples, disagreeing with each other, and building larger ideas from their collective multiple examples.

I structure collective knowledge production in a variety of ways. First, after students have read *The Education of a WASP*, I divide them into three groups to conduct mini-investigations on racism, poverty, and sexism. Beginning with the racism group, I put Fig. 6.2 on the board and ask the class as a whole to generate as many questions as they can about possible current examples of racism at the institutional and cultural levels. As they ask questions, I write them on the board, asking for ideas as to how questions might be investigated. Then each of the students who selected racism volunteers to take a question; I give them a week or two to conduct their investigations. (I repeat the same process with the other two groups, a bit later in the semester.) One of the most effective investigation processes is for students to replicate testing procedures used to investigate housing and job discrimination: to pair with a peer of another race and find out whether they receive the same treatment in a particular context such as bank, real estate agency, retail store, and so forth.

About ten students at a time share what they found out, and usually considerable discussion follows. For example, with respect to poverty, one student acquired published information about available child care for low-income people, then pretended to be a single mother looking for child care and actually made the telephone calls specified; she found out that print descriptions can differ widely from the treatment low-income single women may actually receive. Another assembled paperwork a woman must fill out to receive AFDC. Another looked into local homeless shelters and was shocked to discover how many homeless people the city has. To investigate racism, two young women, one African American and the other white, went shopping together. The white student was shocked to realize that while salespeople helped her, they often followed her African American peer around the store to make sure she did not shoplift. I used to provide much of the information students now bring to class, but realized that when they provide the information, they find it more believable and real, and they also learn where to locate such information for themselves.

A second form of collective knowledge production occurs in the context of ethnographies students read. This is a rather complex assignment, using jigsaw cooperative learning. Each student reads one ethnography of schooling; about ten or twelve different books are available from which to choose. For discussion, I first group together students who have read the same or similar books, to make sure they understand the main ideas in their books. Then I mix students so that four or five books are represented by one student each, per group. I give the groups four to five questions to answer collectively that require them to synthesize the information and ideas in the books; I also encourage students to use their own experience. The questions connect Figure 2 with school issues in the books, such as asking students to examine who benefits most from tracking and why. Sometimes the groups put on a skit illustrating what they learned; other times they collectively write a short paper.

The culminating experience for these two courses is the production and use of a text about issues related to multicultural education. Students are to complete their "why" papers about halfway through the semester. I read them, give students feedback, and give them about two weeks to complete any revisions they wish to make. Then I collect their papers, organize them around common topics or themes, and have them duplicated and bound to form a text that the class uses for the remainder of the semester. At this point, students take control of the production and discussion of knowledge. I participate in discussions with the students, but am no longer "in charge."

I have turned students' "why" papers into a class text three times, after having found that the papers are consistently strong enough to do this effectively. Of all the reading assignments I have ever given, students seemed to take this the most seriously. They told me that they wanted to find out what their peers learned and found important and that this had more meaning to them than any other reading assignment, no matter how interesting other reading assignments may be.

Multicultural teaching is not simply a list of teaching strategies. Rather, it is an orientation to listening to oppressed people, including scholars, with the aims of learning to hear and understand what is being said, of building dialog, and of learning to share decision-making power with oppressed communities. The process of listening, engaging in dialog, and power-sharing is very difficult to learn. Educated whites are very accustomed to believing that we can construct good solutions to other peoples' needs, ourselves. I want students to leave my class having begun a process of listening and dialog; I deliberately reduce my own position as "the" source of information about multicultural teaching. While I do not know the extent to which students continue to seek minority position perspectives for themselves from their students, students' parents, or professionals of color, at least they will have begun this process.

Notes

1. In my current institution, California State University Monterey Bay, an even greater proportion of faculty are of color, and coursework across the university is rooted in marginalized groups' discourses. I edited this chapter to the past tense where necessary so that specific references are accurate but still use similar processes in my current teaching.

2. On occasion I have seen classroom situations deteriorate into unintended emotional side shows, in which the student or guest sharing painful personal experiences breaks down in tears or anger, and the class feels sorry for him or her. One cannot teach about oppression without representing pain, so I try to plan painful experiences in ways that do not violate privacy, as much as possible, such as through the use of films and videos, readings, or talks by individuals who have had some practice discussing painful experiences with a group.

CHAPTER 7

Multicultural Education, Social Positionality, and Whiteness

How much impact can educators make on the worldviews of others? As multicultural educators, how much change can we bring about through the formal education process? In chapters 2 and 3, I stressed the profound impact of our lived experiences and our own societal position on our thinking. In chapter 6, I described how I approach teaching my students, highlighting my own success by getting them to understand someone else's viewpoint. In this chapter, I critique some limits of that success. If we have done our jobs as educators well, when students leave us their perspectives are probably broader, they have more ideas and insights to consider, and they can probably teach more effectively. These are worthwhile goals to strive for. But their lives and entire thought processes probably will not have been transformed.

Recently in one of my Multicultural Education preservice courses, eighteen students (fifteen white, two Latina, and one African American) completed the "why" paper assignment described in the preceding chapter. I had their finished papers duplicated and bound as a text for the last few weeks of class. Having experienced earlier the excitement of students learning to investigate issues from someone else's perspective, this time I also experienced frustration as students filtered new insights through their still taken-for-granted perspectives.

Five of the students' "why" papers addressed school and community problems: dropping out, low-achievement, inadequate parent involvement, gangs, and black-on-black crime. Questions included: "Why do many Hispanic youth drop out of high school?" and "Why do low-income students achieve less well in school than middle-income students?" Ten papers addressed various issues related to curriculum and instruction: culture and communication style, culture and language, and inclusion of people of color and women in textbooks. One paper addressed Title IX, one addressed disability, and one paper (by a white student) addressed racial segregation of local schools, briefly exploring racial politics in the community. Students were encouraged to probe for constructive solutions as well as examinations of why problems exist and I helped students make sure they were obtaining perspectives of members of the groups to whom the questions pertained.

Class discussion of the first five "problem" papers illustrates how whites often process information about issues of oppression. The sources students obtained information from collectively discussed multi-leveled causes of the problems, including poverty and lack of jobs, lack of teacher support, lack of school support, family characteristics, the drug culture, the peer culture, families' attitudes about education, family's socioeconomic status, poor work habits, lack of role models, etc. Exclusion from jobs and from challenging and supportive education were common themes.

In the conclusions of their papers, most students tended to ignore systemic causes they had uncovered in their research and offered solutions that focused largely on constructive, but fairly mild, forms of help. The solutions they suggested for educators included attempting to work with parents (e.g., holding parent-teacher conferences during hours when parents can come), maintaining high expectations for children, reducing tracking, teaching non-violent ways to address problems, matching students with tutors, and offering programs for parents. These are all helpful suggestions. However, they sidestep the larger context of oppression within which problems arise, specifically economic exclusion and systemic racism.

As the class discussed the papers, I tried to push them to consider why jobs are leaving inner cities, how the race of people relates to where they live and to where most jobs are located, actions teachers can take as community citizens, why students of color in low-income communities that are losing employment opportunities might distrust schools, and how teachers could address realities children perceive. The most insightful contributions to the discussion came from one of the Latina students (who discussed vividly the limited future many children of color see for themselves based on the experiences their parents are having currently) and the African American student (who described ways educators demonstrate to children that schools are primarily interested in white children rather than African American children). Most of the white students seemed to have difficulty going beyond a focus on how "we" can help "them," and difficulty thinking of collective political solutions to poverty and racism. Only two white students and two students of color sustained discussions in class about systemic racism. While the rest of the class did not exhibit hostility to discussions about racism (white racism had been a main topic of study in at least one previous class), they were either silent or changed the subject. As one white student commented, she didn't feel she had much to contribute because, "I'm not used to thinking about things from 'downs' perspectives" (referring to an article by Terry, 1993).

Racism and Multicultural Education

As noted in chapter 1, multicultural education grew out of the civil rights movement of the 1960s. As Banks (1992) pointed out, educators with roots in African American studies have been among the most active conceptualizers of multicultural education, viewing it as a discourse community that would advance power-sharing and uplifting communities of color. Having its roots in minority discourses about oppression, multicultural education was part of a larger quest for redistribution of power and economic resources. As such, the field should be advancing strategies to address white racism: white control over most of the wealth, land, and power in the nation. Building on analyses of race, social class, and gender that have been advanced over the past two decades, multicultural education should also direct our attention to concentrations of power and wealth in the hands of a small elite and to manifestations of that concentration in contemporary culture and social institutions. Multicultural education might, for example, help us analyze how schools are situated within a capitalistic structure that continues to transfer wealth to a white elite, while deflecting attention away from itself through various forms of media. Such critique would suggest teaching young people to engage in critical media analysis, to examine the distribution of wealth, to examine social movements that historically have successfully advanced the interests of marginalized groups, and to use political action skills. Such teaching does, in fact, sometimes take place within the field of multicultural education.

However, often multicultural education as a discourse mutes attention to white racism (and usually ignores patriarchy and the class hierarchy), focusing mainly on cultural difference. Culture and cultural difference is certainly important and ought to be a central construct. However, white racism and racial oppression, as well as capitalist and patriarchal oppression, should also be central constructs. Generally they are not, or they disappear from consideration in the minds of white educators. The example of my students is illustrative: although their research suggested unemployment and blocked access to resources as significant underlying causes of problems such as dropping out of school, neither the papers nor class discussions focused much attention on systemic problems—white racism or political responses to economic exclusion.

That multicultural education often skirts around white racism results from white people's reluctance to address it more so than people of color's disregard for it. Those of us who are white usually experience a social reality that does not lead us to critique white racism; rather, we have a vested interest not to "see" it. We are a part of the "norms and models set by white elites" (West, 1993, p. 20) and are accustomed to extending acceptance and approval to educators of color who frame their work within the parameters of our reality and rejection to the ideas of those who do not. The present white understanding of race and ethnicity "emerged into prominence during a period when the civil rights movement was most active and racial minorities were challenging in basic respects the fairness of the American system" (Alba, 1990, p. 317). White society felt threatened and attempted to reframe ethnicity and race within our own worldview and experience. "The thrust of European-American identity is to defend the individualistic view of the American system, because it portrays the system as open to those who are willing to work hard and pull themselves over barriers of poverty and discrimination" (Alba, p. 317).

In what follows, I will examine insights that people who occupy dominant social positions find it very difficult to internalize. Everybody interprets the world from their location in a stratified society. As the work of theorists such as Sandra Harding (1991) and Renato Rosaldo (1989) argue, this means that our understandings are always partial; we always interpret and filter the world through our own life histories and the ideological frameworks we have learned to use.

> Like form and feeling, culture and power are inextricably intertwined. In discussing actors, one must consider their social positions. What are the complexities of the speaker's social identity? What life experiences have shaped it? Does the person speak from a position of relative dominance or relative subordination? (Rosaldo, 1989, p. 167)

This is a broader and deeper issue than charging teachers with "prejudice," which is how audiences sometimes interpret the main idea of this chapter. Usually when one speaks of teacher prejudice, one is speaking of the tendency to prejudge individuals on the basis of stereotypes, before coming to know them as individuals. When one attempts to reduce prejudice, one is attempting to help people view others on their own merits and treat them accordingly. When I speak of worldview, however, I am referring not just to how one interprets and feels about individuals, but also how one frames the contemporary and historic patterns of relationships among sociocultural groups, how one situates humans within a larger cosmology, and how one conceives of human nature itself.

Dominant Viewpoints Rooted in Euro-American Experiences

Four interconnected concepts are discussed that white preservice students find very difficult to grasp, partly because they do not fit white people's daily experience or understanding of our own Euro-American history. Although these concepts have been separated for discussion here, it is important to recognize that they are interconnected and must be addressed as such. Prospective teachers of color probably also need to address issues and concepts discussed below (Montecinos, 1995), but usually in my experience grasp the concepts below much more readily than white prospective teachers because these concepts mesh with their life experiences.

Historic Roots of Racist Opportunity Structures

Euro-Americans often describe the U.S. as a nation of immigrants, but describing it in this way minimizes very important distinctions in groups' historic experiences with opportunity. Ogbu (1991) argues that how a group became a part of the United States defines the trajectory for the group's subsequent experiences and perspectives. European ethnic groups, as well as some Asian and Latino groups, voluntarily, for the most part, immigrated to North America in search of better opportunities, expecting to endure some hardships and discrimination initially. African Americans, indigenous Native people, Puerto Ricans, and Mexican Americans, on the other hand, whom he refers to as "involuntary minorities . . . were brought into their present society through slavery, conquest or colonization" (p. 9). Rather than seeking voluntarily to affiliate with the dominant society to gain opportunities, they were forced to become part of it and in the process lost vast amounts of freedom, land, and economic resources. European groups developed an opportunity structure that allowed for individual upward mobility for whites (a process that did involve considerable conflict among European groups), but until 1954 legally barred groups of color from participating in that structure. These very different histories generated present life conditions and perspectives that diverge to a much greater degree than most white people grasp.

White people in general find it very difficult to appreciate the impact of colonization and slavery on both oppressed groups as well as whites; we tend to prefer to regard everyone as descendants of immigrants. I believe whites retreat from confronting the profound impact of conquest and slavery because doing so calls into question the legitimacy of the very foundation of much of white peoples' lives. The economic legacy of conquest is that whites are indebted to Indian, Mexican, Puerto Rican, and Hawaiian people for the land we inhabit, as well as gold and other resources our ancestors extracted from the land to build industries (Weatherford, 1988). The economic legacy of slavery is that whites owe African Americans about three hundred years of back-wages, money that whites used instead to build profits and profit-generating industries. Economic disparities today are legacies of that history (Roediger, 1991).

However, the view of the United States as a nation of voluntary immigrants is consistent with the family histories of Euro-Americans and affirms the desire of whites to believe that our ancestors earned fairly what we have inherited and that what we control is rightly ours. Generally when acknowledging conquest and slavery, Euro-Americans bracket these off as historic incidents that have little bearing on today. Typical white responses to this history are: "I didn't do it, why punish me?" "My family worked for what they got, we didn't have anything to do with slavery," and "That was a long time ago, can't we just forget all that?" Also, typically white preservice students have only a sketchy idea of the histories of Americans of color and do not situate current issues in a historic context (Lauderdale & Deaton, 1993). Learning history can help to develop a sense of how different the historical experiences have been for voluntary immigrants versus non-voluntary minorities. Yet, white people seem more willing to disconnect history from the present than do many people of color because for whites the present system is fair.

The Nature and Impact of Discrimination

Oppressed groups experience discrimination daily in relationship to individuals and in interaction with institutions; the impact of discrimination is psychological as well as material. This is true of voluntary non-white immigrants (such as Korean Americans) as well as involuntary minority groups, poor whites, women, and gays and lesbians. While immigrants often attribute discrimination they experience to their foreign ways (Ogbu, 1991), involuntary minority group members, particularly African Americans, see systematic racial discrimination as a deep and ongoing problem (Kluegel & Smith, 1986).

Most white teachers greatly minimize the extent and impact of racial (as well as other forms of) discrimination, viewing it as isolated expressions of prejudice that hurt a person's feelings. Americans in general attribute differences in wealth, income, and lifestyle to individual effort on a playing field we assume to be even, particularly with passage of civil rights legislation (Kluegel & Smith, 1986). In fact, many white university students regard legislation such as affirmative action as giving groups of color an unfair advantage, racial discrimination itself having been largely eliminated.

The view that discrimination has minimal impact was illustrated to me in how one of my white students interpreted an exercise. For an assignment, she spent an hour at the mall with an African American friend, then with a white friend, in order to compare the treatment they received. She reported that when she was with the African American friend, two sales clerks seemed more rude than sales clerks normally are to her; aside from these two, she saw no difference in treatment. Her initial conclusion was that discrimination does not happen very often, although when it does, it makes African American people feel bad. I suggested to her that a different interpretation is that her African American friend probably faces some negative treatment everytime he goes to the mall, as well as other places, which may limit where he goes; she had not considered it that way and had some difficulty doing so.

Further, discrimination restricts opportunities, an impact that extends far beyond hurt feelings. For example, racial housing patterns result partially from housing discrimination, which still occurs on a very wide scale despite open housing laws. Where people live affects access to jobs and schools, which in turn affects access to income; exclusionary barriers are, thus, interconnected and have a huge impact on living conditions. But the impact of systematic and persistent discrimination is a very difficult concept for most whites to grasp since we do not experience racial discrimination ourselves. In spite of having spent over an hour of classtime on housing discrimination, for example, the following semester a white student selected as her topic for investigation: Why do many African Americans live in the inner city?

Recently a white former student asked for my help in constructing lessons about discrimination. As we talked, I noticed that she conceptualized discrimination largely as stereotyping and biased interpersonal treatment. When I probed for her understanding of institutional discrimination, she at first drew a blank, then slowly gave a rather vague definition. As we talked, I realized that although she had learned what I taught while in class, when the semester was over she filed much of it away in the recesses of her mind. She did not normally think in terms of systemic racism and had reduced racism to interpersonal tensions and stereotypes.

As noted in chapter 4, women experience sex discrimination, and seem more likely to acknowledge the presence of other forms of discrimination than men. However, most have not engaged in a systematic study of patriarchy and often resist examining how their own lives have been shaped by it. Many white female students view sex discrimination as no more than an annoying patronizing attitude that some males display and that women need to ignore. If this is what discrimination is, they reason, then why can't people of color simply ignore it?

Because they conceptualize discrimination as consisting of isolated acts by prejudiced individuals, most teachers do not explain inequality in terms of systemic discrimination. Mark Ginsburg (1988) interviewed 75 preservice students (75% female, 85% White) to find out how they interpret inequalities in achievement (in both schools and the larger society) and what implications their interpretations had for teaching. A small minority "emphasized the school's role in reproducing inequalities," contextualizing children within a stratified and unjust social structure (p. 167). A much larger second group viewed individuals as freely choosing their own destinies and degree of social mobility; they believed schools neutrally facilitate mobility for everyone. A third group also viewed individuals as freely choosing their own destinies, but believed that people are hindered by individual attitudes and prejudice.

If discrimination consists largely of one-on-one acts by overtly prejudiced people, then the solution must be to be open-minded and accept everyone. If I as a teacher adopt an open attitude, I am not part of a problem. This line of thinking denies a need to learn much that people of color are saying, but it is a common view.

The Significance of Group Membership

The dominant ideology of the U.S. is strongly individualistic, a perspective that teachers commonly share. Americans commonly learn that the United States is a nation in which affiliations are voluntary and people participate in the public arena as individuals. For example, Alan Bloom (1989) wrote that in the American political system, "Class, race, religion, national origin or culture all disappear or become dim when bathed in the light of natural rights, which give men common interests and make them truly brothers" (p. 27). The purpose of schooling is to cultivate reason so that citizens can rise above their own particular circumstances and participate as individuals in a common culture. Similarly, Arthur Schlesinger (1992) described the United States as a nation in which people "escape from origins" (p. 15) and go about "casting off the foreign skin" (p. 112) in order to rise or fall on their own merit and effort as individuals, rather than as members of ascribed groups. This ideology suggests that Americans should not identify themselves with any ascribed group for purposes of public participation and that it is possible and valuable to ignore ascribed group memberships of other people, thus treating them as individuals.

Historically for whites, the significance of ethnic membership has indeed diminished; the ideology above fits family histories. When Europeans immigrated to the United States, ethnicity structured many aspects of their lives such as choice of spouse, job, and location of residence. Today, however, with a few exceptions, European ethnicity is unrelated to life chances and choices (Alba, 1990). The problem is that, while European ethnic group membership no longer structures opportunity to a significant degree, continent of origin does, as do gender and wealth. Insisting on the individual as the main unit of analysis deflects attention away from examination of social responses to visible differences.

As a part of our adherence to the idea that ethnicity does not matter, most whites profess to be colorblind. But in doing so, we cover over the meanings we attach to race, rather than actually dissociating race from meaning. If one conceives of the United States as a nation of voluntary immigrants and the rules of society as essentially fair (with some isolated instances of discrimination still occurring), then why do some groups fare better than others? Typically, most Americans explain group differences in terms of characteristics and desires of group members themselves: for example, women choose low-paying jobs, Mexicans don't want to learn English, low-income people lack the desire to work or keep up their homes. If one asks a white audience to jot down all the negatives they have heard associated with another racial group, then all the positives, the list of negatives is usually much longer. For teachers, trying to be color-blind, therefore, means trying to suppress the application of those negative associations to individual children one is teaching.

Trying to be colorblind also means denying the existence of racial boundaries whites see and usually do not cross. If one asks a white audience how many of them have ever chosen to live in a neighborhood or attend a school or church in which the majority of the people are not white, few hands go up. Whites do see and adhere to racial boundaries, and most feel very uncomfortable crossing them. But whites with at least modest income have many choices (such as where to live, who to associate with) within white domi-nated terrain, and use the range of such choices to deny that race is a factor in their decisions.

Ironically, this failure to think seriously about meanings of race is a part of western culture which Goldberg (1993) argues solid-ifies racism. Race, socially constructed historically for purposes of col-onization, has become a normalized category that most people today accept as fact.

> This deep disjunction between moral idealization and actual racial appeal, between color blindness and racial consciousness, must imply either that morality is irrelevant, that in the case of race it has no force or that liberalism's relative silence concerning racial considerations masks a much more complex set of ideas and expe-riences than commonly acknowledged. (p. 6)

Most white people assume race, but also assume that open acknowl-edgement of race violates the ideal of colorblindness. Paradoxically, this refusal to examine race openly strengthens racialized behavior patterns. To dismantle racism and race as a category, we must first confront race.

Since ethnic and racial identities and cultures are difficult con-cepts to deal with for most white teachers, they tend to reduce mul-ticultural education to a question of individual differences (Good-win, 1994). This, in conjunction with denying institutional racism and its profound consequences, often leads white teachers to frame multicultural education as a depoliticized discourse of differences, in which differences can be reduced to individual variation that have minimal social consequences. We can learn to acknowledge and examine markers of collectives to which we do adhere. The more we critically attend to our behavior, the more guilty many white people feel because we realize the degree to which we adhere to racial boundaries, as well as boundaries of social class, language, and so forth. One could begin to replace guilt with different actions, but this requires some change in how we live, so many of us retreat into the more comfortable position of denying the significance of group membership.

Nature of Culture

Multicultural education is very often reduced to folksongs and folktales, food fairs, holiday celebrations, and information about famous people. Even when teachers are shown more substantive examples of multicultural practice, many still revert to superficial renditions of cultural differences and teach culture as habits and customs frozen in the past, passed on as if they were "genetic inheritance" (Garvey, 1993, p. 21). The popular term "cultural heritage" conveys this image well.

How white teachers often conceptualize culture is rooted in European immigrant backgrounds. In his study of European ethnic identity, Richard Alba (1990) found that the most salient expression of ethnic "culture" among Euro-Americans is eating ethnic foods; Euro-Americans also experience "culture" by using words or phrases of an ancestral language, attending ethnic festivals, and practicing "Old World" holiday customs. Ethnic culture defined in this way consists of remnants of Old World practices that are celebrated and often shared across ethnic groups, at particular times. Alba's description of Euro-Americans' expressions of ethnicity correspond very well to multicultural education as white teachers commonly construct it.

Rosaldo (1989) connects the myth of immigration with what he terms "cultural stripping," in which Euro-Americans believe that immigrants brought culture, but lost it as they assimilated. "Social analysts sat at the 'postcultural' top of a stratified world and looked down the 'cultural' rungs to its 'precultural' bottom" (p. 209). In this conception, "primitive" people lack culture; immigrants brought culture from another country and era, culture consisting of folkways from the past; and mainstream Americans have surpassed the need for culture through technological development.

Culture viewed as folkways becomes romanticized, but culture can also be viewed as pathological. Most white people do not know very much about the daily lives of non-white people, and find it difficult to conceptualize poor white homes and neighborhoods, as well as those of color, in terms of cultural strengths or sensible behavior. Since most of us grow up in race and social class segregated neighborhoods, our firsthand contact with the homes and communities of other groups is very limited. For example, it is difficult to conceptualize how an extended family structure may be highly functional if one has limited contact with close extended families. As a result, if we assume that the context in which people live is fair and neutral, we draw on media images, hearsay, stereotypes, and suppositions to explain differences that we see in who has what. These explanations take the form of group characteristics. Generally we regard these characteristics as descriptions of fact rather than as stereotypes. The degree to which they focus on presumed capabilities or deficiencies is in proportion to the group's status in the broader society. Thus, Anglos will romanticize piñatas and Mexican hat dances, and at the same time argue that characteristics of Mexican culture keep Mexican people from advancing (such as large families, adherence to Spanish language, external locus of control, lack of ambition—mañana, etc.).

This is a very different notion of culture from that advocated in multicultural education. By "culture," I mean the totality of a people's experience: its history, literature, language, philosophy, religion, and so forth. The term "culture" was probably adopted by multicultural education advocates in response to the myth of "cultural deprivation" that was popularized during the early 1960s. All of us grow up in a culture and participate in constructing as well as living culture, everyday.

While my teacher education students can usually grasp the idea intellectually that "culture" refers to the totality of a group's socially-constructed way of carrying on life, most have very little knowledge of the culture of any group other than that into which they were born. And schools have been inducting them since kindergarten into that culture—which they regard not as culture but as given. Without some depth of knowledge of at least one other cultural group and of how another group views one's own taken-for-granted culture, teachers will probably continue to greatly oversimplify the meaning of "culture."

The four concepts discussed above were evident in most of the fifteen white students' viewpoints. Partly as a result of our teaching throughout the teacher education program, they turned more readily to forms of discrimination than to presumed cultural deficiencies to explain differences in groups' attainments. Further, most students developed a degree of facility in thinking about sociocultural groups and identifying themselves as members of groups (e.g., as white). However, their analyses of discrimination usually focused on inter-personal interactions rather than on systems of oppression. Their proposed solutions therefore tended to be simplistic and to appeal to educators and community workers to do the right thing, with little or no reference to the history of white collective behavior or to the desire of a capitalist elite to retain and expand control.

As I listened to my students, I heard silences that became very loud as they persisted. White silence about white racism is a silence that roars, not only from white preservice students but also from white people in general.

White Solidarity and White Silence about Racism

White people talk very little about white racism (Scheurich, 1993). Even those of us involved in multicultural education spend far less energy examining and critiquing how white racism works than we ought. Most whites who read this book are probably aware that racism is an important issue to multicultural education and probably do talk about it from time to time. However, I would suggest that our talk does not delve into racism in very much depth. For example, I can write much more fluently about multicultural curricula or mul-ticultural teacher education than I can about white racism. My own discussions of racism rarely move beyond the introductory level I use with my white students. Other white academics sometimes try to close off discussions of white racism by describing such discussions as "navel gazing," as whites who have "seen the light" bashing other whites, as too politically correct, or as insufficiently poststructural in their essentializing of whiteness.

I first noticed white silence on racism about twenty years ago, although I was not able at the time to name it as such. I recall real-izing one day, after having shared many meals with African Ameri-can friends while teaching in Seattle, that racism and race-related issues were fairly common topics of dinner-table conversation, which African Americans talked about quite openly. It struck me that I could not think of a single instance in which racism had been a topic of dinner-table conversation in white contexts. Race-related issues sometimes came up, but not *racism*. For example, I could remember short discussions about what one would do if a black family moved next door, or about a very bigoted relative, or about policies such as desegregation or immigration. In these discussions, what was viewed as problematic was people of color themselves, changes in policies that relate to race, or outspoken bigots.

White people have developed various strategies that enable us to talk about racial issues while avoiding white supremacy and our own participation in it. One of these strategies, described above, is to equate racism with individual prejudice, thus allowing us to assume that every group is racist and to avoid acknowledging the power differential between whites and groups of color. Another strategy is to focus on cultural difference. Cultural differences do exist, of course; however, whites transmute many issues that are rooted in racism into depoliticized questions of difference, which often take on a "tourist" frame of thinking. For example, a line of action whites could take vis-à-vis Indians, Mexicans, Puerto Ricans, or Hawaiians is to return good land and control over that land. But few of us take such action seriously. Instead, we show interest in such groups by learning about certain cultural artifacts and practices (and then sometimes appropriating them) and paying homage to Indian, Latino, and Hawaiian heroes and contributions to white culture.

Equating ethnicity with race is a related strategy for evading racism. At a women's studies conference I attended, participants were divided into racially homogeneous groups to compile a list of the main concerns facing their group. I was in the European-American group, and it floundered. Participants discussed mainly family history and ethnic immigrant background. By focusing on our ethnic differences, the group tried to place itself on a parallel status with the other racial groups, defining our problems as comparable to theirs. Our whiteness seemed to be invisible to us—we could discuss our religious, ethnic, and social class differences, but not our common whiteness (see Dyer, 1988).

We semantically evade our own role in perpetuating white racism by constructing sentences that allow us to talk about racism while removing ourselves from discussion. One such semantic evasion is to personify racism, making it (rather than ourselves) the subject of sentences. This allows us to say, for example, "Racism forced urban housing to deteriorate." Constructing a sentence in this way hides *who* was responsible for the deterioration of urban housing. We also evade our role semantically by avoiding use of a subject altogether; passive sentence constructions allow us to talk about racism without ever naming our own complicity. For example, consider the following sentence: "Africans were brought to the colonies and forced to labor a lifetime for no wages" (McKissack & McKissack, 1990, p. 16). *Who* brought them and forced them? The sentence does not say.

Whites exert pressure on each other to adhere to common definitions of racial issues. In contexts in which these definitions are contested, one can observe active processes by which whites attempt to maintain racial solidarity. This observation struck me recently, when I watched white teacher education students respond to an issue. The dean had been working with a committee of faculty, school administrators, teachers, and the dean of another institution to create an alternative certification program for prospective teachers of color. When word of this program reached white students in the regular program (actually, a few white students were on the planning committee, but had not regarded the program as a problem needing discussion), a large segment of the white student population mobilized overnight to affirm a common definition of the program: It was racially biased and wrong. When I tried to direct the few students who talked with me about it toward sources of more information about the program and reasons for its need, I realized that these students did not want information; they wanted my validation of their perception of it. In a meeting between the students and the faculty, white students vented openly a degree of racism that caught us off guard, and no white student rose to defend the program (although a few did silently support it). Although part of the students' anger was frustration over the length of the regular teacher education program, part of it was racial.

I began to ask myself: Given the coursework and field experiences the students had (described in chapter 6), why did the white students coalesce so strongly and quickly into a common condemnation of the alternative program? How did they know their peers would support thinly-veiled as well as overt expressions of racial hostility? Why did the supporters of the program decide to keep quiet?

These questions led me to examine "white racial bonding" processes white people engage in everyday, which is one of the processes by which whites attempt to maintain racial solidarity. By "racial bonding," I mean simply interactions in which whites engage that have the purpose of affirming a common stance on race-related issues, legitimating particular interpretations of groups of color, and drawing conspiratorial we-they boundaries. These interaction patterns take such forms as inserts into conversations, race-related "asides" in conversations, strategic eye contact, jokes, and code words. Often they are so short and subtle that they may seem relatively harmless, and we don't remember specific exchanges for very long. I used to regard such utterances as annoying expressions of prejudice or ignorance, but that seems to underestimate their power to demarcate racial lines and communicate solidarity.

Inserts into conversations may go like this. Two white people are talking casually about various things. One comments, "This community is starting to change. A lot of Mexicans have been moving in." This comment serves as an invitation to white bonding, in which the other person is being asked to agree with the implication that Mexicans create problems and do not belong here, although this has not been said directly. The other person could respond very simply, "Yeah, that's a bummer," affirming the first person's viewpoint; this could be the end of a successful exchange. Or, the other person could complain about Mexicans, the ensuing conversation taking the form of Mexican-bashing. In either case, both parties will have communicated agreement that there is a linkage between "Mexicans" and "problems" and will have defined themselves as "insiders" in a network of people who view it as acceptable to articulate a negative valuation of Mexicans. Further, they will have communicated the acceptability of viewing favorably policies limiting Mexican access to the community. Even silence can serve as tacit acquiescence for the purpose of winning approval. Patricia Williams (1991, p. 126–8) described in exquisite detail such an exchange in which she participated passively.

How do I know this kind of exchange serves the purpose of racial bonding? I know because if I do not give the desired response, the other person very often presses the issue much more explicitly; I also may never hear from the other person again (including relatives). For example, if I change the subject, it usually reappears but more forcefully ("Mexicans bring gang problems, you know; I'm really concerned about the future of this community."). Sometimes I give a response I know the other person is not looking for, such as, "Yes, I'm really pleased to see this community becoming more multicultural, I've been working on my Spanish." More often than not, the other person responds with a lecture on problems associated with Mexican American people, and the misguidedness of my judgment. I am usually uncomfortable when people who do not know me well ask what I teach; quite often responses such as "multicultural education" or "urban education" provoke uninvited lectures on race relations or on their own beliefs as a white liberal (hoping that either I will agree or be persuaded to accept their viewpoint).

These kinds of interactions seem to serve the purpose of defining racial lines and inviting individuals to either declare their solidarity or mark themselves as deviant. Depending on degree of deviance, one runs the risk of losing the other individual's approval, friendship, and company. (This usually occurs in the form of feeling "uncomfortable" around the deviant white person.) Many whites who do not support racist beliefs, actions, or policies, but who also do not want to risk social bonds with other whites, simply remain silent. We tacitly agree not to talk about racism.

No white person is exempt from pressures from other white people to "fit in," with the price of conformity to a racial norm very often being approval and friendship. While active anti-racist whites may not be affected by such processes, I would hypothesize that it does affect white educators who are less certain about their own racial beliefs and loyalties. Janet Helms (1990), for example, posited a stage of Reintegration in white racial identity development in which the white person, following coursework and/or experiences that challenged one's previous beliefs about race, returns to those prior, more comfortable and socially acceptable (in white circles) beliefs. We all need affective bonds with people. Given the segregation of our society, the strongest bonds are usually with members of our own race. In a predominantly white teaching profession, white teachers make sure that their peers are "one of us." "Us" may be compassionate, child-oriented, and open-minded, but "us" also defines racial issues from a white vantage point.

Whiteness and the Teaching Profession

As the teaching profession becomes increasingly white and as white educators become increasingly involved in multicultural education, it is likely that what teachers do with multicultural education increasingly will reflect a white worldview. The eighteen students I mentioned at the beginning of this chapter learned to engage with many concepts of multicultural education, and most shaped those concepts to fit their own reality. That reality is one in which social change is not a priority and multicultural education rarely means social reconstruction (Goodwin, 1994). White definitions of multicultural education may become self-perpetuating in schools to the degree that there are few other professionals within the school who bring and articulate alternative perspectives and to the degree that teachers regard themselves as knowing more than the students and parents who might challenge their viewpoints.

Multicultural education ought to be a collaborative process involving dialog and bonding across racial and ethnic boundaries for the purpose of forging greater equality and social justice. This does not mean that white people should be absent from the process, but rather, that we should not dominate or control it.

What is to be done? I can speak most appropriately to what whites should be doing. First, white educators should be engaging in regular dialog and collaborative work with people of color in our own communities, but that dialog and work needs to include regular and continued self-analysis. Dialog is most productive when we are aware of our own biases, limitations, and vested interests that keep us from hearing. Rosaldo (1989) illustrated with his own encounter with Ilongot headhunters:

> This encounter suggests that we ethnographers should be open to asking not only how our descriptions of others would read if applied to ourselves but how we can learn from other people's descriptions of ourselves. In this case I was repositioned through an Ilongot account of one of my culture's central institutions [warfare]. I could no longer speak about headhunting as one of the clean addressing the dirty. My loss of innocence enabled me and the Ilongots to face each other on more nearly equal ground, as members of flawed societies. (p. 64)

Through his experience with Ilongot people, Rosaldo learned at least as much about himself and his own culture as he did about the "Other." As whites learn to hear how Americans of color experience white racism in general and our own actions in particular and as we learn to examine our own worldview in order to identify its boundaries and limitations, we can learn to engage in more productive dialog and action.

Those of us who are white should be spending as much time working on ourselves as attempting to draw in other whites. There is a tendency for white educators, especially those who are new to multicultural education, to proselytize: to attempt to "convert" our friends and colleagues. My students often talk about doing this, while I see them as needing to focus on their own growth. Cornel West (1993) reminds us that, "it is naive to think that being comfortably nested within this very same system [of oppression] . . . does not affect one's work, one's outlook, and most important, one's soul" (p. 21). Multicultural education partly means studying ourselves critically in order to listen more openly. This is not easy, and it takes time and work. My eighteen students had begun the process—they had learned to ask questions that elicited information about racism and exclusion.

Second, the field of multicultural education needs to develop vocabulary and action strategies for addressing white racism and other forms of oppression. When my eighteen students attempted to discuss why jobs are leaving inner-city areas, for example, their limited ability to visualize collective political actions was probably a part of the problem. Educators in general don't usually think in terms of collective political action to make changes; rather, educators tend to conceptualize change strategies in terms of individually persuading other individuals to "do the right thing" (Sleeter, 1992). As a result, many whites don't see what we could be doing differently, and many educators of color become too focused on trying to persuade whites to change when collective pressure politics may be more fruitful. John Garvey (1993) argued that,

> Our most enduring problems will be most satisfactorily addressed by the emergence and growth of a resurgent movement. No one can will that movement into being. But we might assist in its development by establishing situations, within and without formal school settings, for individuals to expand their own political capacities. (p. 85).

History contains numerous examples of white people who have worked collaboratively with oppressed racial groups to combat racist policies and practices (Aptheker, 1992). We are not starting from scratch; we have a history to guide us.

Third, those of us who work to develop teachers' understanding of various forms of oppression must connect teachers with other people who are engaged in active work to dismantle white supremacy and other forms of social injustice. It is naive to believe that one or two university courses will reconstruct an individual's worldview and personal affiliations. My own history attests to the slowness of change and the importance of developing bonds with people who work to challenge racism. Perhaps one form of action we can take is to mentor individuals who have ventured into an unstable stage of racial (or gender or social class) identity development, who are hovering somewhere between tacit acceptance of the status quo and active partnership in struggle. As mentors, we can offer the support and personal care that is needed to help people such as the students discussed here, to stick with the issues and not to turn back.

CHAPTER 8

Race, Class, Gender
and Abandoned Dreams
(with Carl A. Grant)

In 1979, as part of a larger study, we decided to follow longitudinally twenty-four lower-middle-class junior high school students who were of varied racial backgrounds. Initially we were trying to help the school develop a stronger multicultural approach to instruction, but our focus shifted to a study of how culturally diverse adolescents experience school in the context of their lives (see Grant & Sleeter, 1986c). We followed (by observation and interview) these twenty-four students over a seven-year period, through their senior year of high school. School plays a major role in the culture students construct. Like the family and neighborhood, school is a significant context within which students understand and pursue their dreams and aspirations. It provides an institutional ideology, socializing agents, and an experiential context within which students define and shape the way they think about themselves and their personal dreams.

This study examines student culture as it is produced and lived in a particular community. We wanted to understand why students of color, lower-class white students, and female students of all races tend not to succeed in and out of school and tend to assume subordinate roles in society in spite of the fact that school is supposed to serve as an equalizer. We did not assume that schools serve all children equally, since there is abundant evidence that they do not (Anyon, 1981; Oakes, 1985). We believed it would be insufficient to study the school apart from the lives of students, since students are not passive automatons that are simply molded and shaped. Linda Valli (1986) pointed out that too often, in studies of socialization and studies of unequal school processes, process "becomes little more than work upon the raw, inanimate materials of nature; people are objects transformed by processes to which they fall prey and become content enough to fit into the social slots that need to be filled" (p. 15). We saw it as both naive and inaccurate to assume that students do not think about their world and resist attempts to fit them for subordinate social roles.

Student success, or lack of success, can best be understood as a result of interaction between students and the world in which they live, of which the school is a part. One understands how students perceive and act within their world by examining their culture and also by linking it with social-structural inequality as it is manifested in the students' daily experience. Lois Weis (1985) described student cultures as "semiautonomous" and argued that they "arise in relation to structural conditions mediated by both the experience of schooling and the lived experiences of youth in their own communities" (p. 219). Relatively few studies have examined student culture in the way we have, and fewer have integrated race, social class, and gender relationships in their analyses. For example, Michelle Fine (1991), John Ogbu (1984), Charles Payne (1984), Patrick Solomon (1992) and Lois Weis (1985) studied African American lower-class student culture, examining its relationship to racial oppression, very poor quality schooling and the job structure in the community. Signithia Fordham (1988) examined African American students' conceptions of academic success within a context of racial oppression that leads students to view African American identities as being at odds with academic achievement. Robert Everhart (1983), Lois Weis (1990) and Paul Willis (1977) studied working-class white male student culture, analyzing it primarily in terms of its social class context. *They argued that working-class male culture provides* a sense of identity and meaning within a structural context that denies political and economic power to working class men. Linda Valli (1986), R. W. Connell (1982), Angela McRobbie (1978), and Lois Weis (1990) examined white female student culture in relationship to gender and social class relations, showing how schooling contributes partially to the subordination of women. Mary Fuller (1981) examined black girls' resistance to triple subordination based on race, social class, and gender.

These studies show that schooling itself is not equal in quality, and students themselves sometimes recognize and resist this. However, students also perceive and think about opportunities for themselves in the wider society, based on experiences in their own community. Sometimes they shape their behavior in ways that maximize success, often they do not, and often they redefine success to fit the opportunities and roles they believe are open to them.

Exactly what role schools play in this process is not thoroughly understood, particularly for racially mixed schools and for male-female student cultures in interaction with each other. What also has not been investigated sufficiently is how student culture develops and changes over time: At what points do students become aware of, question, and even reject subordinate roles? How do they deal with their own questions, how do they sustain resistance, or how do they reshape their culture to accept eventually their own subordination? Are there critical points when educators could intervene to promote and sustain their success?

These are particularly important questions to address in this era of civil rights rollbacks. As affirmative action, school desegregation, and the remaining shreds of poverty programs are being dismantled, mainstream Americans argue more and more that context does not matter. Subscribing to tenets of political conservatism, they argue that individuals are free to pull themselves up by their own bootstraps, and if they fail, it is their own responsibility. Absent from discussions of social as well as school policy issues are voices of young people themselves, and their perceptions of opportunity, schooling, and the contexts of their lives. In this study, we listened to their voices and to their interpretations of their own realities.

Contexts and Method

The study of these twenty-four students began as a part of a three-year ethnographic study of a multiracial junior high school in a midwestern city in the United States (Grant & Sleeter, 1986c). The community that served as the attendance area for the school was located along a river and historically served as an immigration site for low-income people, particularly people of color, who could not afford to live elsewhere and had often been rejected in other parts of the city. Over the years, as successive waves of Jewish, Lebanese, Syrian, African American, Scandinavian, Native American, and Mexican immigrants moved into the area, an integrated housing pattern developed. In 1980 the mean family income of the community was about $16,000. Residents held such jobs as factory worker, janitor, post-office worker, secretary, and auto mechanic; very few of the twenty-four students' parents had completed college.

The junior high we studied served grades seven through nine. At the time we began this study, school statistics for the racial mix of the 580 junior high students were: white, 67.5 percent; Hispanic, 28.0 percent; Native American, 2.0 percent; African American, 2.0 percent; and Asian, 0.5 percent. On completion of the ninth grade, the junior high students attended a senior high school that was physically connected to the junior high school. A school lunchroom was shared by both schools and served as the architectural connection. Thus, these twenty-four students only had to go through the lunchroom to enter their high school.

The racial composition and the gender count of the twenty-four students were: Mexican, nine (4 male, 5 female); white, eight (5 male, 3 female); African American, two (1 male, 1 female); Puerto Rican, two (2 female); Native American, one (male); Southeast Asian, one (female); Arab-American one (female).

Data were collected over a seven-year period. During the first three years, a team of three researchers made one two-week visit and twenty-three other visits lasting two to three days each. Several methods of data collection were used: observations (including shadowing of students), interviews, and questionnaires. A total of 160 hours were spent observing twenty-three junior high classrooms. During the last four years, two of the three original researchers maintained the vigil on the student population, periodically visiting the school and interviewing the students and a counselor. Phone calls were also made to the counselor in order to keep up with the students' actions. Interview data were recorded and transcribed for analysis. Research bias was partially controlled by rotating interviewers, having all researchers participate in data analysis, and re-asking the same questions in subsequent interviews.

Student Culture and the Abandonment of Dreams

Our title suggests that the students once had optimistic dreams of making it—finishing high school and possibly additional education, getting a good job, making their families proud, and achieving personal satisfaction—but that they slowly abandoned those dreams. To a large extent, this is true. What the title does not delineate, however, is what their dreams were and why they were abandoned. First we will examine the students' dreams for education and work beyond high school. Then we will examine the effect of the school, the family, and the economy on their dreams. Finally their personal identities and their view of the world in which they lived will be considered.

High School and Further Education

(9th grade, April 1981)

Anna:	All the kids in our family who have graduated went on to vocational schools and I want to go to college.
Researcher:	What do you want to be?
Anna:	A lawyer.

(11th grade, May 1983)

R:	What do you plan to do when you graduate?
Anna:	Go to the technical vocational institute.
R:	What influenced you to make these plans?
Anna:	Well, I work at [name of company] Publishing, and they have word processing, so I'll take up that.
R:	Is that what you would like to do most?
Anna:	Not really. I'd rather be a lawyer, but right now I can't afford to go to school.

(9th grade, March 1979)

R:	You still want to be a lawyer, right?
Hazel:	Yeah, but I'm not sure, it's kind of one of my dreams. [It was a dream she talked about with us all year.]

(12th grade, May 1982)

R:	What do you think about doing [next month when you graduate]?
Hazel:	Well, I think about dancing. I don't know if I should go to college right away and start that, or take dramatic arts and communication . . . And I just kinda want to dance for a year or something . . .
R:	You've changed your mind since I talked to you last.
Hazel:	Yeah. That's true, it was law. I kinda gave up on law, I didn't think I had the brains for it.

The students voiced a variety of career goals over the time they were interviewed. Goals they discussed with interest included: lawyer (3 students), teacher (1), professional athlete (2), medical technologist (1), doctor (3), veterinarian (1), computer scientist (1), military (6), mechanic (4), truck driver (1), disc jockey (1), model (2), secretary (2), stewardess (3), beautician (1), and police officer (1). The numbers add up to more than twenty-four because most students changed their minds at least once, or toyed with alternatives. Their degree of conviction about these goals varied, but none of the twenty-four was without some goal.

College was a more immediate concern to many, since their career goals would require college. We asked the students in every interview about career goals and college. Since college is increasingly the "one important escalator" on the "elevation of a people" (Hare, 1971, p. 12), their responses will be discussed in detail.

While in junior high (eighth and ninth grades), thirteen of the twenty-four students said they definitely planned to attend college. Only one definitely said "no" to college; the rest (10) were undecided. The white students tended to voice about the same assurance as others about college: five of the eight white students definitely planned to attend college, and six of the eleven Latino students were definite, with two more discussing professional career goals without specifically discussing college. Of these thirteen, seven were girls and six were boys.

By the end of their senior year, however, only three of the thirteen who said they definitely had college plans were heading for a four-year college. One of these three dropped out his freshman year, leaving only two in college. What happened to the other twenty-one students? Three entered a community college and five planned to enroll in a vocational-technical institute; two of these were part of the thirteen who earlier planned on college, and two more had considered college rather briefly in high school. Three were flirting with the military, one viewing it as a possible career and two hoping to earn money for college. Four more graduated, but were still unsure of plans and talked of taking a "year off." Six did not graduate. Two of these took jobs as mechanics, a goal both had discussed with some interest since junior high. One took a job in a restaurant, a few credits shy of his diploma. One took a minimum wage job and moved in with her boyfriend; we lost track of one; and one dropped out of a school to which he was transferred, was shot on a city street, and now is a quadriplegic in a wheelchair.

What did students say about reasons for their decisions? This can best be answered by providing two representative examples, Carmen and Larry.

Carmen's goals in junior high were very indefinite, although college was a possibility. For Christmas in ninth grade, her father gave her a typewriter. Her parents, both from Puerto Rico, had not graduated from high school and saw secretarial work as a good employment opportunity for Carmen. In tenth grade she started taking clerical courses, receiving encouragement from her business teacher and talking about becoming a legal secretary. By eleventh grade she was thinking about community college to take legal secretarial courses and reported that her accounting and shorthand teachers were very supportive. By her senior year, Carmen was sick of school—boy problems and boring classwork. She wanted just to work for a while—"business, they always need people like clerical workers and stuff." She felt her summer job in a company plus her business courses in high school had prepared her well enough to be a secretary. She simply wanted to be away from the hassles of school.

Larry's four older brothers were in the military. In junior high he figured he would follow suit, although he had not yet given it much thought. In tenth grade he was trying to take some of the harder courses because counselors had said these would help for college, although he was not too sure about college. Money was the main obstacle:

> I know college will be maybe third [choice], after the service and going to a voc. tech.—'cause it's a lot of money. And I ain't got a lot of money. . . . Money just keeps going up and up! So a lot of people find different ways to get around it. Through the service you can get the same schooling for, you know, free.

During his senior year, Larry said he wanted to be a disk jockey. He knew people who had tried and one who made it. If that failed, he did not know; he felt his opportunities to be restricted by his lack of money for college, the unemployment rate, and the poor quality of his secondary schooling. We quote at length because he articulated well the frustration most of our sample felt:

> *Larry:* Every year there's a scarcity of finding jobs. All over the place. . . . If you go to college and have, like, four years, when you get out, there's gotta be something. . . . If you can't get a job, you just wasted a lot of time and a lot of money.
>
> *R:* But many colleges say they usually place 60, 70, 80 percent of their people.
>
> *Larry:* Yeah, but there's always a chance that you ain't that 70, 80 percent that's gonna get a job . . . If you're not a part of that percentage that does get placed, say like me—I'm not a top quality guy in school. I don't think I could handle college right now. I mean, you get a lot of homework, and I haven't had homework for three years now in this school!

Most of the students scaled back on their dreams as they went through school. By their senior year, most who had earlier talked about careers requiring college were no longer talking about college. Most wanted simply to be away from school and working. They felt that they were freely making their own choices about their futures. However, we contextualized their discussions within a particular set of social institutions: the school, the family, and the local economy in the community.

The School

The school can best be described as taking a laissez-faire stand—some resources for college preparation were there, but it was left up to the individual, for the most part, to take advantage of them. In junior high, the academic demand made of students was fairly light. (We have described this in detail in Grant & Sleeter, 1986c.) Most classes gave easy work and no homework; the main person to talk seriously with students about their futures was a counselor who had grown up in the community. When students entered tenth grade, most said that the work was much harder. They were taking academic courses required for graduation (typically English, social studies, math, science, and two electives), and many were receiving homework (typically two or three times per week in math and science). Students also said that teachers explained or helped students with the work less and expected them to figure it out more on their own. Students did not complain much about any of this—they described the high school as treating them more "grown up."

After tenth grade, things changed. We will describe the changes in relationship to what students did when they finished high school. One category of six students entered college or community college after graduation. These students continued to take demanding courses all the way through high school until they graduated (except one who had a half-day of work/study his senior year) and continued to be given some homework. These might be thought of as the college-bound, in that their teachers treated them as if they were bound for college. However, it was often not the school that advised them which courses to take; it was often friends and family who had been to college and knew what preparation was needed. These students made the following kinds of comments about the counseling they received in high school:

(Senior Year)

R: What did [the counselors] tell you that made you take chem-
          istry and physics?
Lin-Su: They didn't tell me anything. I just decided.
R: Did you know that those kinds of things are good for you to
          have if you're going to go to college?
Lin-Su: Yeah, that's why I took them.
R: Who told you you should be taking them in order to go to col-
          lege?
Lin-Su: Some of my teachers. My mom and dad. And my older sis-
          ter—she's going to college and she took those classes.

(Junior Year)

R: Why are you taking so many academic courses?
Rakia: Mm, I don't know. I don't really like gym. I just like classes
          where you can sit and do your work [history, French, algebra,
          trig., computers, biology] . . .
R: Has anyone told you that you need the math and the algebra
          and science courses in order to go to college and become a
          doctor?
Rakia: Yeah, my advisor. They usually ask you, "What do you plan to
          do after high school?" I said, "Go to college." And they said,
          "O.K., you need a lot of math and English and stuff like sci-
          ence."
R: Are most of your friends planning to go to college?
Rakia: . . . Sandra, she wants to be a veterinarian.
R: Is she taking courses like yours?
Rakia: Not at all. . . . I don't think she really talks to people about
          what she's going to do.

(Senior Year)

Rakia: I don't like the counselor. 'Cause instead of boosting up, he'll
          kinda put you down. He said that I wouldn't get in college
          with my test scores. But I did. . . . I just got the letter back
          [from the college] that just proved him wrong.

The picture that emerged was that around tenth grade, counselors asked students what they planned to do after graduation. If
they said "college," they were advised to take more math and science;
three girls told us counselors "made" them stick with math and science at that point. After that, students seemed to be on their own.
Some of their teachers told them which classes to take, and they got

advice from counselors if they purposely sought it, but most of the advice came from outside the school.

A second group of five students consisted of those who were fairly certain they would become secretaries or mechanics. Little academic demand was placed on them in school. They were advised into secretarial or autoshop courses and felt the school was helping them in that sense. These students reported getting advice and being made to work and think in their vocational classes.

The other thirteen students—the largest group—floated through with only minimal demands made on them after tenth grade. Several thought they were going to college, others were unsure. Either way, it appeared that no one in the school seriously thought they were headed for college. The students assumed their needs were being taken care of and so did not seek advice on preparing for life after school. The school took steps mainly to help them fit into the blue-collar labor market. These students reported having little or no homework. Their senior English class was aimed, in one students' words, at "trying to make sure that our grammar's right." Their course schedules were filled with electives such as ceramics, office helper, bookstore worker, chorus, and gym; during their senior year several participated in half-day on-the-job-training programs. They reported that virtually no one in the school talked to them about the future; they were free to select their own courses, and counselors did not talk to them unless they sought out the counselors. There was not even much attempt to let students know what information might be available through the counselors, so few students voluntarily went to ask; one pointed out that counselors "gotta let you know that it's there [information about a college], for you to come and see, you know."

By their senior year, many of these students were bitter, and many were simply bored with school. For example, one who took the easy way through told us the following, one month before graduating:

R: You went through easy.
Pablo: Yeah.
R: Do you ever regret that now?
Pablo: Yeah, 'cause—I feel like I coulda learned more if I went, if I took some harder classes. . . . There's a lot of kids that just, they're smart, but they just take easy classes and not, you know, they're not learning nothing. Once you get into senior high, you don't even have to take math, you know, not at all.

Their experience with school, and particularly the last two years, left many ambivalent about any future schooling: on the one hand, it would help them, but on the other hand it would probably be boring and they were not prepared for it. Some blamed the school for being too lax; others blamed themselves.

We wondered whether the school offered any other kinds of opportunities for learning how to "make it" in society, such as leadership development. We looked for this in our study of the junior high and examined interviews from the senior high for comments. We found very little. The student council was one avenue for developing leadership skills; one of our sample had been president of the junior high student body, and another was senior class president. Even here, however, student leadership did not seem to be taken seriously. The student council did not have authority over anything very important or consequential, and the senior class president spent half of her senior year in on-the-job-training. One social studies teacher made a concerted effort to involve his students in school and community political events, but his singular effort did not seem to make a great impact on the students. The only other comment we found related to leadership development—and it is a weak one at that—was a shy student commenting that English classes that require students to make speeches had helped her learn to speak up more.

The Family

The family was a second institution within which students constructed perceptions of their futures.

> R: How do your parents feel about you going to school in general?
> Alvin: They want me to finish school and get a good education and get good grades, too.

This comment illustrates the way these students' parents felt about school achievement. Discussions with counselors, teachers, administrators, and students on this topic were of one kind: Parents sent their kids to school to learn and expected them not to fool around. Parents were very supportive of the school and left their children's education, guidance, and course selection almost solely in the school's hands. We have reason to assume that because most of the parents had not attended college, and were familiar mostly with traditional blue and pink-collar jobs, they were reluctant to give career advice or to lobby strongly for a certain course selection if they believed the school had endorsed their child's program. There were a few exceptions. For example, Ron's father and uncle were mechanics and encouraged him to follow suit. During the study his goal did not change. Notice his comment in his sophomore year.

> *R:*   What do you want to do when you graduate?
> *Ron:* My Dad tells me I should be a mechanic 'cause he is.

Ron left school in his junior year and is now working as a mechanic.

Juan, who early in the study said he wanted to be a doctor, often spoke of receiving advice from his uncle, who was a doctor, as to which courses to take and the need to work hard in school in order to achieve his goal.

Since most of the students did not have homework on a regular basis, parents did not set up home study hours or have identifiable opportunities to discuss schoolwork with their children. The role that the parents played in helping their children fulfill their academic expectations was very small, which is typical of blue-collar parents who have not been to college themselves and therefore do not know how to help their children advance beyond high school (Lareau, 1989). Besides helping with homework, several ways professional class parents typically help children in academics include providing them with experiences such as museums, plays, and travel, providing lessons and private tutors, and reading books, magazines, and newspapers. Most students when asked reported doing very little of the above either with parents or alone.

The Economy

The local economy was a third institution within which the students constructed beliefs about their future. One important characteristic of the local economy was that neither the students nor their parents had extra money for things like college. This was, in fact, the main barrier to college cited by students. Many also discussed ways of dealing with it. The students' perception of reality may have been limited and even inaccurate, but it was based on available information and guided their behavior.

"Taking a year off" to work was an alternative several mentioned. None laid out a specific plan for doing this, but several felt they needed to work to save some money before they could go to college. Six students were more specific about how they would finance further education: They would join the military and either save their pay for college later or receive their education "free" while in the military. They based this plan on talks given by military recruiters who came to the senior high school. Few students mentioned loans or scholarships for college. We asked them about this in interviews, and they had very little knowledge of this option—it was as if the option did not exist. No one had talked to most of them about it.

Another feature of the local economy that students perceived was the relatively high unemployment rate. It made students feel uncertain about the future and caused several to view four years of college with some skepticism. Although Rakia, for example, enrolled in a community college, she said about the unemployment situation: "I'm kinda worried about it. I don't have a job right now, but that doesn't bother me. But it does worry me because when I get out of college, I don't know what the situation's gonna be like." Other students were more worried about having a job right now and felt some sense of security if they at least had a summer job or were involved in on-the-job-training. The unemployment situation made it risky to give up a job, expect financial support from parents, or incur debt to secure further schooling.

Students' career goals were wide-ranging, but their knowledge of the job market was based on jobs they or their parents actually held. Several distinguished between dreams and reality: One could dream of what one would like to do, but one would have to settle for a job that is really there and that one can really get. Students commented about their own job experience:

R: What do you plan to do when you graduate? [Earlier goal had been veterinarian.]

Linda: I'm going on to the technical-vocational institute. I'm either gonna take computers, or data processing, office fields, general accounting, or accounting.

R: What influenced you to do that?

Linda: I work in 3M, in general accounting, so I'd like to get a job there.

R: Oh. How'd you get the job at 3M?

Linda: Through on-the-job-training.

R: Do you think about the current unemployment rate at all?

Linda: Yes! I'll probably end up being one of them if I don't get some training to keep my job.

Finally, we must consider the peer group itself. When we met the students in junior high school, we were struck by the strong division in their lives between school and the rest of the day. Most of their classwork was boring, but school could be tolerated from

8:00 A.M. to 2:30 P.M. After that, it could be forgotten, especially since few had homework. Students spent their free time either at home, playing sports, or "hanging around" with each other. They cared about passing their classes, but few cared which passing grade they received. It was considered neither "in" nor "out" to be smart—this was viewed in the peer group as irrelevant. Since high school did not offer much change, the peer group did not change much. Students spent less time playing and more time in jobs, but no more time with schoolwork. They became used to investing a prescribed number of hours in a work-type setting and enjoying the rest of the day in social activities. This lifestyle fit the demands placed on them. The students also used each other as sources of information about future plans, quite possibly more than they used the counselors. Thus, their perceptions were widely shared, both because students encountered similar experiences and because they helped each other make sense of their futures.

Personal Identities and View of the World

We wondered how the students viewed their identities as members of particular racial, social class, and gender groups and how they viewed the position of those groups in society. We were interested in the extent to which the students embraced the strengths offered by group membership without being constrained by social stereotypes or stigmas and the extent to which their understanding of oppression developed, if at all. We also wondered what effect views of race, class, and gender had on their dreams. We learned about their personal and group identities by asking about their neighborhood, their views of each other, their views about cultural practices within the home, and their views about choices they made for themselves. We learned about their understanding of racism, classism, and sexism by asking them directly about these things.

Race and Ethnicity

The students identified culturally with their community. The community was composed of working-class people of varied ethnic backgrounds, but the students viewed them as culturally all "the same." Households varied somewhat in menu, religion, strictness, and so forth, but the students did not see the various ethnic groups in the community as culturally distinct from one another. To the students, a distinguishing feature of their community was the fact that its people were different colors—this was seen as positive, and students talked openly and eagerly about it. Culturally, however, they were not different from one another. Over the time of this study, we saw no change in this pattern.

What fascinated us was the extent to which many students disagreed with their parents on this. Several of their parents had moved from elsewhere (such as Puerto Rico, Egypt, Texas, Mexico) and saw different ethnic groups as culturally different. Some of the parents who had lived in the community a long time also saw the groups as different. These parents tended to want their children to date and marry members of their own ethnic group, and some tried to discourage them from associating in any way with a particular ethnic group. The students did not see it this way, for the most part, and some argued with their parents about it. To the students, inter-racial dating and marriage were completely acceptable because color did not matter.

A few students commented on their parents' wanting them to retain their ethnic culture. Some saw this as important, but also saw no conflict between it and marrying someone of another ethnic group. Others did not see it as particularly important. For example, two Mexican-American students whose parents were from Texas told us they were not interested in learning Spanish, even though their parents wanted them to do so.

The students' acceptance of racial diversity seemed almost to interfere with their developing an understanding of racism. Only about half of the students believed any form of racism exists in society, and the examples they described were, with two exceptions, of individual prejudice. For example, a Mexican-American girl said that the students in an all-white school had said they were having an "invasion" when she visited there; a white girl said some of the police were racially prejudiced. A few students described their parents as racially prejudiced, but the only generalization they offered was that times have changed and younger people are not prejudiced any more. Students saw most prejudice away from the community; the main examples of prejudice in the community were offered by a Puerto Rican and an Arab-American (both of whom said people lumped them together with Mexicans, which they resented), and a Viet-namese-American, who commented on prejudice against newly arrived Hmongs.

Only two students attempted to describe institutional racism. One Mexican-American boy said that "just about everything is for white people," explaining that television, for example, is all white. A white boy explained that whites are upper class and Mexicans are lower class because Mexicans have not been able to afford college and therefore do not get good jobs.

The students of color had, as a group, no more understanding of racism than the white students. Nine of the sixteen students of color believed some racial prejudice exists in society, as did four of the eight white students, but the explanations or understandings of prejudice offered by the students of color were no more informed than were those of the white students. Since most students had not experienced overt discrimination in the community and many of the students had not ventured very far outside the community, they assumed race relations in society are similar to race relations in that community. Neither school nor parents taught them much about racism beyond what they experienced. One teacher in the junior high taught about it, and a few students mentioned this while in junior high, but seemed to forget it in high school since the race relations where they lived were positive. We did not study their parents directly to find out what they taught about race relations, but the main thing students ever said about their parents was whether parents were prejudiced against their friends.

Social Class

Students defined themselves as middle class (with the exception of one who said her family was poor, and one who said his was upper middle class). They said they were middle class because, in the words of one student, "We don't make a lot, but then we still have enough to make ends meet." Earlier we described the community as working class but as having two neighborhoods differentiated by racial composition and somewhat by income level; to most of the students, it was all one middle-class community.

The students generated this common self-definition on the basis of several interrelated factors. Geographically, the community was cut off by a river from most of the rest of the city, and residents tended not to venture out. The range of incomes in the community was not great, and the schools served the entire community from kindergarten through graduation. Thus, the students grew up together and associated with others who shared their economic circumstances, their neighborhood, their school. Lacking much firsthand contact with people of diverse social classes, they figured they were middle class since few lived in poverty but none had much money for luxuries.

Their knowledge of the social class structure in society was very thin, even after taking sociology in high school, in which social class was a topic they studied. When we asked students about social class, we often had to explain what we meant, and even then students sometimes did not know how to respond. Students believed anyone could achieve upward mobility by working hard, getting a good education, and—two girls said—marrying well. Most students did not want to move up; a white boy said he would like more money but wanted to stay in the same community. A few others also suggested this.

Gender and Sexism

Students' gender self-definitions were more complex and less shared. The patterns we will describe only very roughly follow ethnic group membership, with the Latino students tending slightly more than whites to adhere to traditional gender identities. All students saw themselves as potential jobholders regardless of sex. Students believed both sexes could hold almost any job, although several ruled out construction for women (they lack the strength) and child care for men (men lack patience). Their aspirations tended to follow sex-stereotypic patterns, particularly as they approached graduation. The aspiring mechanics, truck drivers, and professional football players were male; the aspiring secretaries, stewardesses, and models were female—but the girls also envisioned themselves as lawyers, doctors, and computer technologists, at least until they confronted the problem of paying for college.

Students identified males more than females as providers, and this increased as they got older. Before they started dating, providing was not an issue—when same-sex groups went out, sex did not determine who initiated or paid. Dating changed this. Six of the boys from the time they started dating expected to initiate dates and pay for them, although most were flexible about who could initiate phone calls. By their senior year, the three boys who graduated, plus a fourth who had not dated much, saw themselves as providers for their future families—their wives could work but would not have to, especially if there were children. One boy initially advocated flexible roles, but by his senior year he was paying for all his dates, and referred to a wife's paycheck as "extra money." Interestingly, only two of these eight boys had a firm career goal in mind all during the study; the rest were unsure what they would do. Five of the girls, by high school, also saw the male as the main provider: Their boyfriends initiated and paid for dates, and they expected the man to be the main family breadwinner. This was a relationship they seemed to learn partly through dating; one had offered to pay for dates but the offer was turned down; others thought hypothetically that girls could pay but knew boys preferred it the other way around. Two of these five girls earlier expressed a strong career orientation, but by their senior year were uncertain about their futures. One of them entertained the idea of herself as provider and her husband staying at home, but did not expect this. A sixth girl saw the male as the main provider but was also preparing for a good career in computer science.

On the other hand, three girls and one boy definitely saw initiating and providing as shared responsibilities and had worked this out in date relationships. Two more girls expressed ambivalence about providing: They questioned, but did not reject outright, traditional dating roles and saw themselves as career-bound. The remaining four students did not address this issue.

All students but one saw themselves as present and future workers in the home. Most divided chores by sex; the girls wrestled with this more than the boys. Eleven of the twenty-four students expected and preferred to divide domestic chores by sex and did not debate or question this during the study; four were girls, seven were boys. These tended to be the same students who saw males as providers. Most engaged in these roles at home, although in one boy's home chores were not divided by sex and he thought they should be. Only one boy and two girls completely rejected sex roles at home throughout the study. The two girls were rejecting roles learned at home, and one felt very strongly about this, saying she hated it that guys want women to stay in the house.

The other nine students were less certain. Three (1 boy, 2 girls) simply said it depended on whether the wife holds a job; if she does, they would expect to divide chores fifty-fifty. Four more students (1 boy, 3 girls) questioned domestic roles while in junior high, two girls having been angry about how chores were divided at home; but by their senior year all three of these girls seemed content to adopt traditional sex roles. Two more girls wanted to divide things fifty-fifty but did not expect a man to go along with that.

Students justified role definition primarily based on masculine strength. Eleven students maintained that boys are the stronger sex and therefore better in sports and heavy work; five disagreed, and two girls changed their minds on this during the study. What was particularly interesting was that approximately equal proportions of both sexes defined themselves as athletic, but many boys, and the girls as they got older, defined boys as naturally stronger and more athletic than girls.

With respect to sexism in society, students knew very little. They saw equal opportunity in the work place as an accomplished fact, with the exception of one girl who knew a woman who had filed a sex-discrimination grievance. The fact that many jobs are not sex-balanced was attributed mainly to individual choice or to ability to do the job. Several girls wrestled for a short period with sexism at home, but they saw this as a personal rather than a collective struggle or as something women simply have to put up with. For example, one girl complained that men like to be outside until mealtime and expect to come in and find dinner ready; this was an inconvenient male characteristic more than an arena for struggle. In fact, as students matured, they tended more and more to accept rather than resist sex-divided domestic work roles and supporting sex stereotypes. The only social issue any of the students discussed was whether women should fight in the military. Three boys brought this up, arguing that if women want equal rights, they should be willing to fight in combat. This issue was being debated in the news and seemed to be one of concern to boys who had considered entering the military. The students generated gender self-definitions and their understandings of social relations between the sexes on the basis of several factors. A major one was observation. For example, a boy commented that girls must prefer sewing to cars because he had never seen roles switched, although another said girls in his autoshop class demonstrated that girls could be mechanical. As another example, a girl commented that she had seen traditional sex roles at home all her life. A related factor was doing: All but one student had chores at home, and most became used to and comfortable with those they were assigned, although a few rebelled against them. The local economy seemed to reinforce students' observations—girls were hired as baby sitters and typists, boys as outdoor laborers, paper carriers, janitors, and mechanics. The school was a laissez-faire factor. It made available all courses and activities to both sexes, enabling many girls to develop an interest in sports, but hardly anyone in school (or at home), with the exception of one or two teachers, discussed gender or sexism. So students who questioned or rebelled against roles or expectations had to work these through themselves, and they tended to resolve them in favor of the status quo. A final important factor was the peer group itself. When students began to think about courtship, they began to shape their behavior and expectations in a way that would complement the expectations of the opposite sex. The boys had fewer questions then girls about role and gender-identity, and the girls tended to resolve their own questions by accepting the boys' definition. This facilitated courtship, although it also tended to help reproduce existing gender relations.

Discussion

This study has shown, particularly because it was longitudinal, that race, class, and gender relations in society are not reproduced simply because the young absorb and inherit the status and beliefs of their parents. Nor do individuals make decisions about their lives in a contextual vacuum. It is a more complex process than this. As the young work through their dreams and questions in a particular context, the range of possibilities that seem open and real to them gradually narrows and tends to mirror the lives of their parents and the context in the local community. The culture the young construct from the fabric of everyday life provides a set of answers and a sense of certainty for their questions and dreams. To the extent that everyday life embodies unequal social relationships, the culture students generate and regenerate over time gradually accepts and "explains" existing social relationships. The process may appear inevitable, but it is not. We argue that at least part of the context within which the young grow up can be changed (the school) and can propel them in directions that diverge from the status quo. The school can be the key catalyst in this process. Unfortunately, in our study it did not perform this function well.

Let us review the students' dreams, particularly while they were in junior high and saw their futures as relatively open. In junior high, the students visualized themselves in a wide variety of career roles, unrestricted by race and social class or, for the girls, gender. Over half aspired to college, and only one rejected it. Their dreams of careers and college were, in fact, quite different from the lives of their parents. Elsewhere we have noted that this was particularly true for the girls, whose career goals tended to be more ambitious than those of the boys. In junior high, students seemed to adopt portions of the lives of adults around them that they liked (such as mechanical arts for those who liked working with their hands) and reject that which they did not like (such as housework for those girls who had become fed up with it).

The culture students generated out of everyday life, however, tended to hold them in their community and return them to lives very much like those of their parents. One feature of everyday life they discussed often was their racial diversity. The students generated a common culture among themselves that transcended race. Some of their parents had also done this; others, particularly those who had grown up elsewhere, had not. Rather than adopting their parents' racial prejudice, however, the students resisted it. Their own daily experience with each other convinced them that racism was incorrect. It also tended to convince them that their own community was the best place to live. They frequently told us that schools or neighborhoods of one race would be dull and uninteresting. The students' common culture that transcended race was like a magnet keeping them in their community, and also keeping them somewhat ignorant of race relations in the broader society. In addition, the student culture did not recognize institutional racism; individual prejudice was the main manifestation of racism that the students saw and recognized in their daily lives.

The culture students generated out of everyday life was also nonacademic. Students believed in school and valued education, seeing it as a route to their dreams, but on a day-to-day basis, they invested minimal effort in it. Unwittingly, in fact, they played a role in limiting their academic empowerment, in that they never actively resisted the school's low demand of them. In junior high, for example, they recognized that homework demands were light and several said they thought they should get more homework, but they did nothing about this. We found it interesting to contrast this with students' active resistance toward parents' racism. Why did the students resist their parents' racism but not the school's low expectations of them? Their everyday experience taught them that their parents were wrong, and that racial prejudice would interfere with enjoyment of daily life. (Mexicans aren't lazy because my friend Diego isn't lazy, and if I avoided Diego, I'd lose a good buddy.) Students' everyday experience with school taught them that it was boring and that the content was irrelevant to daily life. School may be important for attaining a career goal, but if the medicine is bitter, why ask for more than the doctor prescribes, especially if more time devoted to school would lessen time with friends? So the students accepted minimal homework and a low involvement with classwork and developed other interests and behavior patterns, centering largely around sports, that filled their time and probably would have caused them to resist a sudden increase in school work (a "what if" they never faced).

The students generated a distorted version of social class, which they used to help answer questions about college as well as goals in general. The inaccuracies and distortions in their beliefs were striking. They believed themselves to be middle class, and when asked many said they did not want to move up in the class structure, particularly if it meant moving away from the community. A white male student put it as follows: "I'd like to probably move upward in money, but not out of the neighborhood." Students seemed to believe middle-class people cannot afford college these days, and since jobs are limited, it is better to get a job now than take a chance that one will find a job after college. They did not seem to see college as improving their chance of obtaining a job, only as opening doors to certain kinds of jobs. The students did not seem to see a great difference in the pay and power that accrue from different occupations. They believed hard work was the best route to upward mobility; the role capital plays in the economy seemed completely unknown. Finally, they seemed to believe that race and gender have nothing to do with one's place in the economic structure. While this belief encouraged them to aspire to any career, it also produced false insights into opportunities available to them. Ultimately, the main beneficiaries of students' beliefs would be local employers: the student culture helped produce workers who were fairly content with their lot and willing to work to maintain their lives.

Everyday life with friends and family provided considerable material for generating an understanding of gender. Most homes placed the young in a sex-divided domestic work role from an early age. This was a role that few of the boys seriously questioned, probably because they grew up in it and it provided routes to attaining some status: being strong, supporting a family, taking a lead in courtship. The boys had experienced only part of this role—supporting a family, which eventually could be difficult for them, was not yet a reality. The girls raised more questions about gender, mainly when they found themselves working while their brothers played outside. Regardless of ethnic background, at one time or another most girls believed it to be unfair and demeaning. There were, however, rewards to adhering to a traditional female role: dates, especially with the popular boys; harmonious relationships at home; and admiration achievable through fashion. Students' questions about gender were never used to help them understand sexism. Thus, they answered their own questions by generating stereotypes (boys are just stronger than girls), accepting things as inevitable (men are just like that, nothing you can do about it), and interpreting conflicts as individual rather than as collective. Many resolved the question of dividing labor by sex by insisting that both partners in a marriage should do as much work, even though the work is different. We stress that there appeared to be little or no relationship between ethnicity and the questions the girls raised. The Latino homes were more likely to adhere to traditional sex roles than the white homes, but Latino girls were just as likely to question their role—temporarily, at any rate—as were white girls raised in traditional homes.

That portion of the context of students' lives that could be changed most readily was the school. In fact, the school had a very important role to play in students' abandonment of their dreams. The school staff, much more so than the parents or the students themselves, knew how the education system works—what kind of preparation is needed for college, how to obtain scholarships and loans, what the differences are between a four-year college degree and job training in the military, and so forth. They also knew more than the students about social class, race relations, and gender. But the school abdicated the job for which they were hired: promoting academic learning.

In spite of students' interest in further education, in spite of their good behavior in school, and in spite of the fact that the majority had normal learning ability, both the junior and senior high school faculty (with the exception of a very few individuals) accepted students' failure to empower themselves through education and in so doing, ensured that they would fail. This was particularly true after the tenth grade. Prior to the tenth grade students were required to take academic courses to meet graduation requirements. While few of these courses rigorously challenged them, at least to a limited degree students were receiving an education. After tenth grade two things happened: the students started raising serious questions about their futures (a major one being whether they could afford college) and the school pulled out of their lives as much as it could, expending its academic energies on only those few who for one reason or another continued to take the more difficult classes. For the majority of the students, advising virtually ceased once graduation requirements had been met, and any homework they might have had in the tenth grade came to an end. The school's main effort became equipping the students to take a minimum-wage job after graduation. The school staff may have viewed it as inevitable that these students would not continue schooling—interviews with the junior high teachers found strong acceptance of this belief—but there was no inevitability here; the school actively helped it to happen.

The school could also have taught more explicitly about race, class, and gender. What the school did was to treat all students as much alike as possible, while teaching a watered-down version of the traditional white, male-dominated curriculum. Students' racial backgrounds were acknowledged mainly through festivals and special programs at certain times during the year, the main one being Cinco de Mayo. One elective course in the junior high—multicultural education—taught about racism, and a few teachers taught isolated lessons about race or sexism, more in the junior than the senior high school. Courses that would have lent themselves particularly well to examining social inequality—money and banking, law and justice, and sociology—were not used for this purpose. To some extent courses affirmed sex roles, in that home economics and industrial arts courses were dominated by one sex. Home economics taught girls how to work with their appearance, and girls' and boys' sports were somewhat different. The main thing we noticed was that the school did not provide much knowledge about the social structure or the students' location in it, yet the teachers had some knowledge, even without doing research. For example, the junior high teachers were well aware of the socioeconomic status of the community, and many were also aware of how sexism affects one's life because in interviews they discussed these issues with respect to their own lives.

The families also played a role in the abandonment of students' dreams, although the family's role interacted with that of the school. Research consistently finds a strong relationship between level of educational attainment and parent occupation (Coleman, 1966). It is often believed that home background limits aspirations and ability to learn in school. We did not find home background to limit students' aspirations or parental interest in school—it limited, rather, the school's aspirations for its clients. What the home background did limit was the help parents could give. They told their children to "get a good education," to do what the teacher says; most did not know that they should have been telling their children which courses to take and demanding that teachers do more teaching. There is, in fact, a paradox here that works against parents of color and lower-class backgrounds.

Students who are white and middle or upper class tend to be taught better and challenged more (Anyon, 1981; Oakes, 1985), regardless, we suspect, of what role the parents might be playing. The higher the social class, the more actively demanding of the school the parents tend to become, but the more likely it is that the school will be trying to empower the students academically anyway. It is those parents who know least about how the education system works and who are most likely to feel intimidated by educators, who have most to gain by involving themselves actively with the school. We are reminded of conversations we had with African American middle-class parents of children attending an upper-class desegregated school. They told us they needed to initiate and maintain contact with the school to let teachers know they, the parents, were educated themselves, and to make sure their children were placed in demanding classes and taught well. The teachers were reluctant to contact them, and many of the teachers expected less of the African American than the white students. The problem was magnified at the school in this study: there was little home-school communication and the parents gave their children what advice they knew how to give and assumed incorrectly that the school was doing the rest. This is a problem that may well grow as teaching staffs become increasingly white and professionalized and, in the process, increasingly removed from lower-class and minority communities.

The students achieved success primarily in their own ethnic self-definitions, in that they learned to embrace their racial diversity while developing a sense of community. Beyond that, they were dismally unsuccessful. What this study has shown is that their lack of success was due in a large part to the very inactive role the school played in their lives. It allowed them to dream and wonder and allowed them to abandon their dreams on their own by failing to provide a strong academic thrust or provide knowledge about their place in the world. One might accuse their homes and the community in general of the same thing, but this does not excuse the school. The students' culture was not simply a mirror reflection of their parents and neighbors. That culture was created as much in the school as elsewhere, and represented an attempt to understand family and community life, as much as it was a perpetuation of it. It is in the school where educators can affect students: by recognizing their dreams, acknowledging their very real attempt to make sense of the immediate world in which they live, and then teaching them accordingly.

As resources for schools and college tuition are being cut, as living-wage jobs are becoming less plentiful, and as various programs attempting to open up access to jobs and schooling are being cut, we would anticipate that more and more students like those we studied here will choose much less than they dream of and blame themselves for their own failures. Educators can affect what happens in schools, but educators also need to be politically active child advocates outside schools. In this era of growing conservatism, as funding for prisons replaces funding for schools and jobs, the need for politically active child advocates is becoming more and more critical.

CHAPTER 9

Teaching Science for Social Justice

In the context of working with an Institute on Multicultural Science Education, I was asked: How can we tell if our science instruction is really multicultural and social reconstructionist? At first I hesitated to reply, since my own science background is not very extensive and some science educators have grappled with this question far more extensively than I have (e.g., Atwater, 1993; Harding, 1994; Hodson, 1993; Reiss, 1993). At the same time, however, in the process of collecting materials for multicultural teaching, I have examined a few science materials that exemplify for me key ideas of multicultural education. In this chapter, I will share my response to the Institute participants by commenting on three curriculum materials for science teaching. In the process, I will clarify what it means to teach for social justice, applying these ideas to a discipline— science—that some would regard as unrelated to multicultural education.

Social Justice and Science

Historically as well as today, Europeans and Euro-Americans have regarded western knowledge, including western approaches to learning about the natural world, as superior to those of other peoples. As Derek Hodson (1993) put it, "The image of the scientist most frequently projected by the curriculum is the western one of a self-assured, technologically powerful manipulator and controller" (p. 703). American children grow up internalizing this image very concretely: if you ask children to draw a scientist, they commonly draw a white man wearing a lab coat and glasses. Hodson pointed out that this image suggests that western scientists engage in a highly rational and objective process of discovering facts. This image suggests further that the "failure" of earlier generations and non-western cultures to unearth the same facts must be a "'failure' of their science" (p. 703).

Europeans and Euro-Americans have used this presumption of scientific superiority as justification for policies of colonization and genocide and have then rendered such policies "legitimate" partly through scientific and pseudo-scientific research, such as craniometry. Historically there has been a strong link between western expansionism and science. Not only have westerners used science to support our presumed superiority, but western science developed primarily to facilitate imperialism. As Sandra Harding (1994) argued,

> European sciences advanced because they focused on describing and explaining those aspects of nature's regularities that permitted the upper classes of Europeans to multiply and thrive, especially through the prospering of their military, imperial, and otherwise expansionist projects. (p. 313)

Funding for science research today still follows much the same pattern in that research projects that support the agendas of the government or of industry are most likely to be supported monetarily.

Science has helped to facilitate colonialism and neo-colonialism, and the idea of western scientific superiority has provided a rationale for expansionist policies. The stance Euro-Americans have taken toward Indian nations is an excellent example. Despite the fact that Euro-Americans learn that our ancestors killed about 90% of the original inhabitants of the North American continent and that many Indian people today live in abject poverty, few of us non-Indians experience a sense of outrage.

> More often, the sentiments expressed by participants [of Columbus Day celebrations] are, quite frankly, that the fate of Native America embodied in Columbus and the Columbian legacy is a matter to be openly enthusiastically applauded as an unrivaled "boon to all mankind." (Churchill, 1994, p. 43)

By constructing ourselves as culturally superior and more advanced than people of color, white people teach ourselves and our children to regard it as unfortunate, perhaps, but for the greater good that "primitive" people and their knowledge are displaced, even destroyed.

By subscribing to the idea of "progress" in humankind's knowledge of the world, Euro-Americans assume that policies of genocide, slavery, and colonization were misguided actions of the past and that the U.S. today would never engage in such actions. However, this assumption is not correct. As Ward Churchill (1994) pointed out, for example, the U.S. spent forty years fighting ratification of the U.N. 1948 Convention on Punishment and Prevention of the Crime of Genocide. Our presumption of cultural superiority leads U.S. citizens, particularly those of us who are white, to support actions and policies that destroy cultural "Others." Science and technology are dimensions of western culture that we learn to value very highly and to see ourselves as having perfected. In the process, we allow the destruction of a good deal of knowledge that we did not invent. Economic and cultural policies of neo-colonialism, often euphemistically referred to as the "spread of western civilization," are leading to the death of numerous cultures and peoples.

> Today, with little notice, more vast archives of knowledge and expertise are spilling into oblivion, leaving humanity in danger of losing its past and perhaps jeopardizing its future as well. Stored in the memories of elders, healers, midwives, farmers, fishermen and hunters in the estimated 15,000 cultures remaining on earth is an enormous trove of wisdom. . . . But the world's tribes are dying out or being absorbed into modern civilization. (Linden, 1991, p. 46)

Western scientists have thoroughly studied only about 1,100 of the earth's 265,000 species of plants, but many species known to tribal healers but not Western science have medicinal value (Linden, 1991, p. 52). The Quechua Indians of South America grow over fifty strains of potatoes; "if these natives switched to modern crops, the global potato industry would lose a crucial line of defense against the threat of insects and disease" (p. 54). In other words, by destroying indigenous cultures or allowing them to die, we are robbing humankind of considerable knowledge and wisdom.

In most cases, we are simply ignorant of people we regard as unimportant. We don't think about them, nor do we attempt to represent them in our curricula at all. However, when indigenous and Third World people are represented, they are usually constructed as being simple, primitive, childlike. For example, many primary-grade teachers incorporate a few Indian stories into their curriculum; high school literature teachers rarely teach Indian literature in much depth, if at all. At the primary level, stories are presented as "cute," and children may be encouraged to make up some "Indian" stories of their own (a practice I have heard teachers describe).

The American public will not demand a reversal to policies of genocide and cultural destruction as long as we learn to justify such policies on the basis of our own assumed superiority. One way to address this presumption of superiority is to teach youngsters to regard "Other" people as equally intelligent as themselves, "Other" cultures as highly complex and rich, and science itself as having been developed historically by a variety of cultures worldwide. Later in this chapter these ideas will be discussed in more detail. While I do not believe that such teaching by itself will change the politics and economics undergirding genocide and neo-colonialism, it can at least undermine the justification most people use to support such policies.

Another way to think about science and social justice is to view scientific knowledge as a tool that can help solve human problems. Science itself does not create or solve problems; people do, and both problems and their solutions are tied to politics. But those who control both the political process and science knowledge are those with the greatest power. As such, those who control science are likely to use science as a tool to advance their own interests. As Hodson (1993) put it,

> Material benefits in the west are sometimes achieved at the expense of those living in the third world. . . . Science and technology serve the rich and powerful in ways that are often prejudicial to the interests and well-being of the poor and powerless, sometimes giving rise to further inequalities and injustices . . . economic exploitation is sustained not only by science but also, albeit indirectly, by science *education*. (p. 704)

Harding (1994) agreed, arguing that "the benefits [of science] are distributed disproportionately to already over-advantaged groups in Europe and elsewhere, and the costs disproportionately to everyone else" (p. 317–318). It is crucial that oppressed peoples gain as much access to scientific knowledge as possible and learn to employ that knowledge to address their own needs and problems.

For example, the problem of toxic waste sites results from a culture of consumption, which ultimately I do not believe we will address without confronting that culture and its economic base. However, at the same time, communities of color and poor communities, including Indian reservations, are disproportionately targets of pollution and toxic waste disposal. Communities with the greatest political resources are able to keep toxic wastes out of their own backyards; communities with the least political clout end up receiving everyone else's toxic wastes, and suffering health consequences (*Minority Trendsletter*, 1991). Those with the greatest vested interest in addressing toxic waste sites—people of color and people from poor communities—are, however, least likely to receive an education that will prepare them to do so. They are not as likely as children from privileged backgrounds to have access to high-quality science instruction (Oakes, 1990), attend college to pursue science training, nor be taught political skills that enable effective participation in public decision-making processes. Thus, while scientific knowledge can enable the development of creative solutions to social problems, that knowledge, and the subsequent use to which it is put, tends to be controlled mainly by those with the most, rather than the least, political clout.

Multicultural science education should help oppressed communities learn to use science as a tool to address their own concerns. This is a political as well as a technical issue. Hodson (1993) writes:

> If "environment" is a social construct, environmental problems are *social* problems, caused by societal practices and structures and justified by society's current values. It follows that solving environmental problems means addressing and changing the social conditions that give rise to them and the values that sustain them. This realization shifts questions of environmental improvement from the *technical* domain into the *sociopolitical* domain. The solution to environmental problems does not lie in quick "technological fix" but in socio-political action. (p. 705)

At issue here are the questions of both access and what counts as science. Modern western science draws a boundary between abstract scientific findings, defined as pure science and presumed to be culturally neutral, versus sociopolitical contexts of the work of scientists, presumed to be not science but rather politics or sociology. While such a boundary may make sense from the point of view of western-trained scientists, it does not make sense to postcolonial theorists who criticize the West for refusing in this way to take responsibility for undesirable consequences of our actions (Harding, 1994).

No single piece of curriculum or teaching strategy will fully address these issues. There is no panacea, and virtually any curriculum resource I might suggest can be critiqued on some ground. However, to the degree that an educator has a vision toward which he/she is working, he/she will use available resources in the service of that vision. Below I will comment on three quite different available resources that teachers might use in the construction of a multicultural science curriculum that attempts to address the social justice issues.

Inspiring and Supporting Achievement in Science

Gifted Hands: The Ben Carson Story (Carson, 1990) is an inspiring autobiography that can be read by middle school or older students. Ben Carson grew up mainly in the inner city of Detroit. He is African American, from an economically poor single-parent family. His mother had attained only a third grade education, although she worked hard and constantly encouraged her boys to achieve: "You weren't born to be a failure, Bennie. You can do it!" (p. 18). As a child, in spite of his mother urging him to do his best, Carson's grades were poor, and he did not take school seriously. Performing at the bottom of a predominantly white class in fifth grade, Carson assumed he was "just dumb" (p. 29) and had little future to look forward to. By the age of 14, he was carrying a knife, which he almost used to kill a friend. That experience was one of the turning points of his life. From that point on, he gradually embarked on a path of achievement. By the time he was 33, Carson had become Director of Pediatric Neurosurgery at Johns Hopkins Hospital and was developing new surgical strategies to save lives. He had transformed his life from what it was at age 14, and rather than using a knife to kill, was very skillfully using it to save people.

Ben Carson provides a model and a source of knowledge for many educationally disenfranchised youth. Although they are 16% of the students in public schools, African American students are only 8% of those in programs for the gifted, but 35% of those labeled "educable mentally retarded," 27% of the "trainable mentally retarded," and 27% of the "severely emotionally disturbed" (Harry, 1992, p. 22). Most African American children enter school wanting to learn, but many teachers interpret their behavior as indicating learning problems. By secondary school a large proportion of them have been placed in special education or tracked into vocational rather than college preparatory programs (Oakes, 1985). Bright African American students in particular, when their capabilities are not recognized and developed in the schools, become bored and often channel their energies and talents into street life, which appears to offer more opportunities and rewards than school (Kunjufu, n.d., p. 51–52).

Partly because schools identify relatively few African American students as high achievers, bright students perceive themselves as having to choose between being Black versus being academically successful (Fordham, 1988). By adulthood, in 1990, 609,000 African American men were in the penal system, while only 436,000 were in college (Mauer, 1990). Yet, as Mary Atwater (1993) speculated, "If students can learn the intricate lyrics of rap songs, then they should surely be able to learn science. The trick is to make science relevant to the students' world" (p. 36).

Dr. Carson has become a role model for young African Americans, encouraging them to envision themselves in the sciences rather than on the streets or attempting to become sports or music stars.

> I realize that particularly for Black people in this country, I represent something that many of them have never seen in their lifetimes—someone in a technical and scientific area who has risen to the top. I'm recognized for my academic and medical achievements instead of for being a sports star or an entertainer. (Carson, p. 231)

As such, a book like this can be very usefully employed in a multicultural science curriculum. By itself, however, it is not a panacea. Many educators explain the failure of students from oppressed groups quite simplistically and therefore use role models such as Carson simplistically.

Teachers who assume that the social system is open to anyone who tries tend to regard role models largely as images children can aspire to and as proof that anyone can become anything. I sometimes hear teachers say that children from low-income backgrounds lack role models and thus lack ideas as to what kinds of futures they can have. If we show them attainments of people like themselves, we can inspire students to try to achieve. There is both truth and fiction in this assumption. While many children from low-income backgrounds have no idea what a pediatric neurosurgeon is and thus do not entertain the idea of becoming one, they are aware of doctors, and while young, some do consider becoming a doctor. One is more likely to aspire to a role in which one has seen people like oneself, but that is not necessarily a prerequisite. For example, in our interviews with junior high students, as noted in chapter 8, Carl Grant and I were struck by the high aspirations of many of the students, particularly the girls. One of the boys we followed in junior high did aspire to become a physician. And yet, by the time they were high school seniors, most had abandoned their dreams, mainly because they were not actively encouraged and prepared, and they did not know how to address barriers they experienced or perceived (such as lack of money for college). The aspiring physician left college during his freshman year.

Role models and books such as *Gifted Hands* can show young people not only what they can become, but also how real people have actually dealt with barriers they encountered. This kind of information is at least as important as particulars about specific roles. I would use a book such as this by asking students to compare Carson's life at a particular age with their own, having them compare his difficulties with theirs, having them identify barriers and difficulties he encountered as he went to college and then medical school, and having them identify strategies he used to address barriers. Used in this way, such a resource becomes instructive, in addition to being inspirational. Of course, a book does not substitute for personal support and encouragement. In Dr. Carson's case, the personal support that mattered most to him came from his mother. As teachers, we can't control what parents do, but we can control the amount of personal support and encouragement we give. Too often we expect far too little and write kids off too easily.

Another issue the book raises involves what constitutes achievement and success. Americans tend to define success in terms of individual acquisition: owning a nice home and a good car, taking good vacations, building up a strong bank account, and so forth. We tend not to define success in terms of giving back to our own (or to other) communities. I thought about this issue recently when one of my white students was completing a field experience at the Urban League. The student brought some computer skills and was put to work straightening out a problem the staff was having with a computer program. The problem he was able to fix was only one of many technology-related problems for which the Urban League staff is constantly seeking help. As my student was providing computer expertise, I felt frustration that while inner-city Kenosha has many children in school, few leave the schools strongly computer-literate, and few people from outside the inner-city think to move there to work. As a result, Kenosha's inner-city, like most inner-cities, lacks computer experts as well as physicians, dentists, engineers, and so forth. The problem is not that most of the few inner-city students who develop science skills leave the inner-city—they should be free to go where they wish. The problem is that so few excel in science in the first place and that those of us from advantaged backgrounds so often prefer to work in economically advantaged areas.

In *Gifted Hands*, Carson talks about "giving back" to the community. He and his wife are establishing a national scholarship for young people with academic talent but no money. He has become actively involved in working with young people to help them set goals and achieve. As such, he illustrates a life in which success is defined not only as individual achievement, but also as collective betterment. This is a model from which *all* of us could learn. While the book does not directly address needs in one's own local community, it provides a jump-off point for doing so. Students could consider what a highly trained person like Dr. Carson might have to offer his or her own community. What does Carson gain for himself and his family by becoming a surgeon? Why does he continue to give back to the community? What kinds of trained professionals does our own community need? In what ways can we link our own personal achievement with community service?

Some science teachers will object that books such as these do not count as science. This objection brings me back to an issue mentioned earlier in this chapter: the tendency of western scientists, and particularly those from advantaged backgrounds, to separate "pure" science from its context.

> Is it any wonder that many of our minority students become so frustrated that they drop out of a world that they have little understanding of and use for—a world that makes it obvious that what counts as knowledge is not what the student knows, but what is presented in a textbook, or what the teacher considers correct science, or what is represented in a national science education framework. (Gallard, 1993, p. 180)

From a multicultural perspective, science is a human endeavor, and addressing human dimensions of science both enriches it as well as helps young people from diverse backgrounds see connections between science and their own lives.

Indigenous Science

Keepers of the Earth (Caduto & Bruchac, 1988) and *Keepers of the Animals* (Caduto & Bruchac, 1991) introduce young people to the natural world from American Indian points of view. Michael Caduto is an ecologist and environmental activist, and Joseph Bruchac is an Abenaki poet, storyteller, and novelist. Together, they framed the scientific study of the earth and its animals within a Native worldview in which humans are an interconnected part of the natural world; humans do not stand above it, but rather relate to it as brother or sister.

> The science of ecology, the study of the interactions between living things and their environments, circles back to the ancient wisdom found in the rich oral traditions of American Indian stories. Time and again the stories have said that all of the living and nonliving parts of the Earth are one and that people are a part of that wholeness. Today, ecological science agrees. (*Keepers of the Earth*, p. 5)

Earlier I mentioned the connection between denigrating non-European cultural traditions and subjugating cultural "Others." There is also a connection between such denigration and broader human and global self-destruction. Consumptive western lifestyles are destroying the natural environment; indeed, the range and scope of that destruction has grown considerably in my lifetime. For example, based on an analysis of smog in the Los Angeles area, Mann (1991) wrote,

> Smog and air toxins are primarily a result of 1) our dependence on an automobile centered, fossil-fuel burning transportation system dominated by the auto, oil, and rubber-tire industries; 2) factories using and emitting dangerous chemicals; and 3) consumer goods produced by the petrochemical industry that pollute our environment. After decades of failed efforts to regulate these industries more fundamental change is needed. (p. 35)

Scientists debate possible long-range effects of environmental destruction, as evidence of short-run effects accumulates. As Euro-Americans scramble for solutions, so far we seem to learn very little from Native American wisdom about how humans should relate to the natural world. For example, the publication *Environment 92/93* (J. L. Allen, 1992) contained thirty-five articles discussing issues and potential solutions to environmental destruction, not one of which referred to Indian knowledge. There are some fruitful alliances between Euro-American environmentalists and indigenous people, but they are few (Gedicks, 1993).

Western science yields a great deal of knowledge, but it is bounded within a western worldview. What Indian people can teach non-Indians is not just techniques for wildlife management or cleaning water, but a worldview and way of living that does not lead humankind down the path of global destruction.

Today the species of Man is facing a question of the very survival of the species. The way of life known as Western Civilization is on a death path on which their own culture has no viable answers. When faced with the reality of their own destructiveness, they can only go forward into areas of more efficient destruction. (Hau de no sau nee, 1977, p. 9)

The worldview indigenous people can teach is one that connects humans with the earth and connects actions with their long-range consequences.

Keepers of the Earth and *Keepers of the Animals* open the door to indigenous science and raise the possibility of viewing human knowledge and the natural world differently. Pamela Colorado, who in 1989 founded the Indigenous Science Network, explained that in western thinking, only the West could have science. The rest of the world's cultures could have culture or philosophy, but not science. But knowledge systems of indigenous people constitute science, if we consider science to be the way people approach knowing. The work of the Indigenous Science Network is to rediscover the ancient wisdom of tribal peoples, particularly wisdom that enabled people to construct sustainable ways of life for thousands of years.

These two books situate scientific investigations within stories that connect humans with the natural world. Indian stories teach people how to view and relate to the natural world; they encode accumulated wisdom of centuries and pass on that wisdom in an engaging and often playful manner. As such, many westerners view the stories as meaningless fiction, since westerners usually encode knowledge in didactic prose and formulas. By viewing Indian stories as "cute" entertainment, we miss the messages they teach. In the foreword to *Keepers of the Earth*, Scott Momaday wrote:

For nearly twenty years I have taught the subject of Native American oral tradition, and I have been a student of that subject for a longer time than that. . . . The stories in the present collection center upon one of the most important of all considerations of human experience: the relationship between man and nature. In the Native American world this relationship is so crucial as to be definitive of the way in which man formulates his own best idea of himself. In the presence of these stories we have an affirmation of the human spirit. (p. xvii)

The books synthesize Indian stories about the natural world with scientific investigations for young people. The entire project of the two books is to teach respect for the earth and its living inhabitants. For example, one unit in a section on water begins with two stories: "How Thunder and Earthquake Made Ocean" (Yurok, California), and "Sedna, the Woman Under the Sea" (Inuit, Arctic). The stories are followed by a discussion of water and marine animals that connects the stories with information about ocean water and marine life. Investigative activities follow, which include learning about marine animals, studying wave action, investigating how salt alters freezing temperature of water, and studying how the Inuit use marine animals for survival.

The book concludes with Bruchac's reflection on his own process of learning and on the power of stories that taught him a way of respecting the natural world. He points out through personal examples that children respond to stories, and to "doing things" rather than being lectured to (p. 194).

> The teachings that have been given to generations of Native American children in stories are ones that need to be understood by all of us. . . . Today, when the secrets of Gluscabi's magical bag, which can catch and destroy all of the animals of the world, are known all too well, it is important for such stories to be told. For ourselves and for our children's children. (p. 196)

Science has never been solely the province of Europeans and Euro-Americans; science has always borrowed cross-culturally. Historically Europeans have failed to acknowledge non-European roots of western science, but many of those roots are being documented (Harding, 1994). *Keepers of the Animals* and *Keepers of the Earth* provide teachers with one avenue for exploring cross-cultural sharing of science and for asking about scientific knowledge that was constructed outside the western tradition. But multicultural education is not trivia about diverse groups. One cannot create a curriculum that is multicultural in spirit by adding in bits and pieces from books such as these. Rather, multicultural teaching means taking seriously the knowledge and worldview of others, which requires immersing ourselves in other worldviews. These books provide a way to begin to do that. By themselves, they do not reconstruct the hierarchical worldview embedded in western notions of science and the natural world; they provide a doorway to an alternative worldview, and one which I believe is vital for all of us to take seriously. Teachers who wish to step further through that doorway can find more help and resources such as the journal *Winds of Change*, published by the American Indian Science and Engineering Society.

This discussion raises a crucial challenge. As noted in chapter 5, it is very difficult for white Americans to learn to engage with Indian (or anyone else's) knowledge without colonizing it. Over the past two decades or so, in our search for meaning, whites have made it fashionable to adopt bits of Indian spiritual teachings, in the process distorting and commercializing them in a manner very similar to what many of us learned to do as children when we played with "Indian" headdresses and tomahawks. This practice is today's extension of our forebearers' practice of taking land, a practice Euro-Americans have not stopped, by the way. (Conflicts between Indian nations and mining companies, or between Indian nations and developers who own or are attempting to buy portions of reservation land are two examples of contemporary contested terrain.)

Ward Churchill (1994) tells us that the first thing Europeans and Euro-Americans must do is to learn to "decolonize" ourselves: "You've become self-colonizing, conditioned to be so self-identified with your own oppression that you've lost your ability to see it for what it is, much less to resist it in any coherent way" (p. 234). He challenges Euro-Americans to look at our own history for what it is and at our own indigenous identities that were taken from us in the construction of a predatory "Europe." As we have internalized identities as "Europeans," and particularly as those of us who are members of the "Euro-diaspora" have been so dislocated from our own histories that we define ourselves "'new people' forging entirely new cultures" (p. 244), we have lost an ability to meet our own human needs in a way that draws on well-grounded ancient wisdom about how to live. Colorado agrees:

> Traditional knowledge and mind cannot possibly flourish in diverse community until Westerners themselves discover their own values and roots. . . . If our species is to survive, Euro-Americans must be supported in their effort to regain the Earth-based knowledge of their ancestors. Native Americans will help. (cited by Simonelli, 1994a, p. 4)

Churchill and Colorado challenge Euro-Americans to construct an identity that departs from the "white" identity rooted in white supremacy discussed earlier in chapter 2.

Many people regard the arguments above as an attack on western culture. The arguments do attack the notion that western people have the best answers for every significant problem, as well as the thread of self-superiority and colonialism woven into European culture (Goldberg, 1993). Advocates of multicultural education do not, however, wish to throw out the best of European cultures and replace them with something else (Banks, 1991/1992). Gates (1992) talks about nurturing a conversation among different voices and cultural traditions, including Euro-Americans. Like all traditions, western science has its "dark side," or blind spots (Simonelli, 1994b). Western science helps us ask and answer some kinds of questions well, but does not help us as much with other kinds of questions such as those having to do with interconnectedness of natural phenomena or moral and spiritual matters. As Colorado sees it, different cultural traditions' systems of knowledge yield essential parts of the whole of human knowledge. Such a union will help to both broaden what counts as science and to generate postcolonial cultural identities for whites as well as people of color.

How would I use *Keepers of the Earth* and *Keepers of the Animals*? The books themselves provide many specific ideas that can be incorporated into a science curriculum fairly easily. The more difficult and important issue is to refrain from viewing them as a way of teaching "about the Indians" and, instead, to allow Indian people (and anti-colonialist whites) to teach me as teacher/student how to live in an ecologically and humanly healthy manner.

Taking Social Action

Exploding the Hunger Myths (Williams, 1987) is written for secondary teachers to use for guiding students in an exploration of why people are hungry both domestically and internationally, of how hunger is connected to our own culture of consumption, and of what concerned citizens can do to help eliminate hunger. The author, Sonja Williams, was a high school and college biology teacher, and this guide grew from her experience teaching students to investigate hunger for themselves, initially in the context of a unit on nutrition. It is written not only for science teachers, however; the lessons are interdisciplinary, and Williams encourages teachers to select those lessons most applicable to their own teaching and students. The guide contains a wealth of resources: self-contained activities, background information and handouts a teacher can use, ideas for student investigations, and lists of recommended supplementary resources.

It is organized around myths about why hunger exists. After the first lesson in which students investigate hunger at an awareness level, the next five lessons are made up of activities enabling students to investigate myths about hunger: 1) food is scarce, 2) there are too many people, 3) technology will solve the problem, 4) the rich world has little connection with the poor world, and 5) foreign aid will take care of the problem. Lessons 7 and 8 engage students in the process of making change, particularly in their own local community.

> This curriculum emphasizes activism and hope—not guilt, apathy, or despair. It counters hopelessness by showing that even small changes can have an impact. It introduces students to the idea that human activities, not acts of nature, are both the root cause and the potential solution to hunger. It is my hope that these teaching materials will be used to foster a new commitment among students to participate in the changes needed to end the injustice of hunger. (Williams, 1987, p. ix)

As I have stressed throughout this book, working for social justice—redistribution of the world's resources—is at the heart of what multicultural education should be about. Within the U.S. currently, the wealthiest 1% of the population earn more than the poorest 40%, and the distribution of wealth is becoming progressively less rather than more equal (Hacker, 1992). Globally, the wealthiest one-fifth of the population take in 83% of the world's income, while the poorest one-fifth earn only 1.4%. The gap in this ratio, also, has been widening steadily (Kellogg, 1994). This poverty and hunger can be tied directly to the neo-imperialism of the U.S. and Europe today.

> From 1970 to 1980, the flow of investment capital from the United States to the Third World amounted to about $8 billion. But the return flow from the Third World to the United States in the form of dividends, interest, branch profits, management fees, and royalties was $63.7 billion. Together, all the multinational corporations and banks in the world take as much as $200 billion every year from the Third World nations. (Parenti, 1994, p. 168)

And neo-imperialism has worked hand-in-hand with expansion of western science (Harding, 1994).

These trends are made concrete in activities such as "The Case of the Disappearing Grain." In this activity, students compare the yield of one-quarter acre of farmland if used to cultivate meat versus grain or soybeans; and they examine the amount of grain needed to produce one pound of beef, pork, or poultry. Students examine their own daily diets, critiquing them as well as broader U.S. patterns of consumption. Students are then helped to develop healthy diets that can be produced on far fewer acres of farmland, and to see their own daily lives as connected to global resource use. (Examples of similar units can also be found in Reiss, 1993.)

It is common for U.S. citizens to view Third World problems as stemming from problems inherent in Third World cultures and solutions to these problems as coming from the expertise of the West. Multicultural education questions this view, directing attention to strengths and resources of Third World cultures and to actions the West has taken that create or exacerbate problems for Third World nations, but that can be changed. As Hodson (1993) put it,

> Discussions of Third World problems of malnutrition, overpopulation, and poor health care must be set within the appropriate religious, cultural, economic, and political context (including western exploitation or indifference) if the often woefully inadequate attempts at solution are not to reinforce prejudiced views about the inferiority of other ethnic groups. (p. 698)

Harding (1994) argues that democratic and sustainable models of science will require people of European descent to learn from and collaborate with Third World people in order to forge solutions to human problems worldwide. To do this, people of European descent will need to "relocate the projects of sciences and science studies that originate in the West on the more accurate historical map created by the new postcolonial studies, instead of on the familiar one charted by Eurocentric accounts of mainly European and U.S. history" (p. 327). *Exploding the Hunger Myths* frames world hunger as a problem that can be solved, but one that requires the West to reform our own consumptive lifestyle, which is within our power to do.

Conclusion

This chapter has not addressed what I view as the heart of the curriculum: the students. Rather, it has addressed knowledge frameworks and curricular materials with which students might engage. But teaching for social justice means not just taking such knowledge frameworks and curricular materials seriously, but, just as importantly, taking seriously the ideas, thought processes, beliefs, and interests of one's own students. As Alejandro Gallard (1993) argued,

> In my view, if the science teacher focuses on learners and learning with the attitude that what they know is not valid and thus must be replaced with appropriate knowledge, then science teaching is meaningless. (p. 171)

It is students of color, students from low-income homes, language minority students, and females who have learned not to assert themselves whose knowledge and voice is most often disregarded in classrooms. Empowering education is constructivist in nature, as I have illustrated in chapter 6.

Constructing a multicultural curriculum in any area is a long-term process that evolves as one digs deeper and deeper into issues of social justice and cultural diversity, and as one pays closer and closer attention to the thinking of children. There are available materials, such as those discussed in this chapter, that provide excellent points of entree in this process of learning, thinking, and re-thinking.

CHAPTER 10

Power and Privilege in White Middle-Class Feminist Discussions of Gender and Education

In education as well as other disciplines, issues are often framed and addressed in ways that set oppressed groups in opposition to each other. When white, heterosexual, economically privileged women think of gender, race, and class as separate issues and choose to challenge only sexism, the effect is to buttress our own relatively privileged position at the expense of women of color or of lower-class backgrounds. For example, schools and universities are often encouraged to hire more "women and minorities," a phrase one encounters in everyday parlance and sometimes in written policies. This phrase lumps the majority of the population into what some people regard as a special interest group that then can be treated as an add-on. When whites use the phrase, we implicitly strip white women of our race and women of color of sex. Similarly, many schools have created programs to encourage more "girls and minorities" to pursue mathematics, science, and computer science. Who predominates in such programs? White daughters of parents of the professional class? African-American, Latino, or Asian boys of middle or professional class parents? What about lower-class students (half of whom are also girls and a disproportionate number of whom are of color)? The thinking behind phrases like "women and minorities" or "girls and minorities" enables educators to believe we have diversified a population if we acquire a few members of that "category"—even when those acquired are mainly white females. At my previous university, the term "diversity" increasingly had replaced the phrase "women and minorities," and many white faculty congratulated themselves on having added "diversity" to the faculty by hiring white women.

When white economically-privileged women frame gender issues around our own experiences, not only do we privilege ourselves, but we also render women invisible who are not white and economically privileged (Zinn, Cannon, Higginbotham, & Dill, 1986). An issue that is often discussed, for example, is the wage gap between men and women. Between 1955 and 1983, full-time working women earned an average of 59 to 64 cents for every dollar full-time working men earned. After 1983, the gap began to close steadily; by 1988, full-time working women were earning 70 cents for every dollar men earned, as growing numbers of women entered jobs traditionally dominated by men (U.S. Bureau of the Census, 1990, p. 409). But it is important to look beyond such a statistic and ask: Were all women sharing equally in progress? The answer is no. At the same time that significant numbers of college-educated women entered fields such as law and medicine, women from low-income backgrounds found it increasingly difficult to finance a college education, the proportion of students of color entering universities fell, and low-income women increasingly entered low-paying service jobs that have traditionally employed large numbers of women. In the nation as a whole, while the gender gap in earnings narrowed, the middle class shrank, the lower class expanded, the number of female-headed households living below the poverty level grew, and the status of Americans of color—both men and women—deteriorated. The wage gap had partially reflected restricted career opportunities for middle-class women; our successful struggles for wider opportunities, however, did not advance the interests or economic status of poor women. When we claim to be closing a gender gap, the gap may be closing mainly for those of us who already are economically privileged.

Much feminist activity purporting to benefit women as a whole often ultimately benefits mainly white middle-class women when it does not address other forms of oppression as well. Gender issues can rarely be separated from race and class issues, and by either ignoring this or arguing that they can and should be dealt with separately, white middle-class women protect our own racial and class privilege. Ironically, the main beneficiaries are white economically privileged men, since a potentially powerful coalition does not form to challenge their control.

Gender, Race, and Class as Separate Topics in Education Research

Most literature about gender in education treats gender, social class, and race as additive rather than integrative forms of oppression, leaving one to choose which forms of oppression to add to one's analysis. Social class oppression, for example, may be added onto gender oppression as a separate layer (McCarthy & Apple, 1989, pp. 24–25). In 1986, Carl Grant and I reviewed seventy-one articles in the education literature published between 1973 and 1983 that addressed race, social class, and/or gender (Grant & Sleeter, 1986b). Sixty-three of the articles addressed primarily one form of oppression; only three addressed gender and race, one addressed gender and social class, one addressed social class and race, and three addressed race, social class, and gender. Further, only one of the studies substantively integrated different forms of oppression, distinguishing among African American, white, and Hispanic males and females of different social class backgrounds (Rumberger, 1983). The rest treated these as separate (e.g., African Americans and women) and additive.

It appears to be mainly white, economically privileged women who consistently interrogate gender either without acknowledging race or social class relations at all or by adding them in a supplementary fashion. Usually women of color must assume the task of confronting race in discussions of gender, and women from working-class backgrounds most often confront class issues. Typically white middle-class women assume that these are someone else's issues and that we have addressed them when we allow women of color and women of working-class origins to join in our work and our conversations. The position that white women often argue is that gender is the major social division they experience as problematic; that women share common experiences resulting from their oppression just as men share common privileges; and that, while race and class oppression are also significant, discussions of gender need to stay focused on gender because bringing in other factors would render discussions too unwieldy and dilute attention to gender.

This problem was illustrated well by Maher and Tetreault (1993), in a case study comparing two feminist college classrooms, one predominantly white and taught by a white professor and the other predominantly African American and taught by an African American professor. In the white classroom, race was rarely named even when students alluded to it, and even when *The Color Purple* was being discussed. Content for discussion came mainly from the students' own experiences that included little or no attention to race. In the African American classroom, racism was a major topic of discussion and was not viewed as separate from gender. When discussing *The Women of Brewster Place*, students engaged in a lively discussion of how a televised version of the novel erased racism and thereby distorted the women's lives.

I see the issue of when and whether to address race and class as a power struggle to define issues for discussion and agendas for action, more than as an academic issue about accuracy. Our analysis of gender is never uninformed by our racial and social class location. Everytime white, economically privileged women presume to speak for all women without engaging a plurality of women in conversation, we are asserting power granted to us by virtue of our racial and social class privilege, tacitly accepting racial and social class relationships as they now exist and, consequently, presenting a distorted picture of whatever we are speaking about. Similarly, when white professional men address equity issues mainly by supporting some demands of white professional women, race and class privileges are being protected.

Power struggles among oppressed groups are at least as old as the thirteen colonies. For example, Angela Davis (1981) described conflicts between African Americans and white women over the vote, showing how white women distanced themselves from black struggles out of fear that African American men might triumph first. In the process, white women excluded African American women from their definition of "women." Today's power struggles over whose voices define women's issues have very long roots; the faces and some of the terms are new, but the issues are not.

A Typology of Integration

Feminist discourse has developed various analyses of how patriarchy marginalizes women. For example, Peggy McIntosh (1987) and Mary Kay Tetreault (1989) posited stages in the integration of content about women into the curriculum, viewing them as a progression from exclusion of women to full inclusion. As Tetreault described them, the stages include: male-defined curriculum, "contribution curriculum," bifocal curriculum, women's curriculum, and gender-balanced curriculum. I will modify this typology to discuss levels of integrating race and class into feminist concerns. This typology is useful for illustrating how discussions of gender often exclude women who are not white and/or economically privileged and how issues may be viewed much more inclusively. I do not view the levels as stages through which one must proceed, but rather as an analytic tool that roughly ranks the degree to which women of diverse racial and social class backgrounds inform any given body of discourse on gender.

Before proceeding, I will relate the political perspectives outlined in chapter 3 to gender (Jaggar, 1983; see also Kuumba, 1994). Liberal feminists uphold individual competition in a hierarchical society, arguing that one's sex should be irrelevant to one's chances for mobility, choice, and personal fulfillment. Radical feminists argue that gender is the most fundamental social category; rather than seeking to make gender irrelevant, radical feminists advocate empowerment of women and valuing that which is feminine. Both liberal and radical feminism have been advanced mainly by white women; that is, neither perspective has given significant attention to race or social class. Radical feminism pays more attention to sexual orientation than do other feminist perspectives. Socialist feminists regard both gender and social class as fundamental categories for social organization, analyzing how women's status is a function of patriarchy and capitalism. Some also view race as equally fundamental; socialist feminists are more racially diverse than the two preceding perspectives. However, none of them necessarily interrogates racism or colonialism as they have differentially positioned women historically. Women who view race as equally important to gender do not, then, fit well within systems that classify white women's thinking (Collins, 1991; Kuumba, 1994).

The main argument of this chapter is that white middle- and upper class women actively support racism and capitalism in our collective refusal to interrogate our own racial and class privileges with the same degree of energy we use to interrogate sexism. As such, the discussion that follows speaks primarily to the blinders that white, economically privileged women wear. Of course, we are not the only women who wear blinders, and one might apply the framework I am using to critiquing other women's thinking. However, to do so here would divert me from the main argument of the chapter.

Level 1. Issues as Defined Only by
White Economically Privileged Women

Writing about the male-defined curriculum, Mary Kay Tetreault (1989) explained that it rests "on the assumption that the male experience is universal, that it is representative of humanity, and that it constitutes a basis for generalizing about all human beings" (p. 125).

While liberal and radical feminists have strongly challenged the assumption that the male experience is universal, many still assume a universal women's experience that revolves around "the minority of women in the world who are white, European, or North American, and middle- or upper-middle class" (Carby, 1990, p. 84). As Elizabeth Spelman (1988) put it, "A measure of the depth of white middle-class privilege is that apparent straightforward and logical points and axioms at the heart of much feminist theory guarantee the direction of its attention to the concerns of white middle-class women" (p. 4).

Gender issues are addressed at Level 1 when most of the women represented in the curriculum are white and middle class, or the only girls to participate in or benefit from a program for girls are white and economically privileged, racism and classism are not discussed at the same time sexism is being discussed, the ideas and frames of reference undergirding a course come almost exclusively from white middle class experiences. Activity at this stage blatantly reproduces race and class privilege: "white women appear 'raceless'. . . [and] the distinct historical experiences of women of color, to the degree they are acknowledged, are credited solely to race" (DuBois & Ruiz, 1990, p. xi).

For example, when educators analyze the history of women in education and the labor force they often discuss women as having "moved increasingly from the family sphere into the wider spheres of economic life" (Greene, 1985, p. 33), which is a theme based on the experiences of white women. In classrooms, when "working women" are discussed in an effort to help girls consider careers, the same assumption is often made—that paid labor outside the home is relatively new to women. However, this assumption holds true mainly for white, economically privileged women. It certainly is not true, for example, of African American women, who have always been highly involved in economic life, although not necessarily paid for their labor, or of white working-class women who also have an active history of wage labor (Dugger, 1991; hooks, 1981; Ladner, 1971).

Analyses of male benefits from sexism in the labor force suffer a similar distortion when gender is the only axis of oppression used. A discussion of the implications of men's and women's economic status for sex equity, for example, noted:

> Historically, women have experienced higher unemployment rates than men, and there is little evidence to indicate that this trend will change significantly in the near future. In 1976, for example, the

unemployment rate for adult women was systematically higher than for men within racial and ethnic categories: 5.9 percent (white men) compared to 8.7 percent (white women); 16.3 percent (Puerto Rican men) compared to 22.3 percent (Puerto Rican women); and 15.9 percent (black men) to 18.9 percent (black women). (Harvey & Noble, 1985, p. 20)

The implication of the entire discussion was that men as a group accrue more benefits than women as a group. But clearly white men were the main ones experiencing the benefits, and white women were benefiting far more than Puerto Ricans or blacks of either sex.

All oppressed groups must spend time and energy focusing primarily on themselves in order to examine their experiences and develop a sense of solidarity. White economically privileged women have needed to do this as much as any other group. The problem arises when one group tries to generalize their experience to other groups, refusing to acknowledge the perspective of others and refusing to acknowledge one's own participation in the oppression of others. It is this arrogance of presuming the white middle class experience to represent *the* women's experience that has bred distrust and blocked coalition building.

Many white women have worked hard, over the past decade or so, to get beyond the myopia women of color repeatedly have pointed out. It may be, however, that each generation has to grapple with racism and classism on its own—one does not simply inherit the advances of older generations nor even those of one's own generation-mates. bell hooks (1993) expressed her dismay with Susan Faludi's (1991) *Backlash: The Undeclared War Against Women*, which "erases any focus on the way in which race is a factor determining degrees of backlash . . . and once again construct[s] women as a monolithic group whose common experiences are more important than our differences" (p. 2). Or again, in the Clarence Thomas hearings, hooks pointed out how "Masses of white women rallied to Anita Hill's defense, all the while insisting that her race was not important and that the 'real' issue was gender"—thus ignoring how racism framed the handling of the entire matter (p. 3). Level 2 presents a common attempt to "fix" the silence of Level 1 on race and social class.

Level 2. Contributions or Exceptions to "the Rule"

Much liberal feminist discourse and many activities attempt to include women who are not white and middle class by inserting them into activities, theoretical constructs, and recommendations that originated in the experiences of white economically privileged women. Contributions to "the rule" add a few women of color; exceptions point out occasional differences between white women and women of color or lower-class women, often in a separate section near the end of the work or course. The main assumption is that women share experiences and perspectives that are largely similar (and can be represented by white middle class women), but that those of women of color or women from lower-class backgrounds differ in some respects. An activity, a piece of curriculum, a discussion, or a group is functioning at this level if most but not all of the women involved or referred to are white and economically privileged. Most textbooks, for example, employ a "contributions" approach to both race and gender. Cosmetically, such work is multicultural; substantively, it is not.

An example of a book that was structured at this level is *A Handbook for Achieving Sex Equity through Education* (Klein, 1985), which is an excellent resource for its concise synthesis of a substantial amount of research on gender in education. However, its chapters were written almost exclusively by white, liberal, feminist scholars, only some of whom acknowledged diversity among women in their chapters, usually by mentioning minority women once or twice. Further, the book relegated women of color to a separate section near the end about "specific populations," assuming that the rest of the chapters apply equally to all women. (The editors did acknowledge having treated women of color and women from low-income backgrounds inadequately, attributing this inadequacy to the state of research on women and girls in general [Murray, 1985, p. 361].)

The author of chapter 19, which focused on sex equity for minority women, explained sex equity priorities of women of color:

> Their priorities tend to be broad-based; they link the goal of sex equity with the goals of liberation, survival, and equity for the total target group and sometimes for oppressed people on a global scale. Moreover, minority women tend to consider various forms of inequity when attempting to achieve equity in a given arena; they do not readily isolate racial, ethnic, cultural, economic, or sex inequity. (Lewis, 1985, p. 366)

But the book implied that white women do not need to consider oppression broadly conceived, since this theme was not woven into other chapters. Even the section on "special populations" did not provide chapters about lower class white women or lesbian women; social class was mentioned occasionally throughout the text, but sexual preference was not. The book also advocated what Jill Conway had described in 1974 as "an educational experience which is critical of many of the assumptions of a male-controlled culture and which takes the female as the norm rather than the deviant exception" (1974, p. 241). However, the handbook took white middle class females as the norm and constructed women of color and women from low-income backgrounds as the "deviant exceptions."

In an effort to address race or class, educators often set up false dichotomies, adding on race or class as separate considerations. As Spelman (1988) pointed out, for example, discussions about whether racism is more important than sexism are nonsense and stem "from the erasure of black women" (p. 120). Consider the educator who wishes to reduce effects of sex role socialization in the home and is confronted with a child of another cultural group in which there appear to be definite sex roles. Does one defer to culture and ignore gender? There are two problems with this question. First, women belonging to the culture in question are often not consulted. Second, the question is framed in a way that ignores the group's location within American social structures of race and class. Discussions of sex role learning focus on processes within the family, such as modeling and differential treatment, and imply that the family is one of the most important sites for creating and reproducing sexism. Many educators point to Mexican-American families as prime examples of patriarchy, viewing machismo as Mexican-style patriarchy. The Anglicized version of this term ("macho") emphasizes male dominance and disrespect for women. Similarly, white male scholars have portrayed African-American families as matriarchal, blaming them for a host of problems that African-Americans experience. Focusing on gender "problems" presumed to arise from within the families of non-white groups neatly removes the dominant society from scrutiny.

Scholars who have examined relationships among race, class, and gender, however, view the construction of sex roles quite differently. In addition to viewing sexism as a cultural phenomenon that may be transmitted through institutions such as the family, socialist feminists situate families within a division of labor that relegates women of different racial and class backgrounds to different places in a stratified system of "women's work." Capitalism and caste work together with patriarchy to create or amplify sex roles, with the main beneficiaries being white, wealthy men (Collins, 1991; Garcia, 1991; Hewitt, 1990; Zinn, 1982). Chicanos have been employed mainly as "cheap labor," restricted to a low social and economic status. Domination of women has become for many men of color a way of gaining status within a fairly closed opportunity structure. As Alfredo Mirande and Evangelina Enriquez (1979) argued, "machismo . . . is a mechanism for shifting the focus away from Anglo oppression to alleged pathologies within Chicano culture" (p. 242). Similarly, Paula Gunn Allen (1986) argued that Native-American communities took on the patriarchal structure of Europeans in the process of being colonized and dispossessed of land. Discussions that consider only gender or that separate sexism from racism and capitalism imply that sexism constitutes a relationship between men and women *within* any social class, racial, or ethnic group, rather than a web of relationships that structure society as a whole.

Work that adds on race and class as "contributions" or "exceptions" is clearly biased, but gives the illusion of inclusiveness. Women working at Level 2 are often puzzled when women of color or socialist feminists show only lukewarm interest in their efforts or criticize those efforts. I speak from experience, having worked at this level myself. For example, years ago I taught a course on Education and Sex Role Socialization. When designing the course, I drew mainly on my own experiences with sexism as well as several texts written by white women. To make the course multicultural, I added one text and some articles by women of color. The first time I taught the course, students enjoyed it, including the few students of color in the course. The second time, students of color as well as lesbian students (whose presence I had not even acknowledged) criticized the course strongly for its white heterosexual framing of gender issues. Their criticism was an important learning experience for me.

To get beyond Level 2, one must first acknowledge that race and class always inform one's analysis of gender. Every knower is situated somewhere in the racial order and class structure; no perspective is nonracial or nonclassed. While one's own experience is a necessary place to start, its limits need to be acknowledged. Hazel Carby (1990) argued, for example, that white women must come to see race as a structure within which whites participate and which shapes white women's identity as much as it shapes African American women's identity. At Level 2, "because the politics of difference work with concepts of diversity rather than structures of dominance, race is a marginalized concept that is wheeled on only when the subjects are Black" (Carby, 1990, p. 85). And even then, as Maher and Tetrault (1993) illustrated, whites still often give priority to gender and tiptoe around race. Examining and questioning one's whiteness and privilege, rather than defining these as irrelevant, is necessary for reconstructing one's understanding of gender and oppression.

Level 3. Bifocal Discourse

Tetreault (1989) defined bifocal discourse as one that dichotomizes women's and men's experiences, examining how they interface and how gender serves as a mode of domination. Applied to the integration of race and class with gender, bifocal discourse contrasts the experiences of white, economically privileged women with those of women who are oppressed on the basis of race and/or class. Rather than placing *any* group of women at the center of consideration, it examines the interfaces among women—how women oppress other women and how different categories of women are oppressed differently. The bifocal approach "shatters the notion of a universal sisterhood. Simply stated, it permits feminist historians to discard celebration for confrontation, and allows them to explore the dynamics through which women have oppressed other women" (DuBois & Ruiz, 1990, p. xii). The main theme of analysis at this level is power and domination. One is asking, "How do white economically privileged women retain privileges over other women and how can this relationship change?" This is very different from asking, as one does at Level 2, how to add in women of color or women who are poor. Consequently, a bifocal approach is very difficult for white economically privileged women to do because it entails confronting our own power and privileges.

Consider a multiracial elementary school in which most of the teachers are white women and most of the parents with whom they have contact are women of color, many of whom are low-income women. At Level 1, a gender concern might be empowerment of the teachers in the school in relationship to the district's bureaucracy, the teachers being mainly women, the administration being mainly men, and the issue being framed in terms of professionalism. What remains unaddressed, however, is the relative position of the teachers and the mothers of students. Quite often teachers as professionals assume a patronizing stance toward mothers of lower status backgrounds, becoming concerned about teaching them how to parent better rather than sharing power with them (Henry, in press). At Level 2, a few parent representatives would be added to a school's management team, giving mothers of color and low-income white mothers a limited voice in the school, but retaining the power of white professionals. At Level 3, the concern is for equal power sharing between white professionals and women who are not white or who are low-income. The power differential is explicitly addressed with the aim of confronting and eliminating it. Clearly Levels 2 and 3 are very different; in fact, white professionals usually perceive Level 3 as threatening.

Bifocal discourse represents an important step forward in integrating race and class with gender because it does not take as normative the white middle-class experience and because it grapples directly with unequal relations of power and privilege among women. I sometimes hear white women speculate that raising consciousness about sexism leads to greater sensitivity for other forms of oppression. I view this as a form of avoidance. For example, in her study of women in the Ku Klux Klan, Kathleen Blee (1991) concluded that "an assumption that women's awareness of their gender interests [which was strong among many Klan women] would lead them to progressive politics on race and social class proved empty" (p. 179). Bifocal discourse that interrogates privileges and power in race and social class relationships among women is necessary.

Bifocal discourse is limited, however, in its bifurcation of the world of women into relatively undifferentiated dominant and subordinate groups.

> The framework itself leads the historian to focus her examination on the relation between a powerful group, almost always white women, and minority women, the varieties of whose experiences are too often obscured. In other words, the historical emphasis is on white power, and women of color have to compete for the role of "other." The historical testimonies of women of color thus tend to be compacted into a single voice. (DuBois & Ruiz, 1990, p. xii)

For this reason, Level 3 is insufficient, even though it presents an important step forward.

Level 4. Discourses About and By Women
Who are Not White and Economically Privileged

Just as much of the scholarship on women starts with the experiences of women rather than men, feminist scholars of color and scholars from lower-class backgrounds start with experiences of women like themselves. Race, sex, and class are not conceptualized as double or triple forms of disadvantage, but rather, as combining to create "distinct social location[s]" (Dugger, 1991, p. 38). Such work does not attempt to enlarge the discourse defined mainly by white economically privileged women as much as it regards that discourse as either peripheral or irrelevant. Patricia Hill Collins (1991) prefaced her analysis of Black feminist thought, for example, by observing:

> I place Black women's ideas and experiences at the center of analysis . . . I have deliberately chosen not to begin with feminist tenets developed from the experiences of white, middle-class, Western women and then insert the ideas and experiences of African American women. (p. xii)

Rich bodies of literature have been produced by women from a variety of racial and social class locations and sexual orientations. Most of it exists outside the field of education, but it is relevant to educators because it reframes questions and practices in education. Literature by and about women of color and/or women of lower-class origins can roughly be classified into three categories: critiques of white liberal and radical feminism (e.g., Carby, 1990; Kuumba, 1994), discussions of the subjective experiences and theoretical positions of one's own group (e.g., Anzaldua, 1987; Asian Women United of California, 1989; Blea, 1988; Chow, 1991; Collins, 1991; hooks, 1990 & 1993; Trinh, 1989), and investigations of a discipline based on the experiences and perspectives of one's own group (e.g., Allen, 1986; Giddings, 1984; Hartsock, 1989; Mirande & Enriquez, 1979).

For example, in an attempt to add Indian women to the curriculum, well-intentioned white feminists (working at Level 2) may simply assume Indian women were subordinate to men in the past, select heroines who they think were significant, focus on assimilation of Indian women into industrial society rather than the preservation and strengthening of Indian communities, or add some Indian women to a white feminist curriculum rather than acknowledging the "red roots of white feminism" (Allen, 1986, p. 209). In contrast, Allen discussed the processes of self-definition that put her own experiences and worldview as a Native American woman at the center, and of reconstructing what she had learned about Indian women from non-Indian sources:

> Whatever I read about Indians I check out with my inner self. Most of what I have read and some things I have said based on that reading is upside down and backward. But my inner self, the self who knows what is true of American Indians because it is one, always warns me when something deceptive is going on. (1986, p. 6–7).

She reconstructed her analysis of Indian women around the themes of Indians as survivors, Indian cultures as woman-centered, white colonization of Indians as stemming from fear of women's power, and tribal cultures as similar around the world.

On many university campuses today, it is fashionable to study women of color. While at first glance this would seem to encourage white women to examine other women's oppression, that examination is often avoided (Maher & Tetreault, 1993). Hazel Carby (1990) noted how easily many white women plunge into literature by and about women of color without coming to grips with their own participation in a racist social structure, defining women of color as "other" and different, not as oppressed. In the process we do not hear the rage of women of color against racial oppression or recognize how deeply white women accept racism and how we socialize our own children to become racists. Several years ago a white student was completing an independent study under my direction, focusing on inclusion of literature by African American women writers in the high school curriculum. After reading several pieces of literature, she commented to me that it expresses much anger and pain and will be better literature once African American women get past their anger and pain, the causes of which she assumed to be historical only. I suggested that she examine what they might be angry about today and what our role as whites continues to be in maintaining their anger.

As white middle-class women, we wish men to stand in our shoes and view patriarchy from our perspective, but we experience great difficulty viewing race, class, and ourselves from the perspectives of women in whose oppression we participate. As Johnnella Butler (1989) put it,

> White women function both as women who share certain similar experiences with women of color and as oppressors of women of color. This is one of the most difficult realities to cope with while maintaining valuable dialogue among women and conducting scholarship. White women who justifiably see themselves as oppressed by white men find it difficult to separate themselves from the effects of shared power with white men. (p. 148)

At Level 4, we shut up and listen, and we do not retreat, but rather work to hear what women in other positions of power are saying about their own identities and experiences and about "the wall" of racism and institutionalized poverty that constricts lives (Maher & Tetreault, 1993).

Level 5. Multicultural Emancipatory Discourse

Tetreault (1989) defined a gender-balanced curriculum as one which recenters knowledge in a discipline in a way that draws on the experiences and scholarship of both men and women equally and in the process transforms our understanding of the social world. Here, I am applying her idea to mean a broadly based, multicultural discourse about education and society that is rooted in the experiences of many groups and that is politically oriented toward equality and emancipation. This level can also be termed "resistance poststructuralism," as discussed in chapter 3. No one group's perspective dominates, and no one group consistently benefits. Power is substantively shared; white professionals do not retain "last say."

Further, a multicultural emancipatory discourse about gender explores how some groups of men are oppressed partly on the basis of gender. Gay men, for example, do not experience the same advantages and privileges as heterosexual men; their oppression is clearly sexual. As Barbara Smith (1990) pointed out, "Recent studies indicate that 30 percent of youth suicides can be attributed to turmoil about sexual orientation and the fear or actual experience of homophobia" (p. 67). One can argue that oppression of either sex based on sexual preference is a consequence of patriarchy, an effort to keep men "men" and women "women."

Young African-American men experience oppression that cannot simply be reduced to race or class, since young women of their race and class fare somewhat better on some indicators: African American women attend college in greater numbers than African American men, are much less likely to be killed or incarcerated, and live longer. Many whites fear the potential power of African American men and, in response, castrate them, either literally or figuratively. Images of violence and rape that whites associate with African American men distinctly revolve around gender and are evoked periodically to play on white racial and sexual fears, such as during the Bush-Dukakis presidential race. Among other things, this sexual oppression helps maintain a wedge between whites and African Americans, which in turn maintains divisions among oppressed groups who might otherwise work together to challenge the social order.

When I have presented this typology to groups, listeners who like Level 5 often ask questions such as, "Which textbooks are at this level?" or "How would you resolve such-and-such a problem in my school at this level?" Such listeners usually wish to bring back to their schools an answer that will solve a problem, a desire with which I can sympathize. However, Level 5 demands some considerations that are difficult and often avoided. First, power is to be shared, and shared with people who usually have been excluded. One person does not hand down "the" answer; answers emerge from collective work. Second, there is no one textbook, curriculum, program, or set of recommendations that can be transferred intact from one setting to another. The curriculum or school program must fit the particular people there and must reflect their concerns and input. One might offer models such as the discussion in chapter 5, but good models cannot simply be imposed. Third, in order to function at Level 5, any professional, and particularly any white professional, must come to grips with her or his own privileged position that results from one's racial, social class, and/or gender status. Without doing so, one will still be functioning in an "add and stir" mode—Level 2—without realizing it.

Building a multicultural emancipatory discourse rests on bridges and coalitions, the building of which requires much work. Albrecht and Brewer's (1990) book, *Bridges of Power: Women's Multicultural Alliances*, speaks directly to the politics of building a multicultural emancipatory discourse. The book emerged from discussions in the 1988 National Women's Studies Association Conference and grapples directly with the work of building alliances among women of different racial and ethnic groups, social class origins, religions, and sexual orientations. It also grapples with the work of furthering alliances with men who are oppressed on the basis of race, class, and sexual orientation. Ironically, at the 1990 National Women's Studies Association Conference, women of color seceded following confrontations with white women over race. Bridges are fragile, indeed. Many women of color actively engage in coalition-building with each other but are reluctant to work with white women because of our track record of pulling back on attempts to address and dismantle racism (Chow, 1992; Garcia, 1991).

Conclusion

The same cross-pressures that hinder the political development of women of color could be a transcending political perspective that adds gender to their other consciousness and thus broadens political activism. (Chow, 1991: 266)

And, one that adds race and class to the consciousness of white economically-privileged women. Ultimately, we should be working toward the emancipation of all oppressed people, but this cannot be done without directly confronting power differences among oppressed groups. For white economically privileged women, participating in multicultural emancipatory discourse will mean learning to renounce our racial and social class privileges and work in coalitions in which we are in the minority. This means facing fears of what we might lose in order to recognize we gain in the process.

CHAPTER 11

Multicultural Education as Social Movement

As argued in chapter 1, multicultural education originated in the context of social movement during the 1960s, the civil rights movement. In the 1990s, however, one commonly finds multicultural education as it is practiced severed from any sort of social movement. This phenomenon struck me forcefully several years ago when I was working with some schools to help them restructure for multicultural education. By restructure, I mean they were not to "add a program" in multicultural education, but to change the schools' processes so that they would better support the concerns, abilities, and perspectives of culturally diverse students.

The change process that my colleagues and I were using involved having a team of teachers investigate and assess structures and processes within their own school, such as placement of students (by race and sex) in remedial and special education, connections between students' interests and the curriculum, relationships between commonly used teaching strategies and students' preferred ways of learning, and the representation of diverse groups in the curriculum. We designed a series of instruments to guide data collection for this self-study. To help teachers interpret their data and plan for change, we gave them a library of literature on multicultural education and had several staff development sessions that focused on issues with which they were grappling. In retrospect, we had packaged multicultural education largely as depoliticized teaching techniques, although at the time did not realize this.

A part of the self-study was to find out more about communities the school served, including community leaders and organizations, issues facing the communities, and community members' feelings about education. The teams in each school seemed to be putting this part of the study off, so my colleagues and I organized an all-day meeting that connected the teachers with various leaders of local communities of color that their schools served. In that meeting, it was apparent that there was little communication between the teachers and communities of color. And in other contexts, as teachers talked about the implications of their findings (such as reasons for racial discrepancies in achievement in their own schools), I saw some large gaps between their interpretations and those of people of color I knew locally.

So, we helped the teachers add community members to their study teams, particularly to help them interpret the data they had collected about their schools and to develop change plans. These efforts helped only minimally, however. The teachers were used to making decisions about the school in-house, and while they did not resist occasional visits by community people, neither did they regard their input as essential to the project. As their reform plans developed, although the plans reflected interests of the teachers, they did not embody a spirit of community renewal and uplift through an education that is multicultural. It was clear to me that multicultural education as conceptualized in these schools had little (if any) connection with community-based movements that aim toward equality and social justice.

This chapter will examine four different metaphors for conceptualizing the form multicultural education often takes: multicultural education as therapy, as teaching techniques, as academic discourse, and as a social movement. I argue that although multicultural education grew out of a social movement, today it usually takes the first three forms. I then suggest the sorts of activities with which we should be engaged if we were to take the social movement metaphor more seriously.

Multicultural Education as Therapy

Multicultural education is viewed as therapy when racism, sexism, heterosexism, or classism are conceptualized as psychological diseases requiring a healing process. Prejudice, stereotypes, hatred, or low self-esteem are its symptoms. Many teachers talk about multicultural issues in ways such as the following, which are interview responses from the same study as reported in chapter 4, in which I asked teachers how multicultural education fit with their teaching goals:

When we were studying Martin Luther King, one of the kids didn't want to study Martin Luther King. They were sick of that holiday and they didn't want Black History Month either. You know, getting rid of that kind of an attitude.

* * * * *

[Kids] need to realize that everybody else needs to belong and to have some self-esteem and that you don't build yourself up by ripping other kids down, and that there's a way that you can all work together and everybody can win instead of winning at so-and-so's expense.

These two comments stressed using multicultural education to eliminate negative attitudes and hurtful behavior such attitudes provoke.

When multicultural education is viewed as a form of therapy for prejudice and stereotyping—which is a very common way it is viewed—teachers or counselors take on the role of therapist, helping students to examine their prejudices and attitudes, to identify negative feelings about themselves and/or others, to identify misconceptions they use to judge people, and to replace negative with positive images. The healing process involves expunging "sick" attitudes from the individual. This is done by helping one to admit one has a problem and confess the sins of one's prejudices, then helping one engage in a long, painful process of healing by examining one's own feelings and working to replace negative feelings with positive ones. (Peck, 1994).

In this view, young children are more easily "cured" than adults, and teachers can prevent prejudice by providing appropriate information and experiences. For example, the authors of *Cultural Awareness for Young Children* explained in the preface that they were concerned about "the lack of acceptance of the diversity of the traditional customs and lifestyles of a culture by many of the citizens of this country" (McNeill, Schmidt, & Allen, 1981, p. 5). They went on to explain that,

> To accomplish an acceptance of diversity, adults working with young children need to be aware of their stereotypic views of cultures and share authentic information about each culture with children. Racist attitudes need to be changed to positive feelings toward others. (p. 5)

To attempt to replace racist attitudes with positive feelings, lessons introduce children to artifacts and customs of traditional non-European people. To develop appreciation of black cultures, for example, children build traditional Zulu houses, make dashikis and masks, and learn some words in Swahili.

Most advocates of multicultural education criticize such "tourist curricula" that exoticize difference (Banks, 1984; Derman-Sparks, 1989). The problem is not that tackling prejudice and stereotypes is a useless endeavor, but rather that this endeavor so often is completely disconnected from political engagement. Such depoliticized approaches to prejudice reduction

> translate the political into the psychological: prejudice and stereotyping are simply operations of human cognition that can be corrected by educating people to new patterns of thinking (with better information, we will reject stereotypes and discard prejudices). (Peck, 1994, p. 101)

Reducing racism, sexism, or institutionalized poverty to psychological feelings and misconceptions that individuals can overcome may help individuals interact with others in a more positive manner and may provide a context for teaching worthwhile concepts. However, this reduction camouflages the main issues and does not necessarily lead to action directed toward real change (Gurnah, 1984).

> In terms of the material conditions of the workless, homeless, school-less, welfare-less blacks of slum city, all this paroxysm of activity [in racial awareness training] has not made the blindest bit of difference. (Sivanandon, 1985, p. 22)

The material conditions with which oppressed groups struggle, in a context of unequal power relations, are a major focus on social justice movements, and a major impetus behind school reform in such communities. The next metaphor focuses more directly than the first on school improvement.

Multicultural Education as Teaching Techniques

Multicultural education is viewed as a set of teaching techniques when it is regarded as a set of curricular and instructional strategies to add to one's classroom repertoire, particularly to use with culturally diverse students. This view can overlap with the therapeutic view above, but it emphasizes the acquisition of particular techniques for teaching "them." And it is also a very common conception among many teachers. Several of the teachers I interviewed about multicultural education responded in terms of teaching techniques to use with children culturally different from themselves. One, for example, articulated an "individual differences" perspective about children, in which teachers make adaptations to individual children's problems or characteristics, culture being one such "problem":

> It doesn't have to be just race, everybody comes in with some sort of, maybe they're left-handed or maybe they have something else, a problem at home or that sort of thing, so I think each child, if you look at each child individually and don't say, Well this is a minority group or this is a Hispanic group or that sort of thing, I think every child has something that's a problem.

Other teachers talked about specific techniques they learned. One emphasized the value of a staff development program teaching

> more about the Hispanic families, the Black families, the Puerto Rican families, but also what incites getting those students happy, how they interact with their parents, what their parents are like when they interact with schools. . . . We have to learn to gear down our languages so that we can communicate effectively when we're dealing with their children.

Another discussed the usefulness of adding teaching strategies to her repertoire:

> More of the cooperative learning activities, I think. By doing more types of hands-on things. . . . Just more types of incorporating, I should say, more of the cooperative learning styles, you know, where they are working together.

As these interviews suggest, multicultural teaching techniques in this view help teachers manage diversity.

Lin Goodwin (1994) surveyed 120 preservice teachers to find out how they conceive of multicultural education. Seventy-one percent discussed it as therapy for racial disharmony; another 16% defined it as a way of addressing individual differences among children. As a whole, the majority described multicultural education as a set of techniques teachers should use to respond to diverse students. "They define it as primarily procedural or technical, requiring knowing and doing something" to adapt the regular curriculum to one's own students (p. 128). Further, the preservice teachers' "emphasis on each child implicitly identifies the individual as the fulcrum of change; multicultural pedagogy becomes idiosyncratic and dependent on the needs of single students" (p. 128).

One certainly cannot argue that teachers should not develop technical skills to respond to students' diversity and teach them effectively. However, Goodwin observed that the vast majority in her study did not connect such skills with broader political issues. Indeed, only one of the 120 preservice teachers argued that multicultural education should include "the ability to look critically at existing political, economic and social structures" (p. 122). Such critical analysis might include critiquing how schools reproduce hierarchies of privilege and advantage (such as through tracking) and working to change such structures and processes. It might also include recognizing that most oppressed people do not wish to remain oppressed and that one should engage in dialog with members of oppressed communities regarding their own wishes for their children's education. This is a very different orientation from one in which a teacher adopts techniques from a book or workshop to apply to children with whom the techniques are supposed to "work" in order to gain greater compliance from them.

Multicultural Education as Academic Discourse

Multicultural education takes the form of academic discourse when intellectuals engage in a great deal of talk about multicultural issues without also actually engaging in social change processes (Platt, 1993). Until recently, multicultural education was rarely a topic of academic debate; over the past few years it has become a hot topic, and in some circles, in vogue. As Gates (1992) put it,

> Academic critics write essays, "readings" of literature, where the bad guys (for example, racism or patriarchy) lose, where the forces of oppression are subverted by the boundless powers of irony and allegory that no prison can contain, and we glow with hard-won triumph. We pay homage to the marginalized and demonized, and it feels almost as if we've righted a real-world injustice. (p. 19)

But engaging in battles of words, by itself, does not necessarily bring social change. Gates commented that, "it sometimes seems that blacks are doing better in the college curriculum than they are in the streets" (p. 19).

Discussions that clarify thinking, share ideas, and persuade are of value. But the frequent substitution of texts and words for genuine dialog and struggle concerns scholar-activists. Carby, for example, asked, "Have we as a society successfully eliminated the desire for achieving integration through political agitation for civil rights and opted instead for knowing each other through cultural texts?" (in Platt, 1993, p. 75).

These observations do not mean that academicians should not work toward the reform of the entire university. Indeed, there is a great deal of work to be done not only to make universities truly multicultural institutions, but also to strengthen their capacity to help us address injustices in the broader society.

> Multiculturalism has to be more than a special project or piece-meal reform to diversify students, faculty, and ideas. We need to engage the whole university in acknowledging that the existing institutions and discourse of race relations are inadequate to the crisis we face. (Platt, 1993, p. 77)

The problem with academic discourse is that it often consists of little more than words and often contributes nothing to improving the real conditions of life for disenfranchised peoples. "The relation between our critical postures and the social struggles they reflect upon is far from transparent. That doesn't mean there's no relation, of course, only that it's a highly mediated one" (Gates, 1992, p. 20).

This book, for example, consists of academic discourse. Academic discourse, like examination of attitudes and development of multicultural teaching skills, is not inherently worthless. The problem is that so often none of these is directly connected with any organized movement for social justice. It is the fourth metaphor, multicultural education as a social movement, that should refocus our energies and actions, and provide the grounding and direction for future work in multicultural education.

Multicultural Education as a Social Movement

If multicultural education were viewed as a movement or as connected with other related social movements, discussions about it would be quite different from those above. Let us examine the various dimensions of social movements, then draw implications of those dimensions for multicultural education.

Dimensions of Social Movements

A social movement is a "sustained challenge to powerholders in the name of a population living under the jurisdiction of those powerholders by means of repeated public displays of that population's numbers, commitment, unity, and worthiness" (Tilly, 1993, p. 7). Movements aim to redistribute power and resources by confronting power relations in which a dominant collective has attained the power to define the society for the masses, to construct an ideology in which that definition makes sense, and to achieve hegemony—to get most people to accept that ideology and act in accordance with it, viewing it as natural (Eyerman & Jamison, 1991; Gramsci, 1971; Touraine, 1988). In a social movement, the goal is not just to effect a particular policy change, but more importantly to shift the power to control decisions, define situations, and allocate resources (Staples, 1984).

Social movement theorists distinguish among four main kinds of actors in a movement: the constituent base, the powerholders, the activists, and the general public who are not directly involved. The base of a social movement consists of a constituency who share common problems or concerns; movements aim toward empowering this base. Initially, would-be members of the constituent base may not necessarily identify with each other, a common set of problems and concerns, or an action agenda. Movements need continued work at building a sense of shared identity and a common definition of shared concerns and at developing networks for communication within the constituency (Eyerman & Jamison, 1991). The movement's constituency can be connected partly through print or electronic media, but regular face-to-face contact through social and cultural organizations serves this purpose most effectively (Aronowitz, 1992; Minkoff, 1993; Shields, 1994). Sometimes a symbol that has meaning to various segments of the constituency is used to represent the whole collective in order to build a common identity; for example, language serves as such as symbol for bridging various Latino communities (Padilla, 1985). But the formal organizational structure of the movement is less important to its success and longevity than are cultural activities that bring people together to cultivate, nurture and sustain solidarity and identification with the movement (Ingalsbee, 1993; Minkoff, 1993; Staggenborg, Eder & Sudderth, 1993).

This constituency stands in opposition to the powerholders who must be confronted in order for the constituent base to achieve better life conditions and self-determination. A movement must have a

clear sense of who the opposition is and what issues differentiate
"them" from "us". Without that, movements tend to dissipate, since
many different sectors, including the dominant society, can articulate
interpretations of problems and recommended agendas for action;
then people who are unclear about the issues and the power differential often end up supporting the regime currently in power (Eyerman & Jamison, 1991; Touraine, 1988). A problem with many recent
"movements" for improvement of life in the U.S. and Western
Europe, such as liberal feminism or populist politics, is that they
are actually attached to the existing political parties and capitalist
structures, rather than opposing these groups and systems
(Aronowitz, 1992; Boggs, 1986).

Movements must differentiate the constituent base from the
opposition, but it is necessary to be aware of problems associated
with binary opposition thinking that constructs each as a monolithic
group (Popkewitz, 1991). Neither the powerholders nor the constituency is a unified monolith, which renders the process of defining
the constituency and the opposition to be quite complex, particularly when we are talking about "multicultural" which articulates
problems defined around race, gender, sexual orientation, social
class, and disability. As argued shortly, it is at this point that multicultural education loses its social movement character.

Activists stand between the constituent base and the powerholders; activists often but not always come from the constituent
base (Tilly, 1993). The role activists play is to organize constituents,
articulate their concerns, and negotiate on their behalf with powerholders. Activists who come from the powerholder group may be listened to more readily by powerholders than those from the constituent base of the movement. In this way, they can be helpful
allies. It is important to realize that activism is a role more so than a
group; one may be an activist in some contexts but not in others.
What one actually does, and with whom one works, identifies one as
an activist.

The primary basis for power of a social movement is its ability
to organize and mobilize the "marching millions" as needed (Staples, 1984). Movement organizers generally mobilize the constituent
base most effectively by networking with existing local political and
cultural groups that identify with the broader movement (Staggenborg, Eder & Sudderth, 1993; Tilly, 1993) Increasingly important
also is a movement's ability to mobilize the general public, who may
identify with neither the movement nor the powerholders. Touraine
(1988) argues that movements today depend more on mobilizing

public opinion than engaging in direct action and that those that grasp importance of public opinion tend to be more successful. To do this, movements must link political advocacy with moral issues and conditions of everyday life, tap into the discontent of large segment of the public, and help them to see connection between the movement's action agenda and their own discontent. In this way, the public can be mobilized as an additional pressure group (Staples, 1984).

At this point, readers should stop and mentally locate themselves as either members of the constituent base of multicultural education, powerholders, activists, or the general public. Quite likely many readers will identify themselves as activists—as educators who are attempting to change other educators on behalf of children from disenfranchised groups. It is possible for activists to evolve into a loose group unto itself, in which they "spend a major part of their energy making claims not on powerholders but on themselves" (Tilly, 1993, p. 15). When this happens, activists move away from direct affiliation with the movement's constituent base, affiliating largely with each other. This is a growing problem in multicultural education, which is a point I will return to later. The connection between activists and the movement's constituents is critical; when this connection breaks down, the movement does also.

Social movements articulate counter-ideologies that frame issues and group identity differently from the dominant ideology. A counter-ideology attempts to situate the group historically in a manner that articulates a group consciousness and redefines its relationship with the dominant society in a way that suggests changing that relationship (Aronowitz, 1992). This includes articulating a vision for the future, goals, and some sort of structure through which to achieve the group's goals. In articulating this counter-ideology, the movement's activists attempt to re-orient the thinking of both the constituency and the dominant society (Touraine, 1988), and to "portray [the movement] as numerous, committed, unitary, and worthy" (Tilly, 1993, p. 17). Movements need someone to do the intellectual work of creating such a counter-ideology although there are debates about who should do this. While some argue that intellectuals should develop the movement's theoretical and ideological underpinnings (e.g., Laclau, 1988, p. 26–27), others are more skeptical, stressing the importance of ideas coming from the movement's constituents—its everyday people—rather than an intellectual elite. As Staples (1984) put it, an organizer "must be able to translate people's dreams for a better life into reality" (p. 8) and those dreams need to come from the people themselves. In fact, many argue that the movement's meaning cannot come from anywhere else except the peoples' day-to-day work and interactions (Ingalsbee, 1993).

A movement develops a repertoire of action strategies, with the long-term aim of shifting power and getting powerholders to act in the direction desired by the constituents (Eyerman & Jamison, 1991; Tilly, 1993). Strategies may include routine advocacy, education and persuasion, negotiation, and non-violent or violent direct action. Movements that use advocacy strategies within routine institutional channels tend to have longer lives than those that use direct action strategies (Minkoff, 1993); activists must weigh the relative advantages and trade-offs of protest as opposed to more routine strategies. Whatever approach is chosen, however, action strategies and pressure tactics must get the constituents directly involved, so that they see a direct connection between their own actions and organization, and results—that is empowerment (Staples, 1984).

The 1960s and the 1990s: Different Decades

As an outgrowth of the civil rights movement, multicultural education arose as a part of struggles by African Americans, then other racial minority groups, to control decisions about education of their own children. In this regard, education was viewed as a social resource connected with other resources such as jobs, power, and community vitality, and the goal was to gain power to define how education for children of oppressed racial groups should be conducted. In the 1960s, communities and educators of color actively demanded or tried to persuade the white education establishment to make specific changes in the conduct of education. Glenn Omatsu (1994), for example, described activism as the Asian American community confronted San Francisco State University during the 1960s. During that time, a coalition of working class Third World students who were closely linked with their communities made specific demands on the university that not only attempted to change education, but also "confronted basic questions of power and oppression in America" (p. 26). This example, plus many others from this time period, were clearly movements in which educational change was part of a larger quest by oppressed communities to gain control over their own lives.

As the social movements of the 1960s became dispersed and marginalized, and conservatism gained ideological ground, links between educational change and community-based movements that began in the 1960s have become obscured. Clearly articulated calls for political changes to benefit large groups have waned; "empower-ment" commonly now means individual advancement rather than collective empowerment and mobility. This is not, of course, simply the fault of educators or activists; many activists have noted the degree to which activism in oppressed communities has taken on the individualism and conservatism of the larger society. For exam-ple, Omatsu (1994) pointed out that while activism in Asian Ameri-can communities during the 1960s was aimed toward empowerment of the community by challenging structures of oppression, today it is oriented toward upward mobility of young Asian professionals who are more concerned about the glass ceiling than about structural racism and poverty. Similarly, Bronski (1994) contrasted the Gay Liberation Front and Stonewall Riots of 1969 with today's gay rights movement. Twenty-five years ago, gay activists confronted restric-tions on sexual behavior; and many also "understood that racism was part of our fight" (p. 22). Today the gay rights movement has shifted away from affirming the right of people to engage in homo-sexual behavior—one can "be" gay in terms of identity, but not nec-essarily "act" gay in behavior; and action confronting racism has been replaced by sporadic talk about "diversity."

Political systems increasingly are closed to social movements; movements need political expression but find it increasingly difficult to connect with any political party (Touraine, 1988). In the U.S., for example, the political system increasingly is controlled by a wealthy elite; ordinary Americans are disaffected from politics, but do not see a clear alternative, and social movements tend to be fractured and marginalized. On a global level, "state-supported global capi-talism" increasingly controls political systems (Brecher, Childs & Cutler, 1993, p. xvi). Partly through control of media, the dominant elite directs discontent and anger of various segments of society against each other, rather than against the existing economic and political system and the elite itself. The current anti-immigrant furor is an example. As people's economic situations have eroded, their frustration has been channeled against immigrants, Americans of color, and poor women rather than against a wealthy elite that has been profiting. As a system for producing and distributing wealth, capitalism has achieved such a degree of hegemony that it is very dif-ficult to organize people around opposition to it (Aronowitz, 1992; Boggs, 1986).

In response to the marginalization of movements, many move-ment activists stress the need to build organic coalitions among grassroots communities who have built a clear sense of their own identity, but also see connections between their own interests and those of other oppressed communities. Childs (1994), for example, calls such coalitions "transcommunal alliances." Further, he and others argue that such grassroots organizations are growing, and many models of effective coalition-building exist (Brecher, Childs, & Cutler, 1993). There is a danger, however, in coalitions becoming "catch-all" parties that attempt to please a wide variety of interests, since these kinds of formations tend to be reabsorbed into existing political structures and ideological formations (Boggs, 1986). Coalitions are necessary, but must retain a clear sense of who and what they are supporting and opposing and what their transformative vision is. For example, coalitions organized around wage improvement, housing improvement and access to jobs and health care can pull very different communities together to address very real, common concerns.

During the early 1970s, multicultural education struggled to be noticed by the education establishment. While its advocates were mainly educators, they were also usually closely connected with community movements and social protest politics. When I began teaching in the early 1970s and first attended multicultural education workshops, I could not distinguish workshop leaders from community activists.

By the mid-1980s, however, as classrooms across the U.S. became more culturally diverse and teachers increasingly began asking for help and as many turned to the growing literature base in multicultural education, more and more Euro-American teachers who had never been involved in social movements took ownership in multicultural education. While some teachers who gravitate toward the field are longtime "boat rockers" (Boyle-Baise & Washburn, 1994), many are simply good people who care about children and who want to improve their effectiveness in teaching the students they now have. By itself, this is not a problem, but it has contributed to a shift in what multicultural education often means. As Euro-American educators who have never been engaged in social activism join the ranks of multicultural education advocates, they filter its meaning through their own ideas about difference and inequality. Further, as multicultural education has adopted an increasingly wide agenda of change, focusing not only on racism but also on gender, social class, disability, and other issues, a still wider array of people have found elements to which they can relate. And by itself this also would not necessarily be a problem. But many have claimed ownership in multicultural education without necessarily taking seriously the needs and claims of other constituents. This leads to the formation of groups of white teachers who are interested in multicultural education (but not in challenging racism), who view it as adding some "diversity" to the day-to-day routines of teaching, and to whom it may not occur to collaborate with community grassroots organizations. Therefore, in the last section of this chapter, I wish to return to the metaphor of multicultural education as a social movement, in order to suggest where our emphases and efforts should be if we were to renew this as the primary metaphor.

Multicultural Education as a Social Movement

Viewing multicultural education as a social movement has implications for how one conceptualizes school change, which in turn has far-reaching ramifications. Most educators do not think in terms of collective action aimed toward institutional change. For example, when I asked sixteen teachers how much power they believed a cadre of teachers had to change schools, only two discussed the change process in terms of organizing to press collectively for change. Most of the others discussed school change as involving a process of attempting to persuade other teachers as individuals to change their attitudes (Sleeter, 1992). As a teacher educator, I find my work structured in this manner; everyday when I enter the classroom, I am trying to persuade future teachers (who are overwhelmingly white and are in the process of becoming professionals) to teach differently.

The social movement metaphor suggests a very different change process from that educators tend to use—that parents and other concerned community people, as well as educators, organize to pressure schools to serve their interests and those of their children. In a thoughtful discussion of neighborhood organizing for urban school reform, Michael Williams (1989) argued that most communities have the potential to bring about significant changes. "This assumption is warranted by the presence in most of these neighborhoods of leaders and organizations already at work on neighborhood problems" (p. 2). However, most communities do not use that potential as well as they could to reform their schools. Williams instructs community people to go into the schools and observe carefully such variables as teachers' attitudes toward students, the handling of disciplinary issues, the handling of homework, and so forth. As community members identify specific problems and generate ideas for school improvement, they should communicate these directly to the school, collectively using pressure to hold the school accountable. He concluded that,

> The goals of organizing for urban school reform are twofold. Neighborhood organizing should promote change in the school as a result of documentation and the application of collective political pressure, and it should build among parents agreement on what their schools should do for their children. (p. 147)

Educators may become resources and collaborators in this process, but should not own the process. Williams' discussion and the social movement metaphor has important ramifications for multicultural education, which this section will elaborate.

Social movements attempt to shift power from powerholders whom the movement opposes, toward the movement's constituent base. Since the 1970s, a distinction between powerholders and the constituent base of multicultural education has become highly blurred, if not lost. We must recapture this distinction and reorient the field in ways that such a distinction suggests.

The constituent base of multicultural education consists of disenfranchised people in this society, particularly parents and children of color and/or of low-income backgrounds; children who are disabled, gay or lesbian, and their parents or adult supporters; and girls. This is a highly diverse lot, including groups who do not identify at all with each other and engage in various forms of exclusion and oppression themselves, a problem that can lead to fragmentation if not addressed directly. I will discuss this issue shortly. However, in many arenas of multicultural activity, predominantly white groups of educators look to ourselves as if we were the constituent base of multicultural education, which misses the entire point of power-redistribution. *Most college-educated white people are not multicultural education's natural constituency.* We can certainly become allies, but we need to recognize the power of our own self-interest and point of view, which often leads us to reshape multicultural education to fit our own needs. In our communities, we need to view children of oppressed groups, their parents, their communities, and their grassroots advocacy organizations as the natural constituency of multicultural education. Multicultural education ought to be about empowering this natural constituency.

Powerholders are mainly the education establishment: administrators, classroom teachers, university professionals, and community constituents who support school policies and practices that multicultural education advocates wish to change. Many readers of this book, as well as its author, could more accurately be thought of as powerholders in education institutions rather than as members of the constituent base of multicultural education. We may be activists and allies to the constituent base, but we do not comprise that base.

The distinction between powerholders and the constituent base of multicultural education is one of relative power and position, rather than strictly one of group membership. Robert Terry (1993) clarified this point very simply and well in his essay "A Parable: The Ups and Downs", writing: "What makes an up an up and a down a down is that an up can do more to a down than a down can do to an up. That's what keeps an up up and a down down" (p. 61). He went on to point out that most people are ups and downs relative to someone else at various times, but some are downs in most relationships while others are ups most of the time. As white women, many of us who are educators are "downs" relative to a patriarchal, bureaucratic education establishment and may see ourselves largely as "downs." We have much more difficulty viewing ourselves *also* as "ups"—as powerholders who someone else would like to change. Yet, relative to our students and their communities, to a large extent, we are powerholders. We may be able to learn to share power and collaborate but must remain vigilant about how our own power and vested interests influences us.

Many readers will regard distinguishing between the constituent base and the powerholders as divisive. Historically in an effort to be inclusive, multicultural activists have offered a wide embrace, arguing that multicultural education is for everyone. While I believe that its ideals *are* for everyone, everyone does not benefit equally from schooling as it currently operates which is what multicultural education is trying to change. Movements dissipate when they lose a sense of who is their constituency and who is the opposition (Boggs, 1986; Touraine, 1988). The argument that multicultural education includes everyone may accurately articulate a long-range vision and help to draw in otherwise reluctant educators and members of the public, but it also obscures analysis of power and the politics of institutional change. As long as power relations are not addressed, those with the least power to change schools remain relatively powerless. And as long as "everyone" can define multicultural education, it will frequently continue to take forms that white middle class people find least threatening.

Locally, the action agenda for multicultural education should come largely from oppressed communities, not from white educators. White educators can be helpful allies, but if we control decision-making, we are the ones who are exercising power. Terry (1993) writes that leadership in social justice issues should come from "downs" much moreso than from "ups." "Ups are too busy trying to maintain the system, rather than generate insight about what's really going on or how to change it. So our source of new insightful information comes from downs, not from ups" (p. 62). The goal is not to get rid of ups, but rather "to get rid of arbitrary up-down power relationships" (p. 63). As educators who are part of a system we are trying to change, we do have a vested interest in protecting our own position and the processes that worked for us. That does not make us bad people, but it does position us differently from the students and parents for whom we advocate. Further, most school systems have the capacity to absorb and contain pressures for change without actually changing in fundamental ways (Skrtic, 1991). Getting rid of arbitrary up-down power relationships means collaborating with oppressed communities. "The neighborhood organization is a political instrument whereby residents can make their educational and other public needs known and have them answered" (Williams, 1989, p. 148). Educators can collaborate with such organizations but cannot tell them what they need.

What about all the many books and articles that have been written over the past twenty-five years, discussing what multicultural education means and how schools should change? Does locating the primary agenda for school change with parents and leaders of oppressed communities mean that we reject the usefulness of this body of knowledge? It does not, although I suggest refocusing its use. Currently such literature—which contains a rich array of conceptual frameworks, research, and specific teaching strategies—often substitutes for dialog between educators and community people, and currently educators have greater access to it than do community people. The reduction of multicultural education to teaching techniques is symptomatic of this gap. In its inception, the action agenda for multicultural education came largely from parents and educators of color, who articulated changes they would like to see in schools. Over time, as academicians have elaborated on that agenda, we have both developed it and to some extent disconnected it from its natural constituent base. Currently, multicultural education is being defined by a wide array of people, including white conservatives (e.g., Bernstein, 1994; Ravitch, 1990a and b; Schlesinger, 1992; Stotsky, 1992). If one depends on professionals to define it, one might be quite bewildered, and even see multicultural education as meaning something contrary to what oppressed groups in one's own community actually want. Further, professional educators use professional knowledge to position ourselves above lay-people. As an activist has pointed out, "school staff can heighten the social distance between themselves and working-class parents by emphasizing that what they teach and how they teach it is beyond the understanding of parents; therefore, parents should stay out of the whole process" (Williams, 1989, p. 130). Professionals may use good ideas with good intentions, but, in an absence of dialog with the communities they serve, still not respond to the concerns of such communities.

The point is that the multicultural education literature should be written for and available to a wider community audience, and oppressed communities should decide for themselves what ideas are most useful. Professionals can help through dialog and information-sharing. Two examples illustrate. A couple of years ago I was talking with an African American parent who was very frustrated about how the school was treating her precocious primary-grade son. As she talked, I suggested that she may be describing cultural differences in learning style between African American and white children and negative reactions that white teachers often have toward African American learning and communication styles. She was completely unaware of this line of argument, so I gave her several articles and books to read. She returned about two weeks later, having devoured that material, and told me that it had given her a vocabulary to describe her concerns, demonstrated that her "gut feelings" were accurate and that she was not "crazy" or imagining things, and suggested ways she might interact more effectively with the teacher. The material I gave her about culture and learning and about multicultural education enriched her own analysis of a problem and strengthened her power to intervene on behalf of her son. (It did not strengthen her power enough to change the teacher or the classroom, however; she eventually transferred her son to another school.)

Concha Delgado-Gaitan (1993) discussed how she worked with a Mexican American parent organization and how this work transformed her understanding of her own position as a scholar. Initially, she viewed her role as an informed, neutral outsider, studying family-school relationships. In the process of meeting with parents to share her research findings, she realized that "not knowing how to connect with the schools had clearly traumatized some of these parents" (p. 397). The parents "tried very hard to do the best for their children, and . . . had the desire and commitment to support their children in their education both at home and at school" (p. 400). What they lacked was the expertise Delgado-Gaitan had about how schools work, what teachers respond to, what program possibilities exist. Over time, she shifted her role with them from researcher to resource. She did not tell the parents what they should want, but rather provided information that could assist them in advocating for themselves. "Although my involvement in their meetings unquestionably influenced their orientation and knowledge base about the schools, the COPLA parents themselves defined their organizational goals and their sociopolitical awareness and identity" (p. 407). In the process, the parents' ability to advocate for themselves grew.

> COPLA moved from conceptualizing change as a list of outcomes, to a list of books they could read to their children, to interacting with each other, to learning the process by which to inquire and access information that would lead them to obtain the resources they desired. (p. 408)

These examples illustrate how the body of knowledge called "multicultural education" can be useful to oppressed communities. The teaching techniques and abstract discourse of multicultural education are not irrelevant. On the contrary, there is a great deal of helpful work available that provides ways of conceptualizing issues, research findings that support what oppressed communities want, and specific practices and materials for classroom use.

At the same time, however, communities must themselves define their own goals and develop the capacity to move the goals forward. As long as this body of literature is controlled primarily by professionals, it is subject to being used as a tool for managing and controlling "diversity" in schools. That is quite different from dialoguing with parents and other community members, using the literature mutually to inform thinking and knowledge of possibilities. Redirected toward parents and community activists from oppressed groups, this literature can serve as an empowering resource.

The flow of ideas in multicultural education has been more toward educators, however, than toward constituent communities. In my own community, for example, I and other local educators occasionally disseminate articles or resource materials through community centers and local organizations such as the Urban League. And I place my teacher education students in community centers for field experiences, where I have them practice listening to and dialoguing with "downs" rather than telling "downs" what to do. However, the networks of communication make it much easier for me to talk about multicultural education with other educators at times, in locations and in discourse styles that exclude multicultural education's natural constituent base.

This is true of conferences as well as professional literature. Viewing multicultural education as a social movement suggests broader uses for conferences and other gatherings than is often the case. I have been involved in many conferences and meetings for multicultural education in which the organizers have lamented that we are simply "preaching to the choir"—that those who need to "hear the message" did not come, reducing the conference's effectiveness. This view suggests that educators who are "for" multicultural education are its constituency and do not need to network among ourselves; that is, we hold gatherings to enlighten the unenlightened. Viewing multicultural education as a social movement suggests that we distinguish among three rather different purposes for gatherings: 1) networking the constituent base for multicultural education (who are mostly non-educators), 2) developing the knowledge-base of educator/activists, and 3) communicating desired changes for schools to powerholders. Some organizations and conferences, such as the National Association for Multicultural Education (NAME) attempt comprehensively to address all three purposes. In addition to such large-scale, comprehensive conferences, other gatherings should be clearly organized based on which purpose they are trying to serve.

For the first purpose, some conferences and meetings might provide opportunities for the much-needed face-to-face contact and identity-building among members of a constituent base. If the constituent base for multicultural education is primarily families and other community members from communities of color and low-income white communities, then such people ought to be actively involved in multicultural education's activities—whether they have education credentials or not. Such involvement would help develop flow of communication between local grass-roots organizations and professional educators, as well as building community empowerment across differences. Face-to-face involvement across differences such as gender, ethnicity, sexual orientation, or language is necessary in order to build a powerful constituency that can function together and work toward the development of a pluralistic, democratic polity. Outside education, there are good models of such grass-roots organizations that bridge differences. For example, Childs (1994) described several "Transcommunal" organizations such as the National Urban Peace and Justice "Gang Truce" Summit in Kansas City and the African American/Korean Alliance in Los Angeles. Many labor organizers are recognizing that "fighting all forms of discrimination is the very foundation of building unity between organized labor and women and people of color" (Oppenheim, 1993, p. vi). Such bridge-building requires that people come to grips with their own prejudices as well as deepen their knowledge about issues of concern to others in their communities, which requires face-to-face contact. As an experienced cross-cultural labor organizer explained,

> People just can't be told to not be racist or to love such-and-such—that's mere polemics. We gotta get out there and DO. Overcoming racial and ethnic divisions starts by asking each other questions, housecalling together, going to events together. (Russo, 1993, p. 41)

Similarly, in a discussion of homophobia within communities of color, activists discussed re-education strategies they use, such as the following:

> We can hold town-house meetings for everyone, not just Indian organizations. I compare it to squaw dances on the rez . . . three-day ceremonies. Everyone from the surrounding area comes and shares. They talk about their lives, what's going on, what's bothering them. . . . We look at the community as a whole. (Garcia, 1994, p. 16)

These are examples of face-to-face cross-difference community-building at local levels. To build capacity for community organizing for school reform, educators should be involved, but not necessarily dominate. I cannot overemphasize the importance of such face-to-face gatherings of members of the constituent base of multicultural education. If the constituent base does not identify with the movement and its action agenda and does not help to move that agenda forward, the experience of social movements indicates that the action agenda and the movement itself will dissipate.

The second purpose for conferences and other gatherings is to deepen educator/activists' analysis of the issues and knowledge of how to make social change. This is rather different from the purpose of community-building, in that it specifically involves seasoned educator/activists and focuses on development of our own knowledge-base and repertoire of strategies for institutional change. Often we are so busy trying to "convert" the "unconverted" that we do not use conferences and other gatherings as well as we might to develop our own knowledge. We assume that those who have become involved in multicultural education know all we need to know about its issues and the processes for making institutional change, when that is rarely the case. One important focus for conferences of activists should be developing our analysis of the political process of making school change, and sharpening our ability to use various political change strategies such as networking and organizing, persuasion, and pressure politics. Another focus could be examining forms of institutional inequality outside the classroom such as tracking and school funding, and developing strategies to address these issues. An example of an organization that uses meetings for this second purpose is the National Coalition of Education Activists.

The third purpose for conferences and meetings is to communicate desired changes in schools to educators and other relevant publics—to the powerholders whom we wish to change, and/or to the broader public at large. From the perspective of the social movement metaphor, in such meetings activists and community representatives communicate specific changes to powerholders, backing up their desire for change with the potential for pressure from the constituent base. An example is a conference in which I was involved in 1991, in which the largest school districts in New York State convened to communicate to textbook publishers that their texts fell far short from a multicultural perspective, and that districts would begin to produce their own materials if publishers did not respond. Workshops may also serve the purpose of trying to change the behavior of powerholders, but too often there is no one—particularly no one outside the schools—holding teachers accountable for using the training they have received.

Finally, viewing multicultural education as a social movement suggests that effort must be expended to cultivate support among segments of the broader public who currently are unaware of or indifferent to multicultural education. Currently the New Right, having control over far greater financial and media resources than progressives have, is educating the public to regard multicultural education as divisive, intellectually weak, and un-American (Sleeter, 1994). Carl Boggs (1986) argued that increasingly, the development of "a viable counterhegemonic politics will depend, in the final analysis, upon essentially subjective factors" which include

> the capacity of disparate groups to unite in a common outlook, and the success of activists in making concrete—making alive—issues that can attract the vast majority of people to the ideal of a democratic, egalitarian, nonviolent world. (p. 249)

Multicultural education activists do need to develop access to mainstream media and do need to connect the goals and processes of multicultural education with the ideals of democracy and justice that most Americans espouse, as well as the public's concerns about a shrinking job market, an uncertain future, and public safety.

Social Movement Metaphor for Classroom Teachers

What does a classroom teacher do who takes the social movement metaphor seriously? This metaphor has several implications for teachers.

First, it suggests that a teacher recognize the ethical dimensions of teaching other people's children, and work to provide them with the highest quality of education one would wish one's own children to have. This means that such a teacher recognizes the aspirations oppressed groups have for their children and the barriers, both interpersonal and institutional, that persistently thwart their efforts. Low teacher expectations and systems such as tracking that institutionalize those expectations are an example of such barriers. Without necessarily meaning to, through our routine participation in schools as institutions, most of us as teachers contribute to the barriers children from oppressed groups face, partly by not recognizing them as barriers. Teachers who take seriously the social movement metaphor find out in what ways the school hinders the success of children from marginalized groups, then work to change processes and structures that serve as barriers.

Second, a teacher who takes the social movement metaphor seriously learns to work as an ally with the community. In the classroom, this means that the teacher shapes pedagogy on the basis of both professional expertise and ongoing dialog with parents and other community members. Professional expertise alone is not enough since perspectives of "experts" sometimes contradict those of marginalized groups. Lisa Delpit's (1988) discussion is an excellent example illustrating a major disjuncture between how African American educators and progressive Euro-American educators view the teaching of language arts to African American children. Delpit calls for dialog and power-sharing so that teachers will use pedagogy that fits the children they are teaching, with the recognition that adults who are members of the community the children grow up in understand a great deal about the children's learning.

The suggestion that teachers share power with marginalized communities is often met with the objection that many parents from marginalized groups have too many problems of their own to be of much help. While this is true, a teacher also should not equate individual parents' abilities to provide for their children with the community's aspirations and resources. Impoverished parents often face debilitating situations and some do not cope well with those situations. However, within the community are networks of strength and resilience, as well as visions of hope for children's futures. The social movement metaphor suggests that teachers seek out these networks; this is, in fact, what successful teachers do (Ladson-Billings, 1994).

Third, taking the social movement seriously by becoming an ally to marginalized communities means acting as an advocate for children from these communities in the broader civic life. This can involve voting for candidates who support the needs of such children and their communities, supporting agencies and social action groups who work on their behalf, persuading other people to support rather than blame adults in the children's lives, and so forth. Allies find out what issues are of concern to the community and how those issues can be supported. For example, some teacher education students whom I have placed in community centers for field experiences have come to realize the lack of recreation opportunities in low-income neighborhoods, and have begun to support local political action aimed toward enriching available recreation activities. In this way, they are beginning to act as advocates for children.

Fourth, a teacher who takes the social movement metaphor seriously teaches children and youth to act politically, to advocate both individually and collectively for themselves and for other marginalized people. Young people can learn to affect their social world quite powerfully. For example, in Nebraska the students of a high school teacher became so interested in learning about American's cultural diversity that they decided to advocate for a state law requiring curricula in Nebraska to be multicultural. With the teacher's guidance, they were able to persuade the state legislature to pass such a law. This is a rather dramatic example of the impact children and youth can have on institutions around them, under the guidance of a politically astute teacher. Children and youth who learn to use the democratic process effectively to advance ideals of social justice can become adults who are able to actualize the ideals of justice and equality through the political process.

Conclusion

Social movements are based on an analysis of vested interests in unequal relations of power. Movement activists assume that, while to a limited degree people will "do the right thing" on moral grounds, people are more likely to act in accordance with their vested interests. Those who have the most obvious and immediate vested interest in school reforms that challenge racism, classism, patriarchy, ablism, and heterosexism, are those highly diverse publics that occupy the "down" side of unequal relations of power in our own local communities.

I believe that concerned educators generally do want to do the right thing for students. However, all of us conceptualize what that means from our own social locations and in the context of an ideological field that shapes meaning. The social locations, vested interests, and ideology of professional educators usually differs in significant ways from that of oppressed communities. Viewing multicultural education as a social movement directs us to look to such communities as the natural constituents of multicultural education, with whom we professional educators may ally ourselves. That alliance, however takes work—work that recognizes the politics of social change in a racist, capitalist, patriarchal society.

CHAPTER 12

Educating the New Majority: A Play

CHARACTERS (All of them are new freshman at State University):

WILLIE, an 18-year-old African American male
SARA, a 19-year-old Mexican American female
ROBIN, an 18-year-old Chippewa Indian female
TOM, a 19-year-old white male

SCENE: The coffee shop of State University campus in September 1999. Students are sitting around tables chatting. Four students enter with soft drinks and sit at a table.

WILLIE: Man, I sure hope this university is more interesting than high school was. At least from their orientation, it looks like they'll treat us like adults.

SARA: Was your high school really boring, too?

WILLIE: Boring is the *only* word for it! Some of my friends thought I was crazy to want to come here and put up with four more years of boredom. (Robin and Tom look at each other.)

ROBIN: Ours wasn't boring at all. At least, my high school wasn't.

SARA: How do you two know each other? I mean, we're from all over the state, but you seem like you are friends already.

TOM: Through a high school project. My school was really interesting, and we had this exchange with Robin's school.

WILLIE: You white boys get all the good stuff. What suburb are you from?

TOM: I'm from this little town over to the west. But you're right, white males do get all kinds of advantages, and that isn't fair. That's partly what we studied in my school.

SARA: You studied that?

WILLIE: Of course they did, everyone studies white men. That's about all we studied in my school, too.

TOM: No, I mean, we studied a lot about racism.

ROBIN: And sexism and poverty, too. I'm from one of the Indian reservations up north. The teachers in our school worked hard to develop our school around Indian culture, so we would get a good grounding in Indian history, the Chippawa language, our traditional religion, our literature, and so forth.

SARA: Wow! They moved me out of bilingual education as soon as I could speak English more or less fluently and treated Spanish as if it was a disease I should get rid of.

WILLIE: Yeah, and then they take mostly white kids when they are fifteen and try to teach them Spanish. Or French or German. But if you grow up speaking another language, it's like you're un-American or something.

SARA: Yeah, you know, I had to learn to read Spanish on my own. Most of my friends didn't bother, they couldn't see where reading Spanish would help them in any way, and they could tell Spanish-speakers with brown skin are looked down on.

ROBIN: But you did learn to read Spanish?

SARA: Yeah, I like stories by Mexican authors. I always liked going to Mexican movies and I like to read, but for a long time all I could read were English stories. My mama helped me get started reading Mexican stories. I'd like to major in Chicano literature . . . if they let me. I love it, once I started reading Chicano literature I couldn't stop!

WILLIE: But it sounds, Robin, like you and Tom got something different in school?

ROBIN: Yeah, our teachers wanted to find a way to expose us to another American group, but in a constructive way. They wanted us to be proud of being Indian, but also be able to understand and relate to another cultural group in America. Lots of Indians hate white people because they keep taking and taking from us. Our teachers were trying to figure out how to help us communicate with white people so we could hold on to what is ours and try to get them to support us rather than continuing to try to destroy us.

TOM: That's where my school comes in. There is a group of teachers at my high school that read this article about a black teacher in Houston and a white teacher in New Hampshire who developed an exchange through the mail (Cobbin & Thomashow, 1994). See, I live in this little rural town and it's pretty isolated. But America is a really diverse and multicultural country. How do you get kids to expand beyond their own little horizons, to have sense of other people we share this country with?

SARA: So your school had an exchange?

TOM: Well, there was more than that. Let me first back up. There's this group of really cool teachers in my school who were concerned about where this country is heading. The poverty, the sexism, the racism, all that. So they decided to re-do our schooling to make us think about those kinds of things. It's a pretty small school, maybe it's easier to re-do a small school than a large school. Anyway, they started by taking heterogeneity and equality seriously. They got rid of tracking—

WILLIE: They got rid of tracking? I thought that was a standard part of all schools.

TOM: Well, it usually is.

ROBIN: Not my school. Indian people aren't into all that hierarchy stuff that white people get into. When Indian people on my reservation threw out the white schools, they set up our school so we all learn together. We help each other learn.

TOM: They call it "cooperative learning."

ROBIN: Whatever. We call it natural.

WILLIE: That's interesting! We call it—maybe teamwork. I used to think how weird it was, you know, that the African American kids in my neighborhood were great at teamwork in athletics. Maybe that's why everyone thinks we're hot athletes, we're really good at teamwork. I wonder why my teachers never picked up on that, there's a lot you could do with teamwork to teach stuff like math or spelling. So your teachers got rid of tracking, then what?

TOM: Well, some of the parents in our community got angry when they got rid of tracking, but that was another interesting thing they did, they got the parents more involved with the school so parents could really see what was going on. When my folks realized we were learning just as well in heterogeneous classrooms using cooperative learning, they stopped complaining. And the lower class parents were happy, because their kids were always thought of as the dumb kids, and now they weren't in dumb classes anymore.

SARA: Wow. Some of my cousins are in the dumb classes, and they aren't dumb at all. And no one asks their parents what they want.

TOM: The next thing they had us do was look around our community to find out how inequality worked there. We started out with sort of non-threatening stuff, but got into some pretty controversial stuff. I remember when they had us look at the newspaper. That was an eye-opener. I always start with the sports pages. Well, did you know about 90% of the people on the sports pages are male, and women get very little coverage?

ROBIN AND SARA: (In unison) Yes.

TOM: Oh, well, I hadn't noticed that before. But that's part of the problem. I just sort of took for granted that men are more athletic than women. So we looked at that stereotype. We looked at current research on athletics and gender. We learned about women athletes. We learned about the struggles women have had to go through to get athletic programs. We learned about how even now, in spite of Title IX, women's teams still tend to get the worst resources and worst playing times. We looked at women's athletics in our own town and, by George, it wasn't equal at all. I had always thought things were equal now, but they aren't. The teachers taught us to ask the oppressed group for their viewpoint, so we interviewed women to find out what they thought about women's athletics, and about sports coverage, and all that. What an eye-opener.

SARA: Someone pointed out the sexism in *Sports Illustrated*'s swimsuit issue, I hope?

TOM: I had never thought about how most sports magazines are written to appeal to men. So then we kids organized a system for equalizing playing times, resources, coaching, news coverage, and all that. We also looked at how the poorer kids get left out of some sports, such as golf, and managed to persuade our parents to use tax money to provide resources for ALL the kids to be able to participate in all the athletic programs, regardless of whether their family could afford equipment or not.

ROBIN: That reminds me of an interesting thing we did. You know all these stereotypes about poor people, like they are lazy and not too smart, and like to go on welfare?

WILLIE: That's what lots of people think about African American people! And we aren't all poor, I never met a poor person until I went to junior high.

ROBIN: Well, listen to this. We did a project in which we interviewed
           poor people to find out how they see things. And we com-
           pared what poor people say about themselves with what's
           in the media. The media hardly ever get it right.

TOM: Yeah. And did you know that poor people have a hard time
           even getting elected to the city council? Most of the people
           on the city council are at least middle class.

WILLIE: And mostly white, where I grew up. In my neighborhood
           this African American business owner, he owns a car deal-
           ership, well, he ran for city council. He's really well quali-
           fied. But three days before the election, the newspaper,
           which wasn't supporting him anyway, ran a front-page
           story about how he supports welfare and abortions and
           stuff. They left out a whole lot of his thinking and just
           zeroed in on these pieces, taken totally out of context. I
           know the dude pretty well. They made him seem like he
           has no sense of responsibility, like he just wants to take
           people's tax dollars and throw them away. So he didn't get
           elected. It sorta makes you not want to bother.

TOM: That's the kind of thing we studied. And not just in social
           studies. Like, in math we worked with statistics to under-
           stand social issues. In science, that was where we looked at
           biology and stereotypes. Oh, and also in science, we got into
           ecology. Did you know that more toxic waste gets dumped
           in neighborhoods of Americans of color than in white neigh-
           borhoods? And in literature we read—

SARA: Wait a minute. Is that true, what he said about toxic waste?

WILLIE: I've heard it is. We sure never studied that. Our textbooks
           just talked about equal opportunity, as if everything was
           really equal and fair now.

ROBIN: It's true. Indian reservations are one of the favorite dump-
           ing sites. Not ours, though. We organized to stop dumping.

SARA: In literature, if I went to your school, would I get to read the
           stuff that excites me?

TOM: Definitely. It was so interesting to realize that there is a
           difference between how westerners construct the narrative
           line in novels and how other groups such as Indians do. We
           read books by people like Amy Tan, David Seales, Leslie
           Silko, Sandra Cisneros, Richard Wright, Toni Morrison—

WILLIE: Shakespeare? Walt Whitman?

TOM: Yeah, them too. The teachers balanced what we read.

WILLIE: You know what happened in my school? I overheard this one
           teacher telling another teacher that the only reason they

included some African American authors was to keep us interested. They had us read "good" literature by white folks, and black stuff just to keep us interested! That's cold. I never took anything from that teacher.

SARA: At least you read some African American literature. In my school we never read anything more than five pages long by a Latino or Latina.

TOM: Wow. You guys really got a deprived education! I had to read probably three Indian novels before I wasn't bothered by the achronological storyline, and could really get into how meaning is built in a nonlinear fashion.

ROBIN: Sort of like Amy Tan's *Joy Luck Club*, huh? I really liked that one.

SARA: Or *How the Garcia Girls Lost Their Accents* (Alvarez, 1991). That was fun to read, have you read it?

ROBIN: No, write it down for me, is it good? Okay, Tom, get back to explaining how your school went.

TOM: Okay, back to the exchange our schools had. Our teachers wanted us to get to really know some people in a different part of the country, or at least the state, from their own viewpoint. That's something I've come to appreciate, people's own viewpoint about themselves. So the teachers in my school happened to meet the teachers in Robin's school at a conference—

ROBIN: And they worked out this plan. Each of our schools would start by putting together a box of material about our own communities. It could be anything we kids thought was important to tell about who we were. They had this idea, that I think is correct, that kids need to learn about each other in terms of what matters to kids. Think about it. I could read a textbook about black history but still never see your point of view. I still might not understand where you are coming from at all because textbooks aren't written how kids think.

WILLIE: But I'd *want* you to read a textbook about black history. And I'd want *me* to read one, too.

ROBIN: We did. It isn't either-or, it's both-and. But you need to get to know real-live people in addition to reading books. That's what our teachers wanted us to do. A lot of teachers don't see how to get kids to know people in other cultural groups when they live far apart geographically. That's what our teachers figured out how to work around.

TOM: So they integrated this community research project into all the subject areas. It was interesting, in fact, to realize that stuff like math can actually be used for something. Math isn't just problems in a book. Anyway, we made a map of the town, found out about how the local economy works, put together a small library of things kids like to read, made videos of stuff we like to do outside school and sort of put together a movie about our town.

ROBIN: We did the same thing, except we didn't make a movie. We wrote a story that tells about our band of Chippewa and our reservation. And we included in the box pictures of our families and pictures of us doing stuff together, a tape recording of us singing, some food, and other interesting things.

TOM: Then we mailed the boxes to each other's school. After our school had received Robin's box and had a chance to read stuff and listen and all that, then they hooked us up by interactive video so we could talk and see each other.

ROBIN: The first time, that was so funny. We just giggled. We didn't know what to say. But by the next time we started really talking.

TOM: We also set up an e-mail exchange. We created a kind of school-to-school bulletin board, so we could send messages and questions back and forth. Some kids actually paired off and started corresponding regularly, others just did it on more of a group basis.

ROBIN: Like I started e-mailing back and forth with this girl, Maggie, in Tom's school. We got to be pretty good friends. And then they would have both classes read the same book or study the same thing in history, then in class talk about it with each other over the video or on the computer. It was really interesting, listening to Tom's class talk about what they got out of *Julius Caesar*.

TOM: Or Robin's class talking about what they got out of *Ceremony* (Silko, 1977). They saw things in it I sure wouldn't have seen.

ROBIN: After we spent all year getting to know each other electronically, then at the end of the school year we went to visit them for a few days. We stayed in their houses and got to know their families. And went to their church on Sunday. Next year, their school will visit our reservation, except Tom and I won't be there because we graduated.

TOM: My teachers are hoping to expand it to include another group
          in another area of the country. My younger sister is lobbying
          for Hawaii. (Laughter)

SARA: Wow. I sure wish I went to a school like that. But tell me
          this. How did you pass the SAT, if you weren't studying
          the stuff everyone else has to study?

ROBIN: Well, to some extent, we were. In history, we studied a mul-
          ticultural version of U.S. history, for example. We had the
          regular textbooks, we just had a lot of other stuff as well.

TOM: And we didn't spend all this time memorizing one boring fact
          after another out of the book. The teacher would select some
          main ideas, and then we would read the section of the text-
          book about that idea, and then talk about whose viewpoint
          was represented. At first that was hard, because I had never
          thought about a textbook having a viewpoint.

SARA: You know when I first really realized that? It was in tenth
          grade, I remember clearly. I was talking about something
          my family did over the weekend, and this Anglo girl says,
          "How come you're always bringing up your culture? I never
          talk about my culture but you always seem to bring up
          yours. Can't we just be people?" I was blown away and just
          stood there. Anglos bring up their culture all the time, but
          they just don't recognize it as culture. I do, when what they
          talk about doesn't pertain to me. Like Madonna or Batman,
          that's their culture.

WILLIE: Amen.

SARA: So anyway, later that day it hit me, what this Anglo girl
          thinks about comes from her culture and experience, so
          what the books and TV and newspapers say comes from a
          culture and experience, too. Before that, I just thought text-
          books were boring. That was when I understood why.

WILLIE: It took you till tenth grade to figure that out?

SARA: To put words around it, it did. Well, Tom, how did you deal
          with that? I mean, once you could see that the textbooks
          come out of somebody's point of view and they aren't the
          word of God, then how do you know what to read? Or do you
          stop reading?

TOM: No, you keep reading, but you don't stop with one viewpoint.
          You get as many as you can. After we read about something
          in the history textbook, then we would reexamine the same
          historical event or time period through other people's expe-
          riences and viewpoints. We did all this in cooperative groups,

and we didn't all read the same material. We shared a lot. So we could cut through a lot of information much more quickly than if we all had to read the same thing. That was another thing that took practice. I remember the first time I had to read something, then share the main ideas with the group, I lost the group after the first sentence. But I got pretty good at reading and reporting on information, and so did the other students.

WILLIE: Now, that sounds like real life. People see things differently all the time. To me, that's interesting. And history taught that way, you could have interesting debates and discussions. And my viewpoint would be okay to express. In my school, I learned to keep my mouth shut because whenever I opened it, what came out wasn't what the teacher had in mind. I like that approach your teachers used.

ROBIN: We did things pretty similarly at my school. We've compared some of what we studied, and it wasn't exactly the same, but similar. We did quite a bit with oral history in our history class. But when we had to start taking the standardized tests, we were familiar with the material they asked about. Actually, I think we knew it better than if we had just read the textbook and listened to boring lectures over stuff in the textbook. And I think more kids from my school graduated and went to college this year than ever before. If they keep teaching like this, Indian kids will want to stay in school and will do well.

SARA: That's part of the reason some of my friends didn't stay in school. They would get so bored listening to teachers talk and reading these books that don't seem to relate to anything, they'd just leave. Go get a job or something. My friend Angela, her parents got so upset when she quit school, and they really wanted her to do well, but she just couldn't put up with the boredom anymore.

WILLIE: You know, listening to you two talk—I never thought about becoming a teacher, but I think I'd really enjoy teaching in a school like the ones you went to.

SARA: Me, too. Maybe that's what we should do, and I just thought of something. There's this graduate student journal I was looking at this morning called *The New Majority*.[1] They called it that because America's new majority will look really diverse, like us, by the year 2010. And we have to be able to talk to each other and deal with the issues that

divide us. We really need teachers that reflect that new
majority. Do you think we could all get in the same school?

ROBIN: Maybe, but we don't have to, to work together. Let's become
teachers and do what my teacher and Tom's did! Isn't that
what they call multicultural education?

The group exits.

Note

1. The New Majority, c/o The Black Graduate Students Association,
Box 94, 226 Kent Student Center, Kent State University, Kent, OH 44242-
0001.

References

Aguilar-San Juan, K., ed. 1994. *The state of Asian America*. Boston: South End Press.

Alba, R. D. 1990. *Ethnic identity*. New Haven: Yale University Press.

Albrecht, L. and Brewer, R. M., eds. 1990. *Bridges of power: Women's multicultural alliances*. Santa Cruz, CA: New Society Publishers.

Allen, J. L., ed. 1992. *Environment 92/93*. Guilford, CT: The Dushkin Publishing Group.

Allen, P. G. 1986. *The sacred hoop*. Boston: Beacon Press.

Allsup, C. 1995. Postmodernism, the "politically correct," and liberatory pedagogy. In *Multicultural education, critical pedagogy, and the politics of difference*, eds. C. E. Sleeter & P. McLaren, pp. 269–290. Albany: SUNY Press.

Alvarez, J. 1991. *How the Garcia girls lost their accents*. New York: Plume.

Anderson, L. M., Evertson, C. M., and Brophy, J. E. 1979. First-grade reading study. *Elementary School Journal*, 79: 193–233.

Andrzejewski, J., ed. 1993. *Oppression and social justice: Critical frameworks*. Needham Heights, MA: Ginn Press.

Anyon, J. 1981. Elementary schooling and distinctions of social class. *Interchange* 12: 118–32.

Anzaldua, G. 1987. *Borderlands/la Frontera*. San Francisco: Spinsters/Aunt Lute.

Apple, M. W. 1982. *Education and power*. Boston: Ark Paperbacks.

Apple, M. W. 1987. Gendered teaching, gendered labor. In *Critical studies in teacher education*, ed. T. S. Popkewitz, pp. 57–84. London: Falmer Press.

253

Applied Population Lab, Department of Rural Sociology. n.d. University of Wisconsin-Madison.

Aptheker, H. 1992. *Anti-racism in U.S. history*. New York: Greenwood Press.

Aronowitz, S. 1992. The politics of identity. New York: Routledge.

Arons, S. 1994. Constitutional implications of national curriculum standards. *The Educational Forum* 58 (4): 353–364.

Asante, M. K. 1990. *Kemet, Afrocentricity and knowledge*. Trenton, NJ: Africa World Press.

Ashton, P. T. & Webb, R. B. 1986. *Making a difference: Teachers' sense of efficacy and student achievement*. New York: Longman.

Asian American Resource Workshop. 1991. *The Asian American Comic Book*. Boston: Asian American Resource Workshop.

Asian Women of California. 1989. *Making waves: An anthology of writings by and about Asian American women*. Boston: Beacon Press.

Atwater, M. 1993. Multicultural science education. *The Science Teacher* 60 (3): 33–37.

Baker, G. C. 1983. *Planning and organizing for multicultural instruction*. Reading, MA: AddisonWesley.

Balch, S. A. 1992. Political correctness or public choice? *Educational Record* 73 (1): 21–24.

Banks, J. A. 1981. *Multiethnic education: Theory and practice*. Boston: Allyn & Bacon.

Banks, J. A. 1984. Multicultural education and its critics: Britain and the United States. *The New Era*, 65: 58–65.

Banks, J. A. 1988. *Multiethnic education*, 2nd ed. Boston: Allyn & Bacon.

Banks, J. A. 1992. African American scholarship and the evolution of multicultural education. *Journal of Negro Education* 61 (3): 273–286.

Bartolome, L. I. 1994. Beyond the methods fetish: Toward a humanizing pedagogy. *Harvard Educational Review* 64 (2): 173–194.

Bennett, C. I. 1986. *Comprehensive multicultural education*. Boston: Allyn & Bacon.

Bennett, L., Jr. 1982. *Before the Mayflower: A history of Black America*, 5th ed. New York: Penguin Books.

Bernal, M. 1987. *Black Athena: The Afroasiatic roots of Western civilization*, Vol. I. New Brunswick, NJ: Rutgers University Press.

Bernstein, R. 1994. *Dictatorship of virtue: Multiculturalism and the battle for American life*. New York: Knopf.

Bigelow, W. 1990. Inside the classroom: Social vision and critical pedagogy. *Teachers College Record* 91 (3): 437–448.

Bigelow, W. & Diamond, N. 1988. *The power in our hands*. New York: Monthly Review Press.

Blea, I. I. 1988. *Toward a Chicano social science*. New York: Praeger.

Blee, K. M. 1991. *Women of the Klan*. Berkeley: University of California Press.

Bloom, A. C. 1989. *The closing of the American mind*. New York: Simon & Schuster.

Boggs, C. 1986. *Social movements and political power*. Philadelphia: Temple University Press.

Bourdieu, P., & Passeron, J. C. 1977. *Reproduction in education, society, and culture*. Beverly Hills: Sage.

Bowles, S., & Gintis, H. 1976. *Schooling in capitalist America*. New York: Basic Books.

Boyle-Baise, L. & Washburn, J. 1994. Coalescing for change: The Coalition for Education that is Multicultural. Unpublished paper.

Brecher, J., Childs, J. B., & Cutler, J. 1993. *Global visions: Beyond the new world order*. Boston: South End Press.

Bronski, M. 1994. Back to the future. *Z Magazine* 7(9): 21–25.

Broudy, H. S. 1975. Cultural pluralism: New wine in old bottles. *Educational Leadership*, 33: 173–175.

Bullivant, B. 1986. Towards radical multiculturalism: Resolving tensions in curriculum and educational planning. In *Multicultural education: The interminable debate*, ed. S. Modgil, et al., pp. 33–47. London: Falmer Press.

Butler, J. 1992. Contingent foundations: Feminism and the question of "postmodernism." In *Feminists theorize the political*, eds. J. Butler & J. Scott, pp. 3–22. New York: Routledge.

Butler, J. E. 1989. Transforming the curriculum: Teaching about women of color. In *Multicultural education: Issues and perspectives*, eds. J. A. Banks & C.A.M. Banks, pp. 145–164. Boston: Allyn & Bacon.

Butler, J. E. 1991. The difficult dialog of curriculum transformation: Ethnic studies and women's studies. In *Transforming the curriculum: Ethnic studies and women's studies*, eds. J. E. Butler & J. C. Walter, pp. 1–20. Albany: SUNY Press.

Caduto, M. J. & Bruchac, J. 1991. *Keepers of the animals*. Golden, CO: Fulcrum.

Caduto, M. J. & Bruchac, J. 1988. *Keepers of the earth*. Golden, CO: Fulcrum.

Carby, H. 1990. The politics of difference. *MS: The World of Women*. 1 (2), 83–85.

Carnoy, M. 1989. Education, state, and culture in American society. In *Critical pedagogy, the state, and cultural struggle*, eds. Henry A. Giroux and Peter McLaren, pp. 3–23. Albany: SUNY Press.

Carson, B. 1990. *Gifted hands: The Ben Carson story* with C. Murphey. Grand Rapids, MI: Zondervan Publishing House.

Checkoway, B. & Norsman, A. 1986. Empowering citizens with disabilities. *Community Development Journal* 21: 270–277.

Cherryholmes, C. H. 1988. *Power and criticism: Poststructural investigations in education*. New York: Teachers College Press.

Childs, J. B. 1993. Towards trans-communality, the highest stage of multiculturalism: Notes on the future of African Americans. *Social Justice* 20 (1): 35–51.

Childs, J. B. 1994. The value of transcommunal identity politics. *Z Magazine* 7 (7/8): 48–51.

Chin, F., Chan, J., Inada, L., & Wong, S. 1991. Asian American literature: Real vs. fake. In *Transforming the curriculum: Ethnic studies and women's studies, eds. J. E. Butler & J. C. Walter, pp. 227–242.* Albany: SUNY Press.

Chomsky, N. 1987. *The Chomsky reader*, ed. James Peck. New York: Pantheon Books.

Chow, E. N. 1991. The development of feminist consciousness among Asian women. In *The social construction of gender*, eds. J. Lorber & S. A. Farrell, pp. 255–268. Newbury Park, CA: Sage.

Chow, R. 1992. Postmodern automatons. In *Feminists theorize the political*, eds. J. Butler & J. Scott, pp. 101–120. New York: Routledge.

Churchill, W. 1992. *Fantasies of the master race: Literature, cinema, and the colonization of American Indians*. Monroe, ME: Common Courage Press.

Churchill, W. 1994. *Indians are us: Culture and genocide in Native North America*. Monroe, ME: Common Courage Press.

Cobbin, J. & Thomashow C. 1984. Breathing life into social studies and language arts. In *Preparing for reflective teaching*, ed. Carl A. Grant, pp. 193–198. Boston: Allyn & Bacon.

Colangelo, N., Foxley, C. H., & Dustin, D., eds. 1979. *Multicultural nonsexist education: A human relations approach*. Dubuque: Kendall Hunt.

Cole, M. 1986. Teaching and learning about racism: A critique of multicultural education in Britain. In *Multicultural education: The interminable debate*, ed. S. Modgil et al., pp. 123–148. London: Falmer Press.

Coleman, J., et al. 1966. *Equality of educational opportunity*, 2 vols. Washington, D.C.: Office of Education, U.S. Department of Health, Education, and Welfare, U.S. Government Printing Office.

Collins, P. H. 1991. *Black feminist thought*. New York: Routledge.

Collins, P. H. 1993. Toward a new vision: Race, class, and gender as categories of analysis and connection. *Race, Sex & Class* 1 (1), 25–46.

Connell, R. W., Ashenden, D. J., Kessler, S. & Dowsett, G. W. 1982. *Making the difference: Schools, families and social division*. Sydney, Australia: Allen and Unwin.

Conway, J. 1974. Coeducation and women's studies: Two approaches to the question of women's place in the contemporary university. *Daedalus* 103 (4), pp. 239–249.

Cornbleth, C. & Waugh, D. 1995. *The great speckled bird: Multicultural politics and education policymaking*. New York: St. Martins Press.

Cortada, R. E. 1974. *Black studies*. Lexington, MA: Xerox College Publishing.

Darder, A. 1991. *Culture and power in the classroom*. New York: Bergin & Garvey.

Davis, A. Y. 1981. *Women, race, and class*. New York: Random House.

Davis, F. J. 1991. *Who is black?* University Park, PA: Penn State University.

Delgado-Gaitan, C. 1993. Researching change and changing the researcher. *Harvard Educational Review* 63 (4): 389–411.

Delpit, L. D. 1988. The silenced dialogue: Power and pedagogy in educating other people's children. *Harvard Educational Review*, 58, 280–298.

Denscombe, M. 1980. The work context of teaching: An analytic framework for the study of teachers in classrooms. *British Journal of Sociology of Education* 1, 279–292.

Densmore, K. 1987. Professionalism, proletarianization and teacher work. In *Critical studies in teacher education*, ed. T. S. Popkewitz, pp. 130–161. London: The Falmer Press,

Derman-Sparks, L. 1989. *The anti-bias curriculum*. Washington, DC: National Association for the Education of Young Children.

DuBois, E. C. & Ruiz, V. L., eds. 1990. *Unequal sisters*. New York: Routledge.

Dugger, K. (1991). Social location and gender role attitudes: A comparison of Black and white women. In J. Lorber & S. A. Farrell, eds. *The social construction of gender* (pp. 38–59). Newbury Park, CA: Sage.

Dyer, R. 1988. White. *Screen* 29, 44–64.

Ebert, T. 1991. Political demiosis in/of American Cultural Studies. *American Journal of Semiotics* 8 (1/2): 113–35.

Editorial: Abolish the white race—by any means necessary. 1993. *Race Traitor* 1, 1–8.

Ellsworth, E. 1989. Why doesn't this feel empowering? Working through the represive myths of critical pedagogy. *Harvard Educational Review* 59 (3), 297–324.

Elshtain, J. B. 1976. The social relations of the classroom: A moral and political perspective. *Telos*, 97–110.

Everhart, R. 1983. *Reading, writing, and resistance*. Boston: Routledge & Kegan Paul.

Eyerman, R. & Jamison, A. 1991. *Social movements: A cognitive approach*. University Park: The Pennsylvania State University Press.

Fairclough, N. 1989. *Language and power*. Harlow: Longman.

Faludi, S. 1991. *Backlash: The undeclared war against American women*. New York: Doubleday.

Fast, H. 1977. *The immigrant*. Boston: Houghton-Mifflin.

Feuer, L. 1991. From pluralism to multiculturalism. *Society* 29 (1), 19–22.

Fine, M. 1992. *Framing dropouts*. Albany: SUNY Press.

Floud, J. & Halsey, A. H. 1958. The sociology of education: A trend report and bibliography. *Current Sociology* 7, 165–235.

Fordham, S. 1988. Raceless as a factor in Black students' school success: Pragmatic strategy or pyrrhic victory? *Harvard Educational Review* 58 (1), 58–88.

French, J. R. P., Jr., & Raven, B. 1959. The bases of social power. In D. Cartwright, ed. *Studies in social power*, pp. 150–167. Ann Arbor: University of Michigan Institute for Social Research.

Freire, P. 1973. *Pedagogy of the oppressed.* New York: Seabury.

Fuller, M. 1981. Black girls in a London comprehensive school. In *Schooling for women's work*, ed. R. Deem, pp. 52–65. London: Routledge & Kegan Paul.

Gaard, G. 1992. Opening up the canon: The importance of teaching lesbian and gay literature. *Feminist Teacher* 6 (2), 30–33.

Gallard, A. J. 1993. Learning science in multicultural environments. In *The practice of constructivism in science education*, ed. K. Tobin, pp. 171–180. Hillsdale, NJ: Lawrence Erlbaum, Associates.

Garcia, A. M. 1991. The development of Chicana feminist discourse. In *The social construction of gender*, eds. J. Lorber & S. A. Farrell, pp. 269–287, Newbury Park, CA: Sage.

Garcia, M. 1994. Roundtable on the religious right and communities of color. *Third Force* 2 (4), 15–17.

Garvey, J. 1993. Reading, 'riting, and race. *Race Traitor* 1 (Winter), 73–87.

Gates, H. L., Jr. 1992. *Loose canons: Notes on the culture wars.* New York: Oxford University Press.

Gay, G. 1983. Multiethnic education: Historical developments and future prospects. *Phi Delta Kappan*, 64, 560–563.

Gay, G. 1995. Mirror images on common issues: Parallels between multicultural education and critical pedagogy. In *Multicultural education, critical pedagogy, and the politics of difference*, eds. C. E. Sleeter and P. L. McLaren, pp. 155–190. Albany: SUNY Press.

Gedicks, A. 1993. *The new resource wars: Native and environmental struggles against multinational corporations.* Boston: South End Press.

Giddens, A. 1979. *Central problems in social theory.* Berkeley: University of California Press.

Giddings, P. 1984. *Where and when I enter: The impact of Black women on race and sex in America.* New York: Bantam Books.

Gilligan, C. 1982. *In a different voice: Psychological theory and women's development.* Cambridge: Harvard University Press.

Ginsburg, M. B. 1988. *Contradictions in teacher education and society: A critical analysis*. London: The Falmer Press.

Giroux, H. A. 1983. *Theory and resistance in education*. South Hadley, MA: Bergin & Garvey.

Giroux, H. A. 1988. *Teachers as intellectuals*. South Hadley, MA: Bergin & Garvey.

Giroux, H. 1992. *Border crossings*. New York: Routledge.

Giroux, H. A. 1993–4. Consuming social change: The "United colors of Benetton." *Cultural Critique* 26, 5–32.

Gitlin, A. 1983. School structure and teachers' work." In *Ideology and practice in schooling*, eds. In M. W. Apple & L. Weis, pp. 192–212. Philadelphia: Temple University Press.

Goldberg, D. T. 1993. *Racist culture: Philosophy and the politics of meaning*. Oxford, UK: Blackwell.

Gollnick, D. M. 1980. Multicultural education. *Viewpoints in Teaching and Learning*, 56, 1–17.

Goodwin, A. L. 1994. Making the transition from self to other: What do pre-service teachers really think about multicultural education? *Journal of Teacher Education* 45 (2), 119–131.

Gore, J. 1992. What we can do for you! What can "we" do for "you"? Struggle over empowerment in critical and feminist pedagogy. In *Feminisms and critical pedagogy*, eds. In C. Luke & J. Gore, pp. 54–73. New York: Routledge.

Gramsci, A. 1971. *Selections from prison notebooks*. New York: International Publications.

Grant, C. A., & Sleeter, C. E. 1985. The literature on multicultural education: Review and analysis. *Educational Review*, 37, 97–118.

Grant, C. A., & Sleeter, C. E. 1986a. Educational equity, education that is multicultural and social reconstructionist. *Journal of Educational Equity and Leadership*, 6, 105–118.

Grant, C. A., & Sleeter, C. E. 1986b. Race, class and gender: An argument for integrative analysis. *Review of Educational Research*, 56, 195–211.

Grant, C. A. & Sleeter, C. E. 1986c. *After the school bell rings*. London: The Falmer Press.

Grant, C. A., Sleeter, C. E., & Anderson, J. E. 1986. The literature on multicultural education: Review and analysis, Part II. *Educational Studies*, 12, 47–71.

Gray, P. 1991. Whose America? *Time* 138 (1), 12–17.

Green, A. 1982. In defense of anti-racist teaching: A reply to recent critiques of multicultural education. *Multiracial Education*, 10, 19–35.

Greene, M. 1985. Sex equity as a philosophical problem. In *Handbook for achieving sex equity through education*, ed. S. S. Klein. Baltimore: Johns Hopkins University Press.

Grossman, H. & Grossman, S. H. 1994. *Gender issues in education*. Boston: Allyn & Bacon.

Grumet, M. R. 1988. *Bitter milk*. Amherst: University of Massachusetts Press.

Gurnah, A. 1984. The politics of racial awareness training. *Critical Social Policy*, 6–20.

Hacker, A. 1992. *Two nations*. New York: Charles Scribner's Sons.

Harding, S. 1994. Is science multicultural? Challenges, resources, opportunities, and uncertainties. *Configurations* 2, 301–330.

Harding, S. 1991. *Whose science? Whose knowledge? Thinking from women's lives*. Ithaca, NY: Cornell University Press.

Harc, N. 1971. What should be the role of Afro-American education in the undergraduate curriculum? In *New perspectives on Black studies*, ed. J.W. Blassingame. Urbana: University of Illinois Press.

Harmon, M. J. 1954. *Political thought: From Plato to the present*. New York: McGraw-Hill.

Harry, B. 1992. *Cultural diversity, families, and the special education system*. New York: Teachers College Press.

Hartsock, N. 1989. *Money, sex and power*. New York: Longman.

Harvey, G. & Noble, E. 1985. Economic considerations for achieving sex equity through education. In *Handbook for achieving sex equity through education*, ed. S. S. Klein. pp. 17-28. Baltimore: Johns Hopkins University Press.

Hatsopoulos, G. N., Krugman, P. R. and Summers, L. H. 1988. U.S. competitiveness: Beyond the trade deficit. *Science* 241: 299–307.

Hau de no sau nee 1977. *A basic call to consciousness*. Mohawk Nation: Akwesasne Notes.

Heller, S. 1992. Worldwide 'diaspora' of peoples poses new challenges for scholars. *Chronicle of Higher Education* 38 (9), A7–9.

Helms, J. E., ed. 1990. *Black and white racial identity: Theory, research, and practice*. Westport, CT: Greenwood Press.

Henry, W. A., III. 1990. Beyond the melting pot. *Time* 135, 9 April, 28–31.

Hewitt, N. A. 1990. Beyond the search for sisterhood: American women's history in the 1980s. In *Unequal sisters*, eds. E. DuBois & V. L. Ruiz, pp. 1–14. New York: Routledge.

Hicks, E. 1981. Cultural Marxism: Nonsynchrony and feminist practice. In *Women and revolution*, ed. L. Sargent, pp. 219–238. Boston: South End Press.

Hirsch, E. D., Jr. 1988. *Cultural literacy: What every American needs to know*. New York: Random House, Vintage Books.

Hodgkinson, H. L. 1985. *All one system: Demographics of education-kindergarten through graduate school*. Washington, DC: Institute for Educational Leadership.

Hodson, D. 1993. In search of a rationale for multicultural science education. *Science Education* 77 (6): 685–711.

Hollins, E. R., King, J. E. & Hayman, W. C., Eds. 1994. *Teaching diverse populations: Formulating a knowledge base*. Albany: SUNY Press.

hooks, b. 1981. *Ain't I a woman?* Boston: South End Press.

hooks, b. 1990. *Yearning*. Boston: South End Press.

hooks, b. 1993. *Sisters of the yam*. Boston: South End Press.

Hoover, K. R. 1987. *Ideology and political life*. Monterey, CA: Brooks/Cole Pub. Company.

Howe, I. 1991. The content of the curriculum: Two views: The value of the canon. *Liberal Education* 77 (3), 8–9.

Ignatiev, N. 1993. Immigrants and whites. *Race Traitor* 2 (Summer), 60–67.

Ingalsbee, T. 1993. Resource and action mobilization theories: The new social-psychological research agenda. *Berkeley Journal of Sociology* 38, 137–155.

Irvine, J. J. 1988. An analysis of the problem of disappearing Black educators. *Elementary School Journal* 88, 503–513.

Jaggar, A. M. 1983. *Feminist politics and human nature*. Totowa, NJ: Rowan & Allanheld.

JanMohamed, A. & Lloyd, D. 1987. Minority discourse: What is to be done? *Cultural Critique* 7, 5–17.

Jiobu, R. M. 1988. *Ethnicity and assimilation*. Albany: SUNY Press.

Jones, P. A. 1991. Educating Black males: Several solutions, but no solution. *Crisis* 98 (8), 12–18.

Jordan, C. 1985. Translating culture: From ethnographic information to educational program. *Anthropology and Education Quarterly*, 16, 105–123.

Kamel, R. 1993. The global factory: Analysis and action for a new economic era. In *Oppression and social justice: Critical frameworks*, ed. J. Andrzejewski, pp. 182–202. Needham Heights, MA: Ginn Press.

Kellogg, P. 1993. The hidden system of neocolonialism. In *Oppression and social justice: Critical frameworks*, ed. J. Andrzejewski, pp. 159–163. Needham Heights, MA: Ginn Press.

Kerr, B. A. 1985. *Smart girls, gifted women*. Dayton: Ohio Psychology Press.

Kessler-Harris, A. 1992. Cultural locations: Positioning American studies in the great debate. *American Quarterly* 44 (3), 299–312.

King, J. E. 1992. Diaspora literacy and consciousness in the struggle against miseducation in the Black community. *Journal of Negro Education* 61 (3): 317–340.

Kipnis, D. 1976. *The powerholders*. Chicago: University of Chicago Press.

Klein, S. S., Ed. 1985. *Handbook for achieving sex equity through education*. Baltimore: Johns Hopkins University Press.

Kluegel, J. R. & Smith, E. R. 1986. *Beliefs about inequality: Americans' views of what is and what ought to be*. New York: Aldine de Gruyter.

Kozol, J. 1991. *Savage inequalities*. New York: Crown Publishers.

Krauthammer, C. 1990. Education: Doing bad and feeling good. *Time* 135 (6), 78.

Kunjufu, J. n.d. *Countering the conspiracy to destroy Black boys*, vol. III. Chicago: African American Images.

Kuumba, M. G. 1994. The limits of feminism: Decolonizing women's liberation/oppression theory. *Race, Sex & Class* 1 (2), 85–100.

Laclau, E. 1988. Building a new left: An interview with Ernesto Laclau. *Strategies*, Fall, 10–28.

Ladner, J. 1971. *Tomorrow's tomorrow*. Garden City, NY: Doubleday.

Ladson-Billings, G. 1994. *The dreamkeepers*. New York: Jossey-Bass.

Lamm, R. 1988. The uncompetitive society. *U.S. News and World Report* 104: 9.

Lareau, A. 1989. *Home advantage*. London: The Falmer Press.

Lather, P. 1991. *Getting smart*. New York: Routledge.

Lather, P. 1992. Postcritical pedagogies: A feminist reading. In *Feminisms and critical pedagogy*, eds. In C. Luke & J. Gore, pp. 120–137. New York: Routledge.

Lauderdale, W. B. & Deaton, W. L. 1993. Future teachers react to past racism. *The Educational Forum* 57 (3), 266–276.

Lauter, P. 1991. *Canons and contexts*. New York: Oxford University Press.

Leo, J. 1991. Multicultural follies. *U.S. News and World Report* 111 (2), 12.

Lewis, S. 1985. Achieving sex equity for minority women. In *Handbook for achieving sex equity through education*, ed. S. S. Klein, ed. Baltimore: Johns Hopkins University Press.

Lerner, G., Ed. 1992. *The female experience: An American documentary*. New York: Oxford University Press.

Linden, E. 1991. Lost tribes, lost knowledge. *Time* 138 (12), 46–56.

Linn, M. C. & Hyde, J. A. 1989. Gender, mathematics and science. *Educational Researcher* 18 (8), 17–27.

Liston, D. P. & Zeichner, K. M. 1987. Critical pedagogy and teacher education. *Journal of Education* 169 (3), 117–137.

Lortie, D. C. 1975. *Schoolteacher*. Chicago: University of Chicago Press.

Maher, F. A. & Tetreault, M. K. 1993. Frames of positionality: Constructing meaningful dialogues about gender and race. *Anthropological Quarterly* 66 (3), 118–126.

Malveaux, J. 1987. The political economy of Black women. In *The year left 2*, eds. M. Davis, M. Marable, F. Pfeil, & M. Sprinker, pp. 52–72. London: Verso.

Mann, E. 1991. *L.A.'s lethal air*. Los Angeles: A Labor/Community Strategy Center Book.

Marable, M. 1987. The contradictory contours of Black political culture. In *The year left 2*, eds. M. Davis, M. Marable, F. Pfeil, & M. Sprinker, pp. 1–17. London: Verso.

Martin, B. 1993. Lesbian identity and autobiographical difference[s]. In *The gay and lesbian studies reader*, eds. H. Abelove, M. A. Barale, & D. M. Halperin, pp. 274–293. New York: Routledge.

Martinez, E. 1993. Latino politics: Scapegoating immigrants. *Z Magazine* 6 (12), 22–27.

Mattai, P. R. 1992. Rethinking the nature of multicultural education: Has it lost its focus or is it being misused? *Journal of Negro Education* 61 (1), 65–77.

Mauer, M. 1990. Young black men and the criminal justice system. *Chicago Tribune*, March 4, Section 4, p. 3.

Mazumdar, S. 1989. A woman-centered perspective on Asian American history. In *Making waves: An anthology of writings by and about Asian American women*, eds. Asian Women United of California, pp. 1–24. Boston: Beacon Press.

McCarthy, C. 1988. Rethinking liberal and radical perspectives on racial inequality in schooling: Making the case for nonsynchrony. *Harvard Educational Review*, 58, 265–279.

McCarthy, C. 1995. The problem with origins: Race and the contrapuntal nature of the educational experience. In *Multicultural education, critical pedagogy, and the politics of difference*, eds. C. E. Sleeter & P. McLaren, pp. 245–268. Albany: SUNY Press.

McCarthy, C. and Apple, M. W. 1989. Race, class, and gender in American educational research: Toward a nonsynchronous parallelist position. In *Class, race, and gender in American education*, ed. L. Weis, pp. 9–42. Albany: SUNY Press.

McCarthy, C. & Crichlow, W. 1993. Introduction: Theories of identity, theories of representation, theories of race. In *Race, identity and representation in education*, eds. C. McCarthy & W. Crichlow, pp. xiii–xxix. New York: Routledge.

McIntosh, P. M. 1987. Curricular revision: The new knowledge for a new age. In *Educating the majority: Women challenge tradition in higher education*, eds. C. S. Pearson, D. L. Shavlik & J. G. Touchton, pp. 406–412. New York: Macmillan.

McKissack, P. & McKissack, F. 1990. *Taking a stand against racism and racial discrimination*. New York: Franklin Watts.

McLaren, P. 1994. Multiculturalism and the postmodern critique: Toward a pedagogy of resistance and transformation. In *Between borders: Pedagogy and the politics of cultural studies*, eds. H. A. Giroux & P. McLaren, pp. 192–222. New York: Routledge.

McLaren, P. & Hammer, R. 1989. Critical pedagogy and the postmodern challenge: Toward a critical postmodernist pedagogy of liberation. *Educational Foundations*, Fall, 29–62.

McNeill, E., Schmidt, V. & Allen, J. 1981. *Cultural awareness for young children*. Dallas: The Learning Tree.

McRobbie, A. 1978. Working class girls and the culture of feminity. In *Women take issue*, eds. Women's Studies Group, pp. 96–108. London: Hutchinson.

Minkoff, D. 1993. The organization of survival: Women's and racial-ethnic voluntarist and activist organizations, 1955–1985. *Social Forces* 71 (4): 887–908.

Minority Trendsletter 1991. Special issue on "Toxics and communities of color," Vol. 4, No. 4.

Mirande, A. & Enriquez, E. 1979. *La Chicana*. Chicago: University of Chicago Press.

Montecinos, C. 1995. Culture as an on-going dialog: Implications for multicultural teacher education. In *Multicultural education, critical pedagogy, and the politics of difference*, eds. C. E. Sleeter & P. McLaren, pp. 96–108. Albany: SUNY Press.

Mudimbe, V. Y. 1988. *The invention of Africa: Gnosis, philosophy, and the order of knowledge*. Bloomington: Indiana University Press.

Muñoz, C., Jr. 1987. Chicano politics: The current conjuncture. In *The year left 2*, eds. M. Davis, M. Marable, F. Pfeil, & M. Sprinker, pp. 35–51. London: Verso.

Murray, C. 1984. *Losing ground: American social policy, 1950–1980*. New York: Basic Books.

Murray, S. R. 1985. Sex equity strategies for specific populations. In *Handbook for achieving sex equity through education*, ed. S. S. Klein. Baltimore: Johns Hopkins University Press.

Nasar, S. 1988. America's competitive revival. *Fortune* 117, 44–50.

Nicholson, L. J. 1990. *Feminism/postmodernism*. New York: Routledge.

Nieto, S. 1992. *Affirming diversity*. New York: Longman.

Oakes, J. 1985. *Keeping track*. New Haven, Conn.: Yale University Press.

Oakes, J. 1990. *Multiplying inequalities: Opportunities to learn in mathematics and science*. Santa Monica, CA: Rand.

Ogbu, J. U. 1974. *The next generation*. New York: Academic Press.

Ogbu, J. U. 1991. Immigrant and involuntary minorities in comparative perspective. In *Minority status and schooling*, eds. M. A. Gibson & J. U. Ogbu, pp. 3–33. New York: Garland.

Olguin, R. A. 1991. Towards an epistomology of ethnic studies: African american studies and Chicano studies contributions. In *Transforming the curriculum: Ethnic studies and women's studies*, eds. In J. E. Butler & J. C. Walter, pp. 149–168. Albany: SUNY Press.

Oliver, M. 1986. Social policy and disability: Some theoretical issues. *Disability, Handicap & Society* 1 (1), 5–18.

Olneck, M. 1990. The recurring dream: Symbolism and ideology in intercultural and multicultural education. *American Journal of Education*, 98(2), 147–174.

Omatsu, G. 1994. The four "prisons" and the movements of liberation: Asian American activism from the 1960's to the 1990's. In *The State of Asian America*, ed. K. Aguilar-San Juan, pp. 19–70. Boston: South End Press.

Omi, M., & Winant, H. 1986. *Racial formation in the United States*. New York: Routledge & Kegan Paul.

Oppenheim, L. 1993. Editor's introduction. *Labor Research Review* #20 12 (1): vi.

Orner, M. 1992. Interrupting calls for student voice in "liberatory" pedagogy: A feminist poststructuralist perspective. In *Feminisms and critical pedagogy*, eds. C. Luke & J. Gore, pp. 74–89. New York: Routledge.

Outlaw, L. 1987. On race and class, or, on the prospects of "rainbow socialism" In *The year left 2*, eds. M. Davis, M. Marable, F. Pfeil, & M. Sprinker, pp. 106–121. London: Verso.

Padden, C. & Humphries, T. 1988. *Deaf in America: Voices from a culture*. Cambridge, MA: Harvard University Press.

Padilla, F. M. 1985. *Latino ethnic consciousness*. Notre Dame, IN: University of Notre Dame Press.

Pagano, J. A. 1990. *Exiles and communities*. Albany: SUNY Press.

Parenti, M. 1978. *Power and the powerless*. New York: St. Martin's Press.

Parenti, M. 1988. *Democracy for the few*. New York: St. Martin's Press.

Parenti, M. 1993. From *The sword and the dollar*. In *Oppression and social justice: Critical frameworks*, ed. J. Andrzejewski, pp. 164–181. Needham Heights, MA: Ginn Press.

Payne, C. N. 1984. *Getting what we ask for*. Westport, Conn.: Greenwood Press.

Peck, J. 1994. Talk about racism: Framing a popular discourse of race on Oprah Winfrey. *Cultural Critique* 27, Spring, 89–126.

Perez-Torres, R. 1994. Nomads and migrants: Negotiating a multicultural postmodernism. *Cultural Critique* 26, 161–190.

Perry, N. J. 1988. The education crisis: What business can do. *Fortune* 118: 70–73.

Platt, A. 1992. Defenders of the Canon: What's behind the attack on multiculturalism. *Social Justice* 19 (2), 122–141.

Platt, A. M. 1993. Beyond the canon, with great difficulty. *Social Justice* 20 (1–2), 72–81.

Popkewitz, T. S. 1988. Culture, pedagogy, and power: Issues in the production of values and colonialization. *Journal of Education* 170 (2), 77–90.

Popkewitz, T. S. 1991. *A political sociology of educational reform*. New York: Teachers College Press.

Price, H. B. 1992. Multiculturalism: Myths and realities. *Phi Delta Kappan* 74 (3), 208–213.

Raskin, J. B. 1995. Affirmative action and racial reaction. *Z Magazine* 8 (5), 33–41.

Ravitch, D. 1990a. Diversity and democracy: Multicultural education in America. *American Educator* 14 (1), 16–20, 46–68.

Ravitch, D. 1990b. Multiculturalism: E pluribus plures. *The American Scholar* 59 (3), 337–354.

Reiss, M. 1993. *Science education for a pluralistic society*. Philadelphia, PA: Open University Press.

Reyes, M. de la Luz. 1992. Challenging venerable assumptions: Literacy instruction for linguistically different students. *Harvard Educational Review* 62 (4), 427–446.

Richardson, V., Casanova, U., Placier, P. & Guilfoyle, K. 1989. *School children at risk*. London: The Falmer Press.

Roediger, D. R. 1991. *The wages of whiteness*. London: Verso.

Rosaldo, R. 1989. *Culture and truth: The remaking of social analysis*. Boston: Beacon Press.

Rubin, G. S. 1993. Thinking sex: Notes for a radical theory of the politics of sexuality. In *The lesbian and gay studies reader*, eds. H. Abelove, M. A. Barale, & D. Halperin, pp. 3–44. New York: Routledge.

Rumberger, R. W. 1983. Dropping out of high school: The influence of race, sex, and family background. *American Educational Research Journal* 20 (2), 199–220.

Russo, M. 1993. This world called Miami. *Labor Research Review #20* 12 (1): 37–49.

San Juan, Jr., E. 1992. *Articulations of power in ethnic and racial studies in the United States*. Atlantic Heights, NJ: Humanities Press.

Scheurich, J. 1993. Toward a white discourse on white racism. *Educational Researcher* 22 (8): 5–10.

Scheurich, J. 1994. Policy archaeology: A new policy studies methodology. *Journal of Educational Policy* 9 (4), 297–316.

Schlesinger, A. M., Jr. 1991a. The disuniting of America: What we all stand to lose if multicultural education takes the wrong approach. *American Educator* 15 (3), 14, 21–33.

Schlesinger, A. M., Jr. Dec. 30, 1991b. Writing, and rewriting, history. *The New Leader*, 12–14.

Schlesinger, A. M., Jr. 1992. *The disuniting of America*. New York: Norton.

Schniedewind, N., & Davidson, E. 1983. *Open minds to equality*. Englewood Cliffs, NJ: Prentice-Hall.

Scott, J. 1992. Experience. *Feminists theorize the political*, eds. J. Butler & J. Scott, pp. 22–40. New York: Routledge.

Sears, J. T. 1992. The impact of culture and ideology on the construction of gender and sexual identities. In *Sexuality and the curriculum*, ed. J. T. Sears, pp. 139–156. New York: Teachers College.

Shade, B. 1989. *Culture, style, and the educative process*. Springfield, IL: Charles C. Thomas.

Shanley, K. 1991. Time and time again: Notes toward an understanding of radical elements in American Indian fiction. In *Transforming the curriculum: Ethnic studies and women's studies*, eds. J. E. Butler & J. C. Walter, pp. 243–256. Albany: SUNY Press.

Shields, K. 1994. *In the tiger's mouth: An empowerment guide for social action*. Philadelphia: New Society Publishers.

Shirts, G. 1969. *Star power*. La Jolla, CA: Western Behavioral Sciences Institute.

Shor, I. 1982. *Critical teaching and everyday life*. Boston: South End Press.

Shor, I. 1986. *Culture wars: School and society in the conservative restoration 1969–1984*. Boston: Routledge & Kegan Paul.

Silber, J. 1988. Education and national survival. *Vital Speeches* 54: 215–219.

Silko, L. M. 1977. *Ceremony*. New York: The New American Library.

Simonelli, R. 1994a. Traditional knowledge leads to a Ph.D. *Winds of Change*, 9 (4): 43–47.

Simonelli, R. 1994b. Finding balance by looking beyond the scientific method. *Winds of Change*, 9 (4): 106–112.

Simpson, A. W. & Erickson, M. T. 1983. Teachers' verbal and nonverbal communication patterns as a function of teacher race, student gender, and student race. *American Educational Research Journal* 20, 183–198.

Sivanandon, A. 1985. RAT and the degradation of black struggle. *Race & Class* 26 (4): 1–33.

Skrtic, T. M. 1991. The special education paradox: Equity as the way to excellence. *Harvard Educational Review* 61 (2): 148–206.

Sleeter, C. E. 1992. *Keepers of the American dream*. London: The Falmer Press.

Sleeter, C. E. 1995a. An analysis of critiques of multicultural education. In *Handbook of research on multicultural education*, eds. J. A. Banks & C. M. Banks, pp. 81–96. New York: Macmillan.

Sleeter, C. E. (1995b). Teaching whites about racism. In R. Martin, Ed. *Practicing what we teach*, ed. R. J. Martin, pp. 117–130. Albany: SUNY Press.

Sleeter, C. E., & Grant, C. A. 1987. An analysis of multicultural education in the United States. *Harvard Educational Review*, 57, 421–444.

Sleeter, C. E. & Grant, C. A. 1991. Race, class, gender, and disability in current textbooks. In *The politics of the textbook*, eds. M. W. Apple & L. K. Christian-Smith, pp. 78–110. New York: Routledge.

Sleeter, C. E., & Grant, C. A. 1992. *Making choices for multicultural education*, 2nd ed.. Columbus: Merrill/Macmillan.

Sleeter, C. E. & McLaren, P., eds. 1995. *Multicultural education, critical pedagogy, and the politics of difference*. Albany: SUNY Press.

Smith, Barbara. 1990. The NEA is the least of it. *Ms: The World of Women*. 1 (3), 67.

Smyth, J. 1992. Teachers' work and the politics of reflection. *American Educational Research Journal* 29 (2), 267–300.

Solomon, R. P. 1992. *Black resistance in high school*. Albany: SUNY Press.

Solorzano, D. G. 1989. Teaching and social change—Reflections on a Freirean approach in a college classroom. *Teaching Sociology* 17, 218–225.

Spelman, E. V. 1988. *Inessential woman*. Boston: Beacon Press.

Spivak, G. C. 1990. *The post-colonial critic: Interviews, strategies, dialogues*. New York: Routledge.

Staggenborg, S., Eder, D. & Sudderth, L. 1993. Women's culture and social change: Evidence from the National Women's Music Festival. *Berkeley Journal of Sociology* 38, 31–56.

Stalvey, L. M. 1989. *The education of a WASP*. Madison, WI: University of Wisconsin Press.

Stanley, W. B. 1992. *Curriculum for utopia*. Albany: SUNY Press.

Staples, L. 1984. *Roots to power*. New York: Praeger.

Stone, M. 1993. From *Three thousand years of racism*. In *Human relations: The study of oppression and human rights*, 3rd edition, ed. J. Andrzejewski, pp. 293–296. Needham Heights, MA: Ginn Press.

Stotsky, S. 1991. Cultural politics. *American School Board Journal* 178 (10), 26–28.

Stotsky, S. March 1992. Academic vs. ideological multicultural education in the classroom. *The Education Digest*, 64–66.

Suzuki, B. H. 1984. Curriculum transformation for multicultural education. *Education and Urban Society*, 16, 294–322.

Suzuki, B. H. 1989. Asian Americans as the "model minority." *Change* 21 (Nov/Dec): 13–19.

Takaki, R. 1989a. *Strangers from a different shore: A history of Asian Americans*. New York: Penguin Books.

Takaki, R. 1989b. The fourth iron cage: Race and political economy in the 1990s. Paper presented at the Green Bay Colloquium on Ethnicity in Public Policy, Green Bay, WI.

Tan, A. 1989. *The joy luck club*. New York: Ivy Books.

Tatum, B. D. 1992. Talking about race, learning about racism: The application of racial identity development theory in the classroom. *Harvard Educational Review* 62 (1), 1–24.

Teens less healthy than parents were, report says. 1990. *Racine Journal Times* 134 (160): 1.

Terkel, S. 1980. *American dreams lost and found*. New York: Pantheon Books.

Terry, B. 1993. A parable: The ups and downs. In *Oppression and social justice: Critical frameworks*, 3rd edition, ed. J. Andrzejewski, pp. 61–63. Needham Heights, MA: Ginn Press.

Tetreault, M. K. T. 1989. Integrating content about women and gender into the curriculum. In *Multicultural education: Issues and perspectives*, eds. Banks, J. A. & Banks, C. A. M., pp. 124–144. Boston: Allyn & Bacon.

Tiedt, P., & Tiedt, I. 1986. *Multicultural teaching: A handbook of activities, information and resources*. Boston: Allyn & Bacon.

Tilly, C. 1993. Social movements as historically specific clusters of political performances. *Berkeley Journal of Sociology* 38, 1–30.

Touraine, A. 1988. *Return of the actor: Social theory in a postindustrial society*. Minneapolis: University of Minnesota Press.

Trinh, T. Minh-ha. 1989. *Woman native other*. Bloomington: University of Indiana Press.

Trinh, T. M. 1991. *When the moon waxes red*. New York: Routledge.

Troyna, B., ed. 1987. *Racial inequality in education*. London: Tavistock.

Trueba, H. 1988. Culturally based explanations of minority students' academic achievement. *Anthropology and Education Quarterly*, 19, 270–281.

U. S. Bureau of the Census 1990. *Statistical abstract of the United States 1990*, 110th ed. Washington, DC: U.S. Government Printing Office, p. 409.

Valli, L. 1986. *Becoming clerical workers*. Boston: Routledge & Kegan Paul.

Van Dijk, T.A. 1993. *Elite discourse and racism*. Newbury Park, CA: Sage Publications.

Watrous, S. 1993. Making waves along Lake Michigan. *Z Magazine* 6 (6), 14–15.

Weatherford, J. 1988. *Indian givers*. New York: Fawcett Columbine.

Weiler, K. 1988. *Women teaching for a change*. South Hadley, MA: Bergin and Garvey.

Weis, L. 1985. *Between two worlds*. Boston: Routledge & Kegan Paul.

Weis, L. 1990. *Working class without work*. New York: Routledge.

Wellman, D. T. 1977. *Portraits of white racism*. Cambridge, MA: Cambridge University Press.

West, C. 1987. Race and social theory: Towards a genealogical materialist analysis. In *The Year Left 2: An American Socialist Yearbook*, eds. M. Davis, M. Marable, F. Pfeil, & M. Sprinker, pp. 73–89. London: Verso.

West, C. 1993. The new cultural politics of difference. In *Race, identity, and representation in education*, eds. C. McCarthy & W. Crichlow, pp. 11–23. New York: Routledge.

Wexler, P. 1982. Structure, text, and subject: A critical sociology of school knowledge. In *Cultural and economic reproduction in education: Essays on class, ideology and the state*, ed. M. W. Apple, pp. 275–303. Boston: Routledge & Kegan Paul.

White, C. J. 1988. Conversation as text. *Educational Foundations* Fall: 87–105.

White, G. 1993. Gay news: Colorado's gay salute. *Z Magazine* 6 (4), 7–9.

Whitty, G. 1985. *Sociology and school knowledge*. London: Methuen.

Williams, M. R. 1989. *Neighborhood organizing for urban school reform*. New York: Teachers College Press.

Williams, P. 1991. *The alchemy of race and rights*. Cambridge: Harvard University Press.

Williams, S. 1987. *Exploding the hunger myths*. San Francisco: The Institute for Food and Development Policy.

Williams, W. A. 1991. Empire as a way of life. *Radical History* 50, 71–102.

Willis, P. 1977. *Learning to labour*. Westmead, England: Saxon House Press.

Wolf, N. 1991. *The beauty myth*. New York: Morrow.

Wrong, D. H. 1979. *Power: Its forms, bases and uses*. South Hampton, Britain: Basil Blackwell.

Yadav, A. 1993/94. Nationalism and contemporaneity: Political economy of a discourse. *Cultural Critique* 26, 191–229.

Yamane, D. 1994. Personal communication.

Zinn, M. B. 1982. Mexican-American women in the social sciences. *Signs: Journal of Women and Culture in Society* 8, pp. 259–272.

Zinn, M. B., Cannon, L. W., Higginbotham, E. & Dill, B. 1986. The cost of exclusionary practices in women's studies. *Signs: Journal of Women and Culture in Society* 11: 190–303.

Index

275